P9-DOC-952

AVON PUBLIC LIBRARY
BOX 977 / 200 BENCHMARK RD.
AVON, CO 81620

FAIL UNTIL YOU DON'T

ALSO BY BOBBY BONES

Bare Bones: I'm Not Lonely If You're Reading This Book

FAIL UNTIL YOU DON'T

Fight Grind Repeat

BOBBY BONES

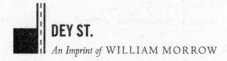

DEY ST.
An Imprint of WILLIAM MORROW

FAIL UNTIL YOU DON'T. Copyright © 2018 by Austin Bones, Inc. All rights reserved. Printed in the United States of America. No part of this book may be used or reproduced in any manner whatsoever without written permission except in the case of brief quotations embodied in critical articles and reviews. For information, address HarperCollins Publishers, 195 Broadway, New York, NY 10007.

HarperCollins books may be purchased for educational, business, or sales promotional use. For information, please email the Special Markets Department at SPsales@harpercollins.com.

FIRST DEY STREET HARDCOVER PUBLISHED 2018

FIRST EDITION

Designed by Paula Russell Szafranski

Library of Congress Cataloging-in-Publication Data has been applied for.

ISBN 978-0-06-279581-6
ISBN 978-0-06-287755-0 (B&N signed edition)
ISBN 978-0-06-287756-7 (BAM signed edition)
ISBN 978-0-06-285323-3 (PMI and Parnassus signed edition)

18 19 20 21 22 LSC 10 9 8 7 6 5 4 3 2 1

To my dog, Dusty. Sadly, you'll never get to read this.

Mostly because you didn't know how to read.

Because you were a dog.

RIP, buddy: 2003–2018.

CONTENTS

INTRODUCTION

Fight, Grind, Repeat or . . .

Your Motivational Guide to Being Less Terrible at Life

When I decided to write another book (even though I didn't know if I had another chapter in me, let alone a whole new book in me), I wanted to write about how to face your fears. I figured I'd describe a lot of the fears I've felt in my life and how I faced them all—like the superhero that I am. But, to be honest, that would be a load of crap. And my fans are quick to smell the BS. (It's weird to call my people "fans." When I think of "fans," I picture a Green Bay Packers diehard with face paint and no shirt fighting the elements in subzero temperatures. My people aren't fanatical about me. They understand me—or at least can stomach me for relatively large amounts of time. That's all I really need. And I appreciate that.)

So instead of hitting you with a fake face-your-fears-it's-amazing read, I'm going to tell you the story of when I faced my biggest fear. And I'm writing this just a few hours after it actually happened. Basically, this is the book version of an NFL instant replay. Except not so instant, because you're reading it months after it happened, because these books take *forever* to get published.

Rest assured, the details are still fresh in my brain as I sit here in the Little Rock airport, a familiar and comfortable setting. I'm surrounded by nice folks decked out in Arkansas Razorbacks hats and T-shirts. About ten people have already stopped to tell me that they listen to my show. I appreciate when anyone stops me to say they tune in to the morning show I've been doing in some shape or form for nearly twenty years. (Man, I'm getting old. I know I started radio at seventeen, but twenty years? So, my career is as old as some of the girls I've considered dating. I mean, I know twenty is too young for me. They can't even get into a casino. But I'll start taking rejections at age twenty-five or so.)

Although my morning show is nationally syndicated, it's always cool when someone from where you grew up says they listen. It's especially sweet in Arkansas, my first home (with Austin and Nashville coming in second and third). Despite all that good stuff, my cage is a little rattled right now. Mostly because of that fear I just mentioned. (You know, the one we discussed before debating openly if I'd still date a college sophomore. To reiterate, I don't think I would.)

Before I reveal the mysterious fear, a little backstory.

You know all about this if you read my memmmmmwarrrrrr (a.k.a. memoir), *Bare Bones* by Bobby Bones (that's me); or have listened to my radio show, where I talk a lot about myself; or have stood anywhere within twenty feet of me in the last hundred months. But just in case you don't fit into any of those categories, here's a quick version—I don't know my biological father. I mean, I know *who* he is, like his name and where he comes from. It's the same place I came from. (Not the same vagina. That would make him my "brother-dad," and I'd have a reality show on TLC right about now.) But that's about it.

This stranger, otherwise known as my dad, left my mom and me around the time that my memories started being formed. So I have only fleeting impressions of him sort of being there, but no full-on memories. No ball playing. No whuppins. No "you'll eventually get girls to like you," or "you can't date that many girls at once." (Amy, my cohost and moral compass, set me straight on that one.)

So, yeah. I don't know my dad. He's never been a part of my life. It's sad. So sad that I decided to turn it into a joke for my stand-up act. Here it is:

THE SADDEST JOKE I'VE EVER WRITTEN

*I was on Facebook yesterday looking at the tab of **People You May Know** and my biological father popped up.* (Long pause for effect.) *I didn't.*

I'd now like to do an impression of my biological father . . . (Then I walk offstage.)

(In my mind, that joke was a real hit, even though it just confused the audience. But I love it. I love creating any sort of emotion. I love to make people confused and question if they are supposed to laugh. I love to make people feel, which often means taking them out of their comfort zone.)

Jokes aside, when it comes to not having a dad, I've been sad, angry, resentful, apathetic (having repressed all the previous feelings), and then sad again. That's a cycle I've repeated for about the last thirty years of my life. And, as I was thinking of the scariest things I've ever done—you know, for a relatable and engaging anecdote to open my new book—I felt like it would be hypocritical not to describe my biggest fear. And that is . . . meeting the person I've turned into the ultimate villain in my mind. My dad.

I let my anger and fear keep me from ever reaching out. I thought I was punishing him for not being around when I was a kid. In reality, though, I was punishing myself. It wasn't until I started thinking of the central ideas of what I wanted this book to be about that I felt I finally had to take that polar plunge. (That's the stupid group of people who jump into the water in winter because they say it's so invigorating. But most of the time, I think they just end up with pneumonia.) Although I might have been subconsciously looking for any reason, I decided to reach out to my dad after all these years because I didn't want to feel like a hypocrite when I wrote about all the positive results that come from facing fear.

The adventure started with a text to my cousin Mary asking if she had his number. She did. Crap! Now I had to reach out. Again, if I wanted to lecture you about chasing your biggest fear, you would come back at me about why I hadn't done mine. So I was in it to win it. Or, as they say on the streets, "I was in it because I was writing a book about failure and didn't want the whole thing to be a farce." Yeah, that's street lingo.

"Hey. It's Bobby Estell," I texted, thinking if I just wrote "Bobby" he probably wouldn't know who it was. (I nearly texted,

"It's your long-lost son Bobby." But I wasn't sure he would get the sarcasm.)

"I'm going to be in town," I continued, "and wanted to know if we can meet up."

Then I waited for a text back.

One hour—nothing.

Two hours—nothing.

I assumed he wasn't like me, the guy who keeps his phone in his hand the entire day, but it was still nerve-racking to not get a text back after a few hours. I had really put myself out there by sending that message. The least I would expect was an answer, even if it was "No."

I was traveling that day, so I didn't have a lot to do except stare at my phone, which made time drag by even slower and my anxiety ramp up even more. I began to think he wasn't going to text me back at all. Rejected again.

Finally, about four hours and twenty-three minutes later (but who's counting?), I got: "That sounds good. Let me know."

What did that mean? "Sounds good"? And "let me know"? AND why did he take four hours to get back to me? Was he on a job site, getting an MRI, trapped in a well? Or did it actually sound *not* good to him . . . I don't know what I was expecting. "WOWOWOWOWOW!!! 😎 Glad to hear from you. I've been meaning to text you for the last 30 years but I couldn't find your number. ☺"

Nahhhh.

But still.

Over the next few days, I distanced myself from my nagging doubts. If there were an Olympic sport in compartmentalizing emotions, I'd take down Muhammad Ali or Michael Phelps as being the greatest of all time. Right then, I separated myself from it. *Bam!* Much like doing the Tide Pod Challenge, I acted like I didn't want to go through with it, but secretly I wanted to see what all the fuss was about (both meeting my dad and eating Tide Pods). (By the way, WTF are people thinking eating those small packets of washing detergent? And by people, I mean adults who are smart enough to put videos on YouTube. There's no reason we need to do PSAs for twenty-three-year-old Internet attention whores who choose to eat soap. For moms with babies, I get it. "Hey, new moms! Watch out that little Katie doesn't eat those packets that look a lot like candy . . ." But for adults to learn on the news: "Don't eat detergent, because you can die." They already know that! To report on the obvious is to do nothing but compel fools to continue eating the clothes-cleaning poison. That's right: I blame you, *Today* show!!! Sorry. I'm just dealing with a lot of Tide Pod stories right now. Onward.)

The trip to see my father became just a date on the calendar. I booked my flight from Austin to Little Rock and carried on with my life. *Nothing to see here.* (Imagine me whistling after I say, "Nothing to see here," like they always do on television from the fifties. Yeah, that was me playing it cool.)

It wasn't until I was on the flight to Little Rock that it thumped me in the ear: I was going to meet the man who helped bring me into this world, then disappeared over thirty years ago, and for all that time hid in plain sight. He lived no more than a few miles from me for a lot of the time I was growing up, but for that story you'll have to read my first book.

One of my favorite creatures is the butterfly. (It's not my absolute favorite. That would be dogs, with koalas coming in a close second. I got to hold a koala in Australia, and he didn't bite or take a crap on me, so I was pretty pumped. After that, the koala shot up the favorites list very fast.) I say I love butterflies because I love that feeling of butterflies in your stomach that you get when you're nervous. We don't have a lot of times in our lives when we get to be genuinely nervous about a potentially positive outcome. Being nervous is uncommon; it's uncomfortable; it's stressful. That's why it's awesome. Being nervous is how I feel alive. To me, it's a rush. A mental bungee jump.

On the plane to meet my dad, though, I wasn't nervous. At least not in the awesome way. I was overwhelmed with thoughts about where this whole thing would lead. I wondered if my father was suspicious of my motives. I'm the one who has yelled on the radio and written in a book that I was pissed about his sudden departure all those years ago. And yet here I was initiating contact by texting him out of the blue. What could he be imagining—that I wanted to beat him up? Or be best friends? Did I need a kidney?

I was trying to get into his head more than I was worried about what was going on in my own. This was no doubt an intellectual defense mechanism, because I knew that a few layers down, I was petrified.

As soon as my flight landed in Arkansas, I texted him that we should meet for lunch the following day at a BBQ restaurant I had found online and chosen for its convenient location. I had initially thought about meeting in a park or just on a bench somewhere, but then reconsidered. That was just too weird. If someone who I hadn't seen in years told me to meet him at a park in the middle of the day, I'd instantly assume it was because he wanted to jump me for money . . . maybe to buy that new kidney I was talking about.

The next day, at exactly noon, I drove into the parking lot of the BBQ joint and—*bam*—there he was, sitting inside his truck. I knew it was him because I had seen him in a couple of pictures over the years. And I also could just tell. He looked like me more than anyone else I'd ever met. Or should I say, I looked like him.

Now, I had purposely showed up right on time in order to avoid this situation. I hoped he'd be early and inside waiting on me. Not the opposite. This was now turning into a first-date-with-a-hot-chick experience. Except instead of a hot chick, insert "the man who abandoned me thirty years ago."

I turned off the gray Jeep Cherokee I had rented, got out, and walked directly into the restaurant. I didn't want to walk inside *with* him.

Who opens the door for who? Pass on that situation.

The awkward talk and walk, side by side? Pass on that, too.

The BBQ place was the kind where you order from a counter, get a number, seat yourself, and wait for your food. I was looking up at the menu above the counter when he walked in and stood right behind me. He was wearing a blue work uniform. Blue on blue, and extremely white tennis shoes. Let me commend his white shoes, by the way, because I know those were probably work shoes, and they were as clean as could be. I got a pair of white Yeezys and before I could get them out of the box, somehow they looked like they had been in a charcoal bath. White shoes are THAT hard to keep clean. So I respected that. He also had on a camouflage ball cap on top of his long hair.

With my dad too close to ignore and continue ordering, I

turned to him. "Hey, man. Good to see you," I said, reaching out my hand to shake his and thinking, Please don't try to hug me.

He didn't. He shook my hand and said it was good to see me as well. We had a brief, uncomfortable conversation about what to eat. (Luckily, I already knew what I wanted. I know what I want to eat before I get to a restaurant almost every time I go to one. I prepare for the menu as if it were a driving test. Although I don't have to cheat with menus like I do with driving tests. I've never NOT cheated the eyesight part of the driving test. You see, I *can't* see. I have one eye that simply doesn't work. My right eye only sees light and fuzzy shapes. And when I look into that machine with said eye, I see nothing but a bright yellow stain mocking my inadequacy. If you google the right things, you can memorize that current test. I shall say no more for fear of having my driver's license revoked, but, yes, I'm always trying to game the system.) Then I put in our order and sat in the back of the restaurant.

He was smaller than me. I liked that, because if things got ugly I knew I could take him to beatdown town, except for the small fact that I've never actually punched anyone. Still, I liked that I was bigger. My brain started to draw complex maps of the unknown terrain ahead.

What do I say first?

Did I really use the phrase "beatdown town"?

I'm such a loser.

I decided to go with thanking him for taking off work to meet me as an opener. Then I asked *the* most important question first. I mean, sitting in front of me was someone who was supposed to be the most important man in my life and I hadn't seen him in thirty years. Now was my chance to find out what I wanted to know more than anything else. So I just went for it. I asked it. Straight up.

"Will you pull your hat back?" I asked. "Do you still have all your hair?" He let out a nervous chuckle and pulled his hat back.

"I've still got it all," he said.

He wasn't bald! Or even losing his hair! As a matter of fact, he has lots and lots of it. He basically looks like everyone from Lynyrd Skynyrd. That was awesome, and I was grateful. He may not have bought school supplies, taught me how to shave, or awkwardly told me it was "normal for men to play with themselves," but he did give me good hair genes. And before you tell me, "Hair is all on your mom's side," that's BS. It's been proven 123,413,232 times that it can come from either or both. I have a lot of friends who are just as bald as their dad. So, hair. Check!

The food came. I noticed his hand was shaking when he took a bite of his sandwich—and that was pretty much the only bite he took. However nervous I felt on the plane yesterday or even in the parking lot a few minutes earlier, it was clear my dad was way more nervous. There was something about seeing how rattled he was that settled me down. When crazy situations arise, most of us fall into roles. Mine was the calm one. He hardly touched his food, but I was devouring mine. As I went through an entire rack of ribs, I had them bring me an extra plate for the bones and more paper towels.

We talked about what he does now (he works with my cousin Josh, who runs a roofing company) and about how he had been sober for a while.

"I'd really like to drink," I said, "but it doesn't seem to be a good spot for any of us with our genetics." He agreed and urged me to stay away from it since I've gone this long without touching the stuff.

He talked a lot about his horses. "I get back to my land whenever I can to make sure they are fed and taken care of," he said with obvious pride. I was happy to hear that.

I wanted to talk about jail. See, a lot of my family has been to jail and I wanted to know why. He told me he had only done a "few rounds" for dumb stuff, and for very small amounts of time. We talked about my cousin Derrick, who made the national news a couple of years earlier for escaping prison.

"I couldn't believe that it was on *Good Morning America*," I said. "The cops were calling asking if I knew anything."

He said the same thing happened to him. I think they showed up at the house of pretty much every Estell to see if Derrick was there. By the way, google "Derrick Estell prison escape." That's my first cousin!

I don't remember my dad asking me any questions. Part of me thinks that he listens to the show and reads things like this book, so he has a good idea of what's happening with me. Part of me thinks he was just too freaked out. Either way I was okay, because being in his physical presence was enough.

For once in my life, I just wanted to sit across from my dad and have a conversation, even if it was about nothing. And for forty-five minutes, over lunch, I did. Sure, he'll never be my "dad" in the way most people use the word, but by not reaching out to him because I was scared of rejection I wasn't giving either one of us a chance to change the story. As a defense mechanism, I had turned him into the Joker or Bane, a supervillain out to destroy my life. By avoiding him, I had made him into something much larger than he actually was—someone who has screwed up a lot, someone who is extremely flawed, someone just like me.

The End.

Except . . . not really. That was the perfect ending for this section: dramatic and heart-wrenching, with a hint of self-reflection. But I don't go down like that.

Can I first say how awkward it was for me to write the word "dad" in reference to the man I had lunch with? I just got tired of writing "biological father" in every paragraph. I wouldn't call him "dad" to anyone, except for the fact that I'm a lazy writer. I also won't call Kid Rock "Bob." (His real name is Robert Ritchie, and his friends call him Bob.) I've spent some time with Kid Rock recently through work, and everyone keeps telling me to call him "Bob." Even Kid Rock says, "Call me Bob." Won't do it. I nod and say, "You got it, Kid Rock!" He will always be freaking Kid Rock. And I'm a huge dork.

The real end of the story with my—gulp—"dad" is a lot less dramatic. We've exchanged a few texts since that lunch, and I plan to reach out next time I'm home. I never thought we were going to turn into Andy Griffith and his son, Opie. The greatest outcome from that lunch is that I will no longer NOT go home because he is around. This fairy-tale ending is still growing its wings. Hopefully nobody dies!

What I hope you take away from this is that sometimes we assign completely false narratives to stories because they make life easier to understand. I did. I imagined my real dad lying in bed at night, laughing like a maniac about how he had wronged his son. Totally false. He didn't like it any more than I did. But it was easier for me to believe that over the truth, because it allowed me to make him the bad guy. The truth is that he is just flawed.

I am also flawed, and I hope people can understand and forgive me like I have my dad.

HOW THE HECK IS THIS A SELF-HELP BOOK?

By now, you're probably wondering how this depressing story about a deadbeat dad and his neurotic son is going to lead to self-improvement, right?

I'll be honest. At first, I wasn't sure I wanted to write this book. I'm not a guy who looks for signs in the universe to tell him things. I believe that if you search hard enough for the answer you already know, you will find it. As human beings, we generally follow an instinct but still chase affirmation from something bigger than us to tell us that instinct is right. But I'm not a normal human being, and I'm not going to do that. I don't believe in luck. I don't believe in destiny. Instead, I believe that our lives are powered by countless microdecisions. Some dude found a million-dollar lottery ticket on the sidewalk walking to work one day. What if he hadn't gone to work? What if he hadn't chosen that sidewalk? What if he hadn't looked down at the ground? All of these are factors that we assign to luck. But I believe every single thing that happens to us, good or bad, is affected by decisions we make.

The title of this book should be a tip-off that this isn't going to be some think-positive-thoughts-to-success kind of program. I always come to things from an underdog's point of view, and who am I to offer any kind of "program," anyway? My preferred place to start is the bottom, where, as they say, you have nowhere to go but up. And when you start from the bottom and succeed, you also have a theme song. Cue Drake's "Started from the Bottom."

The point of the lunch-with-my-dad story isn't even that I had faced my biggest fear. For years and years, I had thought about meeting him, even at times obsessed over it, but I never, ever made a single attempt. As those years kept ticking by, the act of trying just got bigger and harder—and so I had to turn my dad into a villain to explain my inaction.

By giving the act of meeting my dad one legitimate, full-hearted try, I knew that no matter what happened, I wouldn't fail. At least not in the long run.

In my book (both literally and figuratively), failing isn't bad. Oftentimes, people won't try things because they're afraid to fail, but my philosophy in life is all about *winning by losing*. That might sound like a foreign concept, because the general rule is that if people are good at something, they win. But really, from all I've learned, the biggest winners are also the biggest losers. And I definitely put myself in the biggest loser category. Not to be confused with the TV show *The Biggest Loser*. The only episodes I've seen are the ones where the contestants bust through the paper of their old selves and *poof*, they are one hundred pounds lighter. That show makes losing a hundred pounds look pretty easy, even though obviously it isn't. I'd like to equate the finale of *The Biggest Loser* with your life. Most people will just see you bust through the paper in whatever transformation you've made and think, "Ah, that was so easy for you." But they don't know you've been grinding on a treadmill for hours when the cameras were off. They don't know you've been getting yelled at by Jillian Michaels for licking the plastic wrapping on a cookie a few too many times. They don't know! But I do know, because I'm someone who has failed so often that eventually I learned something useful to break the cycle. And I plan to give you the information to turn heartbreak and failure into inspiration.

I developed the strategies I lay out in this book (including embracing failure) out of necessity. I had a dysfunctional upbringing that lacked any of the resources—financial or cultural—that people typically need to succeed. And yet, I had big dreams for myself. I wanted to do more than follow the example of my parents and peers in my small, poor, dying Arkansas town. I wanted to beat my very bad odds. When you're trying to beat bad odds, you have to do more than what's expected (like going to college and working hard). A lot more. And you have to be your own champion.

None of that's easy, which is why I came up with these strategies to help me along. But let me say, they weren't right the first or second or ninety-third time I implemented them. And they continue to be partially wrong even today. I have figured out that you never completely figure it out. If that makes me sound like the Aristotle of Arkansas, so be it. Everything in life is a moving target. I set absolute goals (e.g., I'd like for my show to be heard in one hundred cities or to make my next romantic relationship last for more than eight whole days), but regardless of the result, I learn from it and keep going. Too many people in my life just blow in the wind and change what they want as the weather picks up. I'm basically Jim Cantore from the Weather Channel; I stand out in the hurricane and take it on to see what happens on the other side.

Take, for instance, this Category 3 hurricane that blew in just today, conveniently, as my deadline arrived to commit to writing this next piece of literary genius. My latest inspiration in the winning-by-losing game came just two hours ago in the form of being rejected *yet again* for a television show. If you haven't read my first book (*Bare Bones* by Bobby Bones, in case you already forgot), I should give some more backstory. That book started with me auditioning for a TV show. And ended many months later with me landing the part (yay!) but the network ultimately not picking up the show (boo!). And lots of life stories, both happy and sad in the middle . . .

Here we are. Again. I got a no on another TV show. But at least you didn't have to wait through an entire book to find out the ending. And it motivated me to start this book right.

(For your visual consideration: I'm sitting at a red desk, wearing a pair of blue shorts and a fake vintage AC/DC T-shirt—even though, for the most part, I think fake vintage shirts are so cornball. The problem I have with fake vintage shirts is that people wear them to look way cooler than they really are. Someone with real style or passion for a vintage band or piece of clothing would have many options to find a legitimate, authentic band shirt: eBay, thrift shops, Etsy. But nah, instead we find it at the mall or Target, buy it, and Wikipedia JUST enough about the band or album in case anyone asks us about it. My light blue AC/DC shirt that I'm wearing right now says 1974 JAILBREAK. I wasn't even born in 1974. I admit to being a cornball, but I would like to establish a new rule about wearing music T-shirts to simply look cool. If you are wearing an artist on your shirt, and you don't know at least five of the artist's songs when someone asks, you owe a five-dollar donation to the charity of that person's choice. With this rule now in place, either people will learn more about Merle Haggard or puppies will get fed! Either way, it's a win.)

So back to my latest rejection, which arrived in an e-mail, notifying me that a show I was executive producing had been turned down by a major network. This was one that I felt pretty sure was going to work (and I'm a very pessimistic person). It was about a couple of people in the country music world and their family life. Nothing earth-shattering, but we weren't trying to be groundbreaking here. The finished product was warm, funny, and not puke-inducingly fake. In reality-show terms, that's the best you can hope for. The network's test audiences gave it great reviews. And even so—*bam!*—nope.

My response could have been to curl up into a ball and binge-watch *The Walking Dead*, but I have a general rule: the bigger the disappointment, the harder I keep trying. A wise man once said, "Instead of crying, I keep on trying." And that wise man is me, because I just made that up. I think. Quote me on that unless you see it in a meme somewhere where Billy Graham or Gandhi said it. Otherwise, yeah. I just made that up.

I'm not going to give up or let this setback stop me from getting lots of TV shows on the air (and right now "lots" means one). So here I am, hours after being told NO to yet another TV show, taking a few notes on what I've learned this time around, and bouncing back with the knowledge that if I keep trying and getting better at making television, something will actually work—and I'll Win by Losing.

Now, I can imagine you may *not* be very inspired by this kind of advice from a guy like me. I'm no longer broke, I have radio's biggest country music morning show, wrote a bestselling book, and front a band that has also had a number-one record and song—and here I am patting myself on the back for recovering after not *also* getting a TV show. But if you knew where I came from, you might understand the power of my mindset and see how it has helped to get me to where I am today. Like many other people, I grew up with so much adversity and negativity, it would have been easy to get overwhelmed and give in. But by turning negatives into positives, losing into a journey to winning, I have been able to overcome the odds that were against me and change them into motivation for my success. It's that mentality I hope to pass on in this book to others who are struggling.

I was raised in the small town of Mountain Pine, Arkansas (population seven hundred—and that's optimistic). Typical of a company mill town after the mill shuts down, it's an impoverished place. When I was growing up there, money wasn't a thing people missed, because no one had any of it. If you give a sixteen-year-old a BMW, take it away from him, and replace it with a Kia, he's probably going to be upset. We didn't even know BMWs existed. It was the same with options in life. Hardly anyone left Mountain Pine to pursue his or her own dreams. We didn't even know BIG dreams were allowed to happen. The folks who I grew up with weren't mad about that; we just knew our place. And we knew it because we saw it every day all around us. No one told us we were stuck. But no one told us we weren't, either. Suffice it to say, my hometown was not conducive for a kid's dreams of creating his own media empire.

Yet, even within this poor community, I always felt that I was coming from a disadvantage. My mom, who struggled her entire life with alcohol and drug addiction, had a hard time holding down a job and often left me in the care of my grandmother for long stretches. For years I resented the fact that I was a food-stamps kid, a head-lice student, a connoisseur of the finest welfare checks. I hated it. I blamed everyone around me, and I loathed other kids with the flimsiest of safety nets, because I had none. I never saw this uncertainty for the strength it gave me.

It wasn't until much later that I realized the dividends all those years of suffering and struggling have paid. Starting from zero meant I had nothing to lose. Most important, though, having no options kept me focused in a way that would have been impossible otherwise. There was no plan B for me. I didn't have the luxury of a fallback career. My only choice was to keep plugging away even as I failed. And failed. And failed.

But I didn't just fail; I also kept notes. And learned from my mistakes. And kept my head in the game. As my stepdad used to say to me when I was in my teens, "You can't catch a fish if your hook isn't in the water." I kept my freaking hook in the water. All the time. Even until this day. My hook is *never* coming out of the water.

John Mayer once told me that he figured out the world was "bendable" when he was around nineteen years old. Although I had never used his fascinating term for the experience he was describing, I knew exactly what he was talking about. I didn't discover I could move around in the world freely until my early twenties.

Around the time I graduated from college, I realized that it wasn't just me who felt insecure and at times defeated; most people didn't know what they were doing, either. They were also figuring it out as they went—and that's nothing to be ashamed of. If I just showed confidence in a direction I had chosen (false confidence or not), that was good enough. I didn't need to have any special knowledge or power to give something I wanted to try a shot. I just needed to do it—and there's a lot of freedom in that line of thinking.

I believe with all my heart that if you want something bad enough, with the right life choices and work ethic, you can get it. (Unless it's physically impossible to attain, so don't hit me with "I want to dunk a basketball but I'm an overweight five foot three." It's not going to happen for you, dude.)

WHEN YOU'RE STARTING OUT NOT AT HOMEPLATE BUT OUTSIDE THE BALLPARK

I didn't come from the toughest background of all time. I understand that I had privileges others didn't. I met a guy a couple of months ago who had been homeless all the way through high school. Still, he graduated, went on to college, and even earned an advanced degree. So, when I say the privileged have it easier, we are all a little more privileged than somebody else. It doesn't just go one way.

The reason I talk about where I come from is because I come from the same type of background that a lot of America comes from: small town; week-to-week paycheck; some sort of not-so-pleasant family situation that may or may not include a lot of illegal substances. You may be a rich kid who had a terrible family situation. We all have our baggage. I'm not the only one. Mine's bad. Others have worse. Who is capable of judging on that kind of scale? I used to build seawalls (one of the many jobs I've done—you'll read more about those later), and the worst part of that was carrying large white buckets of wet concrete up a hill. They'd bruise your legs, hurt your hands, and there was always another waiting for you at the bottom of the hill. We all have our different buckets of concrete.

I know there are a lot of people out there who can relate to me. And it's for folks who don't have anyone to say, "Not only do

I know where you come from, but *you can do this,*" that I'm writing this book.

When you are coming from less (and there's a lot of us), you have to give more to get equal to the rest of the world. It's not fair. But the fact that we have to fight our way to the top makes us so much stronger when we eventually get there. How counterintuitive is that? When we start from worse, it can make us better! But it's a real advantage if we use it the right way.

FAILING UPWARD

If we take a look at some of the most successful people in our culture, you'd be surprised how often they failed. I could give you a million examples, because I've studied this. But here are just a few striking ones:

WALT DISNEY

Walt Disney was one of the most creative and innovative minds of the twentieth century. He created freakin' Mickey Mouse! He dreamed up Disney World! He produced over six hundred animated movies! No way he ever sucked! Right? Wrong.

- He was fired from a local newspaper because he lacked creativity. (Can you believe that someone thought this dude lacked creativity? That's like me getting fired because I don't have enough *B*s in my name.)
- His first business went bankrupt.
- He was told his little mouse was a terrible idea because it would terrify women.

- More than three hundred people turned down investing in his crazy theme park about that same terrifying mouse.

But Walt believed, and now there's probably not a person on the globe who doesn't know the name Disney. Because he kept on, that "terrible idea" turned into a global multibillion-dollar corporation of parks and resorts; broadcast, cable, and radio stations; a killer movie studio; toys; apps; clothing. . . . And I think his head is still frozen somewhere, regardless of what anyone says. (Okay, so maybe not *all* of Walt's ideas were winners, but you get the point.)

STEVE JOBS

Whenever you read articles or books that talk about the cofounder of Apple, they always bring up that he, like Bill Gates, dropped out of college—and still became one of the most successful people in the universe. But that was just one of his "failures." The man, who basically created the way we talk to each other now through technologies like the iPhone and iPad, had a whole bunch of massive product failures with that company he started in his garage. Even after he became a success, he was fired as an executive from the company he created! People took many things away from the famous biography of him by Walter Isaacson—that he was controlling, that he had a big ego—but what I saw was a guy who people considered nuts and who wouldn't give up when it came to his vision. I hope to be considered as crazy one day.

STEPHEN KING

Writers, like actors, are famous for getting rejected. It goes with the territory. But the bestselling horror writer took rejection to a whole other level. "By the time I was fourteen the nail in my wall would no longer support the weight of the rejection slips impaled upon it," he wrote in *On Writing: A Memoir of the Craft.* "I replaced the nail with a spike and went on writing." Still, when his first book, *Carrie,* was rejected by thirty publishers, even he got discouraged. You can't blame him for throwing the manuscript in the trash, which is what he did. Luckily for him, his wife fished it out and encouraged him to give it one last shot. I guess the thirty-first time was the charm, because it was accepted and became a runaway bestseller. Since then he's sold more than 350 million copies of his books worldwide, many of which have been made into movies that scare the crap out of kids everywhere. And by kids, I also mean adult men in their thirties who wear dark-rimmed glasses.

ELVIS PRESLEY

Let's talk about him for a minute. We know him as pretty much the first great American solo artist. But when he went to the Grand Ole Opry, they basically said, "Dude, don't come back. You can't sing." Then they advised him to go back to being a gravedigger, which is what he had been doing to make money. He couldn't even get into an a cappella group—and nobody likes a cappella. Except Pentatonix. Pentatonix! You're cool.

"Ode to Failure," My Poem-ish Thing from My Tedx Talk in Nashville

Even Disney got fired
The opposite of winning . . .
Now we love that cartoon couple
Mickey Mouse and Minnie.

Honest Abe failed at business
How much lower can you get?
He dusted it off, got up again
Became our sixteenth president.
Do you know how many Jobs . . .
Steve was fired from?
Now we're all swiping Apples
So much it hurts our thumbs.
Oprah was let go as a reporter
At the age of twenty-three.
Oprah Winfrey in the daytime
Highest-paid host on TV.
The Beatles were turned down
By some record label jerk.
You tell McCartney or Lennon
That his music wouldn't work?
And I don't stand here before you
As the picture of success.
I just got real good at losing
And held out longer than the rest.

The pattern is real; the people who make it are the ones who don't quit. They are borderline crazy about what they are trying to achieve. They fail. But they don't quit.

That's been true in my life as well. Out of thirty radio jobs I applied to in my career, I only got three of them. And thirty is a low estimate. Those are the ones I can remember not getting. Still, one in ten—that's a lot of freakin' rejection. Sometimes a formal rejection was the best thing that could have happened. Want to feel like you really suck? Send a full package—your résumé, tapes, the full thing—and hear *nothing* back. Not even crickets to keep me company. That happened to me more times than I was told no.

I wanted a job so badly that one time I placed a tape of my radio show, my résumé, and my picture in a pizza box. Then I put on some khakis and a button-up shirt to deliver the pizza box to the station myself. I figured if the program director thought it was pizza, he would open it and take note of my ability to go the extra mile creatively. I walked into the station and the program director was in the reception area! Jackpot! "This is for Peter Cottontail," I announced. (Not his real name, duh.) Freaking Peter Cottontail opened the box, excitedly looked inside, and then mumbled, "This isn't even pizza. This is an f-ing demo tape." That was right before he threw it into the garbage. Needless to say, I moonwalked out of that place and did the ol' "nothing to see here" whistling trick until I got far away!

Do I enjoy bombing out? No, of course not. But I've learned far more from my failures than I have from my successes. It's almost a feather-in-the-cap-type thing when you mess up and can figure out what went wrong, because then hopefully you won't make the same mistake again. The next time, I sent a pizza with the demo tape. I still didn't get the job, though. It's like the baby that touches the stove. Most babies don't give that stove a second grab. I try not to give boneheaded moves a second grab. And rarely a third. (If you keep making the same mistake over and over, it's time to call a shrink—because there's some hidden cog in your brain that's sabotaging your best intentions, and you gotta work that crap out. See: every relationship I've ever been in.)

University of Alabama head football coach Nick Saban once said, "I don't want to waste a failure." That struck me. Every failure is some kind of opportunity in disguise. In fact, I'm only writing this book because I failed at pitching a children's book.

True story. I went from publisher's office to publisher's office, selling my idea for a kids' book. Except no one was buying. Finally someone (my wonderful publisher) decided that I should do a kids' book "later" (still waiting) and begin my career as an author with a motivational memoir instead.

I was petrified to write that thing, and, frankly, at first I didn't think it was very good. I wasn't sure if my stories were relatable, inspirational, or at all entertaining to anyone. Particularly smart folks like you, who read real-life books!

Smash cut to my first book making the *New York Times* bestseller list. And it never would have happened if I hadn't failed at writing a children's book. It's unbelievable looking back at the turn of events that led to *Bare Bones* and all the awesome people I met during the process. Turns out readers not only sympathized but mostly empathized with my stories. My whole perspective on my own life story changed because I failed.

Fail. Learn. Repeat. Fail. Learn. Repeat. Keep failing, until you don't.

Don't believe me? I get it. I'm just a radio dork/barely decent comedian/mediocre musician. Why would you take my word for it? I am about to get all smart on you and reference something pretty amazing. How about a Stanford professor and one of the world's leading researchers in the area of motivation, who has spent her life studying the secret to success? After decades of researching how people achieve, psychology professor Carol Dweck discovered a simple but revolutionary concept she calls "mindset." Basically, she breaks mindset into two different types—fixed and growth. Those who have a fixed mindset think that their ability and intelligence are fixed and that talent is the biggest predictor of success. If you have a growth mindset, on the other hand, you believe you can improve any of your natural skills through "dedication and hard work." As the good professor writes: "Brains and talent don't bring success. . . . They can stand in the way of it."

That's really something coming from a lady who's taught at Harvard, which is ground zero for brains! But I get what she is saying. Knowing you can improve is a highly undervalued form of intelligence. Some of the smartest people I knew in high school and college have struggled. But the folks who always worked their faces off are all doing fine. There is no genius in effort. There is no genius in fortitude. I've found that the most successful self-made people are those who are great at chasing an idea hard, screwing it up, learning from it, and getting right back into the chase. It's about keeping up the hustle. I love the hustle.

Dweck is a huge fan of effort, arguing that you can always improve no matter where you are starting from, and that mindset "creates a love of learning and a resilience essential for great accomplishment. Virtually all great people have had these qualities." In her book *Mindset: The New Psychology of Success,* she shares how her research began with a desire to figure out how people deal with failure. She created a study where kids were presented with puzzles that got increasingly harder. Some kids simply gave up, while others embraced the challenge and got psyched on the struggle so they could get better at doing puzzles. "I always thought you coped with failure or you didn't," she wrote. "I never thought anyone loved failure. Were these alien children or were they on to something?"

It seems those kids were on to something and so was Dweck, whose theory has had wide-ranging implications for the fields of business, sports, and education. "Failure is information," Dweck later told *Forbes*. "We label it failure, but it's more like, 'This didn't work, and I'm a problem solver, so I'll try something else.'"

That gives us failures some real hope! As long as we can find the resilience to bounce back from defeat and the consciousness to learn from it, we can achieve "success." According to people who study this stuff, a lot of it depends on your attitude toward whatever you find hard. If you think that you're a loser *because* you didn't get math, the girl, or the job, you're probably going to have an even harder time making a go of it next time. *If* there's a next time. But if you can flip the idea of rejection on its head and turn it into a chance to improve your algebra or your pickup lines, then you aren't stuck at the bottom of the heap but at the beginning of a long, optimistic hike up the mountain.

If failure is information, according to Dweck, I got a huge data dump on me during my network TV debut, when I was tasked with interviewing Jason Aldean on an awards show.

The plan was for the chart-topping singer and me to talk for a solid two minutes, which is an eternity for live TV/radio/anything. Look in your mirror and just try to talk for two minutes straight. Then come back to reading this, and you'll have a lot more empathy for this story.

With microphone in hand and a ton of questions and witty comments in my head, I waited backstage with Jason for our cue. Moments before we were set to take the stage, a producer yelled, "We have fifteen seconds! Not two minutes." Fifteen seconds! That is hardly enough time to say "Jason Aldean." This was no longer an interview but an intro. Before I could process the information, the producer had counted me down and I was onstage. Away I went, and by "away I went," I mean I screamed like a parrot. If I could write how my intro sounded, it would go something like this: "Jason Aldeaaaan is neeext, babyyy, wooooooooosadfsldkfaljsdflsd." And then the camera shut off, someone grabbed my mic, and I was led to my seat.

You can always tell when you don't do a good job, because no one wants to talk to you afterward. Sometimes people will talk to you—but not about the presentation you just gave in the office or your performance in a community theater production but about something totally random. While I walked back to my seat, a friend said, "Man, your jacket looked great on camera." He might as well have said, "You sucked, and I need something else to compliment you on because otherwise I'm gonna feel really awkward."

No one would have blamed me if I chose to ignore the whole embarrassing moment where I choked on national TV. Instead, when I was back on the radio Monday, I played my parrot imitation over and over. Everyone laughed, which is always the aim of my morning show, but I was doing something for myself. By repeatedly exposing my screw-ups, no matter how painful, I minimize my chance of repeating them. I can promise you I'll never sound like a wounded chicken on national TV again.

MY BIGGEST FAILURE: ANDY RODDICK

I don't want you thinking I'm the only one who fails big time. That's why I asked some of today's top talents in sports, entertainment, and media to share their biggest failures.

First up is one of my best friends, Andy Roddick. He also happened to be one of the top tennis players in the world before he retired in 2012. He's an athlete with heart, having established the Andy Roddick Foundation, which since 2001 has raised more than ten million dollars to provide education and sports-based mentoring to low-income youth. Whether on the court or advocating for kids, Andy is a true fighter. As *Tennis* magazine described Andy: "He kept working, kept searching for new ways to win, kept listening to new voices and kept himself near the top of the game."

"My biggest failure is not winning Wimbledon. I lost to Roger Federer in three finals and, for better or worse, that defeat defines me to most of the public. I have been the number-one-ranked tennis player in the world; won the U.S. Open; finished in the Top 10 of ATP's rankings for nine straight years—but the only thing people want to talk about at Starbucks is 'that match with Roger.' While I still have moments where I feel sick to my stomach when I think of how close I was to beating the greatest ever in a Wimbledon final, that match completely changed my relationship with tennis fans—for the better. Viewing me through a different lens, they began to always pull for me, say hello, or tell me where they were for 'that match.' I went from a temperamental, polarizing, arrogant, sometimes misunderstood (by my own doing) figure, to simply . . . Andy. Press was easier. Public practices were more fun. I was now flawed and relatable. My biggest failure created thousands of these mini moments, simple interactions that meant so much to me. I don't know if I would have appreciated that kind of human attention if I had won that match. I might have taken self-absorption to another level. Who knows? I love where I'm at now—and I wouldn't be here if I hadn't lost at Wimbledon."

WHAT THIS BOOK IS NOT ABOUT

Life is weird. Or maybe, better put, frustrating. Or how about this? Unfair. A hundred right decisions might not make you a success, but one really bad decision can ruin you.

I was at the gym today and a guy there started talking to me about his brother, who had crashed into a tree because he was driving drunk. Now he's in the hospital on a ventilator. Doctors aren't sure he's going to make it. The guy was naturally upset because of his brother's condition, but he was also surprised that his brother had been drinking and driving. He had never known him to drink that much, let alone get into a car drunk. The only thing he could be thankful for was that his brother didn't hit anyone else.

I don't drink, never have. My parents' own struggles with booze have scared me straight. But I could still relate to the scenario. That one decision to drink and get behind the wheel, which may change the course of his life forever—if he lives—probably all came down to a single moment of at best, not thinking clearly, and at worst, making a stupid choice.

Drinking and driving and almost dying is a morbid example of how with just one bad decision you can lose everything.

So I want to make a *very clear* distinction between failure and screwing up. Failure is when you're working toward a positive goal and you either have a setback or have to start from square one. Screwing up is when you're *not thinking* or when you're making excuses for why something's okay when you know it really isn't. This has nothing to do with risk. Sometimes you have to take risks. I've taken many, but they've all been calculated. There's a big difference between calculated risk and risky behavior. Risk is what billionaire hedge fund managers assess before making a stock trade. Risky behavior is what teenagers do in the back of parked cars.

Rewards are much harder to come by than consequences. It's not a fair fight. But "fair" is just a fairy tale anyway. Don't let that be your excuse to throw it all away with one stupid choice. Keep fighting and you'll get there (in one piece).

HOW TO DO THIS THING
(OR AT LEAST MY WAY OF DOING IT)

I'm fully aware that it's way easier to type these words than to actually do what they spell out. When you get divorced or let go from your job, it feels like crap. In those moments, it's hard to find a positive takeaway.

I do a lot of speaking, especially at schools. Whenever I do, the kids ask some version of the question "How do I become successful?"

It's such a big idea that it's almost meaningless. Except that it's the most meaningful question in the world. They're asking me what we all want to know: Am I going to do something with my life? Am I going to matter? Am I going to be all right? I wish I had an answer that made life easier, because if I did I'd use it for myself.

I'm still working on and learning about myself all the time. I think about my revelation after recently meeting my dad. As we were walking out of the BBQ place, I thanked him again for taking off from work and meeting with me.

"You're welcome," he said, turning to look me in the eye. "It was weird having a day off."

"You don't take many days off?" I asked.

"Hardly ever. I end up thinking about sad sh** too much."

In that moment, I saw a mirror of myself and realized that the man I had turned into a supervillain was just a flawed and vulnerable person like me—and like most of us.

Unless you are a sociopath or a Tim Tebow, basically we are all the same: normal freaking humans. When I put myself in my dad's position (he was sixteen and in a bad place when he had me), I had more compassion for who he was and the decisions he had made in his life.

There are no easy answers, and that's kind of the point. I want people to feel better about the struggle. So when those kids in the auditorium ask me how to be successful, I ask them the same thing that I'll ask you in this book.

Can you fight, grind, and repeat?

Fight. Grind. Repeat. This isn't just something I use in my speeches at schools. I say it over and over again on the radio. I say it to myself. I have these words written on the wall at home; on many of my workout shirts; and on my chair at work (thanks, Garth). I even have them tattooed on my scrotum. (Okay, that last one's a lie. I'm not that tough.)

Because this phrase is such a huge part of my identity, people often ask me how I came up with it. Here's what I can tell you: it wasn't something I gave a lot of thought. Once I get past stage one of thinking, I start to overthink. That's when things get murky, and I usually land in trouble. "Fight, grind, repeat" was born one day after I'd worked fifty-three days in a row doing radio shows, comedy sets, shows with my band, and a few TV appearances.

I was exhausted to the depths of my soul (and I'm someone who has to wake up every morning at 3 A.M. for work, so that's saying something). To get through the last few days of this grueling stretch I needed something to hang on to, something to say. I needed a reminder of why I was doing all of this. There's nothing like a half-empty theater where the few people who are there aren't laughing at your jokes to make you want to call it quits for good. (Especially if you're running on three hours of sleep a night.)

Fight. Grind. Repeat. Those three simple words were enough to shift my psychological state from defeat to, if not victory, at least the will to stay in the game.

Fight: Because every day is a fight. In some form or other. It could be a fight from within to push yourself to a new limit, or it could be against one of the many people in this world who want to tell you no.

Grind: The thing is, when a fight starts out, there's a lot of adrenaline. But that's quickly drained and what you're left with is technique and stamina. This is the everyday stuff that's not cool or interesting or all that brave. It's waking up at 3 A.M. so that you're never late (if you're me) or sitting down to fill out those college applications. The little details of working toward what will most likely be failure (at least for a while)—that's the Grind. This is where it gets hard.

Repeat: Now take the Fight, the Grind, the failure—and then do it all again. And again. And again. The Repeat is truly the only way to separate yourself from the pack, and where it gets really hard. It's also where you'll find true success.

I'm going to tell you lots of stories about my being really crappy at things until I wasn't anymore. To add some variety, I'm also going to share stories about cool and influential people such as Charles Esten and Walker Hayes who were told they weren't so hot, either. Hopefully, we'll all learn something. If not, at least you'll get a chuckle out of my ability to muck things up.

Ready? Let's do this.

Welcome to my somewhat motivational, somewhat humorous, but very reasonably priced book, *Fail Until You Don't*. And if you're listening to the audiobook, thanks for buying it! With my last book, I thought the audiobook was just part of the deal, meaning I'd have to read many hours as part of my contract. NOPE! They paid me extra to read it. Bonus!! Here's to a positive attitude, and hopefully another audiobook.

WHAT ARE YOUR FIGHTING WORDS?

There isn't anything earth-shattering about the three words "Fight, Grind, Repeat." They are just the ones that work for me. Like a mantra, I say them out loud at times when I'm just not feeling "it," or when that alarm goes off and I didn't get to sleep until midnight the night before. I'll say them before a single eye opens. I believe in them.

If they work for you, too, go for it and use them. But maybe you just aren't feeling them. If not, find three different words that work for you.

Take out your smartphone, computer, pad and paper—whatever is easiest for you to put ideas down. Brainstorm a bunch of words for each category. Maybe less negative words work for you (like "Dream, Hard Work, Revision"). Or maybe you go for humor ("Crap, Crappier, Crappiest").

The actual words don't matter; it's the concepts behind them. Whatever words stick in your head and stay in your heart are the ones you should use to know that you'll be bad at stuff when you first start out and that that shouldn't stop you from pursuing your dreams. In other words, it's okay to suck—just don't give up.

Just a warning: this book is going to seem really negative at times. And at times it's going to be quite inspirational. I struggle with that balance even in life. And you could argue with me about every single point in this book. Because in the end, we are all wrong, all the time. See how negative that sounds? Get ready for a master class in Bobby's life theory.

Part 1

FIGHT

1

WHAT IS THE FIGHT?

I exercise a lot. I try to do it for at least an hour, five or six days a week. And I *hate* exercising. It's the worst. There's not a moment of working out where I think, Oh, this is just fine. Nope. Torture. Every minute. For me, it's like waking up at three o'clock in the morning—something I've done for the last fourteen years, thanks to the fact that I run a national morning radio show. I hate waking up way before the crack of dawn, too, but I do it because otherwise I wouldn't get to keep my radio show. So, the long-term payoff is way nicer than the momentary pain. It's the same with working out. The feeling of muscle exhaustion and mental victory when I'm done is so much better than the pain I went through to get there. (Plus, working out is how I maintain my girlish figure.)

But because I exercise a lot—and hate it—I'm always on the

lookout for new workouts. I've tried everything from jogging to lifting to spending all my money on those Billy Blanks DVDs. Yes, I was once an avid Tae Bo disciple (which, I may add, made me quite popular with the middle-aged moms I worked out with at the gym in my apartment complex). I'll do something a ton, get bored, and then move on.

Bored was the state I was in when, several months ago, I noticed a boxing gym near where I live in Nashville. I didn't know anyone at the gym or anything about it, but I decided to give it a go. (Trained as I am in the Blanks method of martial arts on steroids, my hands are lethal weapons. Okay, not really, but I figured the gym would probably just be a lot of moms toning their arms and taking out their frustrations in the ring. It was my kind of place.) I called the number in the window one weekend and said, "Hey, I want to come in and box."

What I didn't realize when I made an appointment was that I had booked a one-on-one session with a boxing coach. I thought I was signing up for a group class with the ladies. Instead I met a former trainer of pro boxers and other professional athletes, who looked like he could be one himself. Boxing was the hardest physical activity I'd ever done. And I was immediately hooked. (Although, don't get me wrong; I still much prefer *after* I'm done boxing to before I've started my boxing workout.) I immediately booked three sessions, then nine, then twenty. Ever since I walked into that gym, I've been boxing so much that I'm now considering opening a gym of my own. (If you know anything about me, you know I'm a person of extremes.)

You're probably wondering what makes boxing so great, particularly for a guy who isn't fond of physical exertion and only brags about going to beatdown town. Simply put, boxing is a challenge, and I like to be challenged. Whether it's performing onstage, interviewing famous musicians, or exercising, I actually enjoy the uncomfortable feeling when something is unfamiliar and hard enough to make me consider quitting. And boxing, if nothing else, is really hard. It's by far the most grueling exercise I've ever done. And I've done them all. I did an Olympic-distance triathlon, cheated during a marathon, got into the cult of Cross-Fit, considered myself a recreational bodybuilder, stretched it out in yoga. Well, that's not ALL of them, but it's a lot. And boxing is the most mentally and physically taxing of them all. Before I got into the ring, I thought the sport was just about who can punch the other person in the face the most. Now I understand it's about muscular strength, cardiovascular endurance, agility, strategy, and pain tolerance.

I'm not a boxer. I'm not even pretending to be one. Come on, I'm skinny and wear glasses. I'm never going to get in the ring and try to fight another human in any kind of real way. When I talk about training, I'm not paying money for someone to punch me in the face fifty times. The goal isn't to front that I'm something I'm not—or lose any teeth. (I saved a long time to pay for these teeth, which were once terrible due to the fact that when I was a kid growing up poor in Arkansas, the dentist was as foreign a concept as the queen of England. Since earning a decent paycheck, I've become very well acquainted with the field of dentistry. My new teeth are amazing, and I have no shame whatsoever about telling you that they are bought and paid for. Shout-out to Dr. Cutbirth. That was not a paid shout-out, by the way. Although maybe I can get some sort of rebate by throwing his name in here.)

Back to boxing . . . The kind of boxing I do means I won't lose my teeth, but I can still take some pretty nasty blows that result in big old bruises. In order to avoid getting hurt in the ring, even in the mildest of training sessions (the ones that are over an hour of nonstop cardio, with added weights and core work thrown in, and barely time to get a drink of water or towel off your eyeballs covered in sweat), you have to work not only on your conditioning and footwork but also on how best to position your body to minimize the impact of your opponent's punches.

Because, just like in life, you are going to get hit in the ring. So you need to plant your body at the right angle so you are only grazed instead of absorbing a full shot to the nose.

How do you put yourself in the best position to succeed?

That's not just my boxing coach talking. That is the perfect metaphor for the Fight. It begins with setting up the right foundation so you can feel your strongest.

I'm constantly working on my footwork and rhythm when I'm in the ring, which isn't all that different from how I think about my regular life. Whether it's being on time for work or how I talk to people in meetings, these are the disciplined, small actions that become the sum total of my behavior. Each step counts, even if they are easily forgotten or dismissed for a million different reasons.

Maintaining your stamina and confidence is that much harder when you get punched in the side of the head. No one wants to get into a fight and be outmaneuvered. But it happens. When hits are coming at you quickly, how do you regain your composure and find the spot where you can take a punch and turn it back over again? Like Mike Tyson said, "Everyone has a plan until they get punched in the mouth."

Whether it's boxing, work, or love, my plan is always to plan to get punched in the mouth. In my life, when my radio show has bad ratings, a theater full of people don't laugh at a joke, or another relationship falls apart, it feels like I'm getting punched in the face. During those times, I deflect the shot as much as I can, learn from it, and use that knowledge to my *advantage*. That, for me, is the Fight.

IT'S ALL RIGHT TO FIGHT

Fighting is usually thought of as a bad thing. When you're a kid, your parents and teachers tell you not to fight and get mad at you if you do. As an adult, there are the folks for whom everything is a fight. You know, the guy who honks his horn as soon as the light turns green, then speeds up alongside your car to make sure you fully understand how much he doesn't appreciate your driving skills right before he cuts in front of you. Or the person who sends back every dish at every restaurant, blaming the poor waiter or waitress for never getting it right. Constantly battling the entire world because you have some deeper issue you're not facing is no way to live. That's exhausting for you and everyone you come in contact with—and it's *not* the kind of fighting I'm talking about.

My kind of Fight isn't about negativity. It is about survival. It is in my DNA.

It all goes back to that small, poor kid who grew up in a small, poor town just trying to keep his head above water. Fighting might have been part of my nature from birth, but it was also how I nurtured myself into something better than what I was born into. Socioeconomically, I had to work extra hard to catch up to my peers. I had jobs before anyone else my age. I'm not bragging that I was some kind of business genius. I didn't create a state-of-the-art lemonade stand or invent the gluten-free Bitcoin. I was just out raking leaves as soon as school was over until it got dark. No, I was never the one with the brilliant idea; I was just the one out doing *anything* I could for a dollar.

Money wasn't the only area of struggle. Physically, I also had to do more just to meet the average. Athletically, I was never the fastest runner. Never had the best hands. Nor could I hit the ball the farthest. Heck, I only have one working eyeball. (My right eye only sees light. It's never been able to perceive color or any real definition, so my brain doesn't even try. I wore a patch as a kid to try to fix it, but no dice. Hence my life of cheating on those driving tests we talked about earlier.) I made up for my lack of visual depth perception and puny frame by putting in hours of training. I would get to practice first, or beg to get in the field house to work out even when we didn't have practice. The effort paid off; I was drafted third overall by the Chicago Cubs in the 1999 baseball draft. HA! Kidding! But I was an all-conference first baseman and named to the all-district tournament team as well as defensive player of the year. And don't get me started on my football accolades (mostly because there aren't very many).

I've always felt like I had to work harder in life—and despite all that's gone right, I still feel that way. I'm constantly fighting to improve.

Every day is a fight to get ahead. There are the internal fights with myself: to prepare for the best show possible; to land jokes funnier for my stand-up act; to write better songs for my band. There are also my constant fights with the rest of the world: with others who want to take my job, to beat me in the ratings, or generally to see me fail.

My battles are not only self-interested. I also fight for causes I am passionate about: St. Jude Children's Research Hospital, which treats kids with cancer and other life-threatening diseases; the Andy Roddick Foundation, launched by my good friend, which gives children from disadvantaged backgrounds awesome after-school experiences; and Austin Pets Alive, a no-kill animal shelter that does amazing work in Central Texas. I might not be the most articulate defender of these organizations, but I'll be the loudest, screaming on the radio, from the stage, in interviews, or in the pages of my books.

Enthusiasm is my way of combating the fact that I'm never the most talented, smartest, or anything-est person in the room—or profession, while we're at it. (I was just recently inducted into the National Radio Hall of Fame at age thirty-seven, making me the youngest member in the organization's history, and I started my speech with those exact words, "I'm not the . . . *est* person at anything." I didn't say a word, just *est*. Now that I think about it, I don't know if it made sense to anyone but me.)

My mediocrity has only become more obvious as I've gained a little bit of fame and entered arenas where everyone and their uncle are endowed with incredible gifts.

Take awesome artist Walker Hayes, who for my band The Raging Idiots cowrote with me and produced the song "Na-maste," which was the number-one comedy song for weeks on the *Billboard* chart. Working with him in the studio, I couldn't keep up with how his brain processed music. It was like listening to someone speak a language I didn't know existed.

I didn't get defensive or freaked out when all I could do was sit like a dummy by Walker's side as he worked his magic. I'm able to enjoy myself in moments like that, because I've had a lot of practice. I'm used to being out of my depth, which happens all the time. It's a natural by-product of constantly trying to get better.

I was definitely out of my league when I did podcasts with John Mayer and the songwriter and record producer Busbee. These two guys went on about philosophy and art in a way that made it clear they were on a totally different plane than me intellectually. Although I pride myself on having learned a lot about music and culture from my surroundings, moments like when John described the sounds, tones, and overall recording of "Gravity" blew my mind. Where I just heard a good song, he heard the micro details that come from having a hypertrained and talented ear. As confused as I might have been, I was just happy to hear experts talk in a way they would only talk to other experts. It was as if someone got to an advanced level of Super Mario Bros. and then handed me the controller. I wasn't good enough at the video game to get there myself, but to experience what the super pro gamers feel like was really freaking cool.

FIGHTER IN THE SPOTLIGHT: WALKER HAYES

This talented singer-songwriter is the dictionary definition of a fighter. After his two debut singles didn't do what his record company hoped they would, he was dropped by his label. Meanwhile his wife, Laney, was pregnant with their fifth child! The music business doesn't care how many mouths you have to feed. If you don't hit the charts high, that's it, game over. So Walker took a job doing the graveyard shift at Costco. His hours—4 A.M. to 10 A.M.—meant he could still pursue his dreams during regular business hours. While he struggled with paying the mortgage, he also struggled with alcoholism. Eventually, not only did he get sober but he also used the struggle as inspiration for one of the songs ("Beer in the Fridge") that got him signed to a new label and named one of *Rolling Stone's* 2017 "10 New Country Artists You Need to Know."

"I draw strength from a bunch of stuff. The example I wanna set for my kids. The husband I wanna be to my wife. The son I wanna be for my parents. The singer-songwriter I wanna be for this town. The man I wanna be for myself. I have been given gifts, and it's my responsibility to share them in order to leave this world better than I found it," Walker says. "I feel like 'life' should be spelled F I G H T. Success and sobriety aren't all they are cracked up to be. Success just makes me want more success, and even though I'm not getting messed up, I'm still pretty messed up. It's always a fight."

I'm never the guy who tries to be intimidating because of my skills or good looks (okay, stop laughing at that last one). I'm just the guy who shows up. If I have any talent at all, it is the willingness to fight. But I don't know that I can even call it a talent, since I've worked on that, too.

I pride myself on not being the best. Never have been. Everything and anything I'm halfway decent at now, I really sucked at during some point in my life. Sometimes I continue to suck and still do it. Case in point: my radio career. I have a job where I make a great living talking—and I'm not even a good speaker! I speak in broken sentences. I speak too fast. My speech pattern is technically "bad." (This is all according to serious professionals.) And yet I get paid (handsomely, I may add) to talk to millions of people every morning.

It might seem counterintuitive, but because I'm not naturally good at stuff, I have to make my presence bigger whenever I try something I want to do. I have to try harder and make the stakes higher when I put myself out there. Don't believe me? How about this: I get paid to sing, and I can't sing! My band, The Raging Idiots, is one of my coolest examples of what you can do when you engage in the Fight.

I started The Raging Idiots as a teenager with some friends in high school. Our band's original name was the Concubines, but we were told to change it if we wanted to play at local churches and family-friendly events. (We were fine with that since we didn't really know what "concubine" meant.) The first incarnation of the band fizzled after people actually saw us play and realized that we did indeed suck as much as people thought we would.

I brought The Raging Idiots back as an accompanying band to my stand-up act. "Bobby Bones and his hilarious band The Raging Idiots" wound up being me doing seven minutes of bad comedy and then, after grabbing a guitar, becoming a one-man, one-instrument band. The rest of the band was always "sick" or on tour with Lou Bega, who was at the height of his "Mambo No. 5" fame.

I reappropriated the name of my high school band whenever I wrote song parodies or spoofs that I played on my radio show with my producer, Eddie, on guitar and backing vocals. The audience reaction was good enough that I dreamed up a plan to make The Raging Idiots a legitimate band. Smash cut: four years later, we have a number-one comedy record, a number-one kids' record, and a Top 5 country album. We're playing main slots at major festivals. We're headlining big theaters. We're making millions for charity.

And did I mention I'm a C+ singer at best? By the way, that's up from the D+ level I started at. I've not only worked hard to improve my singing, I also surround myself with awesome-r people. (Pro tip: this is a must. Drop the ego and put better people around you.)

So how did I turn my parody-playing group with a lousy front man into a band that sells out shows to thousands of people? The success of The Raging Idiots goes back to how we started by playing the kind of bars where people don't need the music to be good to enjoy it. The audience (and I use that term "audience" generously) might not have cared if we were funny or in tune, but from the first Raging Idiots "concert" I was convinced I could market our group into something much bigger than it was. I might have been rocking out in the back room of a burrito joint, but I was captivated by the idea of creating an act worth seeing by convincing people it was worth seeing. I knew if I could get momentum going through excitement, our band would rise to the challenge by improving as we went along. The Raging Idiots was my version of a science experiment, with the added benefit of doing some good for good causes.

From the moment I committed to this concept, I wanted to figure out how I could make my band seem much cooler than it really was and get bigger as fast as possible. It wasn't about money (at the time)—all of that was going to charity. Remember, I come from a family with serious addiction issues. While I might not drink or do drugs, I do have the same drive for wanting more and more. This drive can be used for good or for evil; I hope that I choose a good way more often than not.

Back to my rock 'n' roll master plan. What I did was book these tiny rooms (fifty-person-maximum-capacity tiny), simply because I knew they'd sell out immediately. This wasn't an exercise in ego boosting. I knew our sold-out shows had nothing to do with our talent and everything to do with the size of the room. It was a marketing ploy. If I brought home the message that we were selling out, it didn't matter how small the venues—just that we were selling them out. I kept ratcheting up the size bit by bit. We graduated from one-hundred-capacity rooms to two hundred and so on, until today, when we're playing two- to three-thousand-person venues.

Now that I've achieved my goal of growing the audience of The Raging Idiots, I have to live up to my original promise to myself of actually becoming a really good band. Because we kept selling out the festival and theater dates we booked, promoters kept giving us bigger and more prominent venues. The proof was in the ticket sales. The success of the radio show has helped with promotion and we've gotten better, but in my estimation, we're still not as good as the huge stages that we play. So the new Fight is figuring out how to grow into our rooms.

The Fight—a quality I've been blessed with and nurtured into an amazing tool—is a way to level the playing field of life.

You may think I'm the unfunniest guy on earth and the worst

musician. You may hate my radio show and my politics. You may think I'm stupid and stupid looking. But the one thing nobody can say about me is that I was born with an easy pass to life. When I started my career in a radio market so small it was unrated, it was a huge achievement for me. I knew no one and had no money. Every move I made was a risk. Some of my gambles failed. A lot didn't. But no matter, for over a decade, I always showed up—for twelve-, fourteen-, eighteen-hour workdays.

Maybe you weren't born on third base either. Or maybe you were, but, for whatever reason, you don't feel like it. I've learned, as my life has evolved, that it is never *not* a struggle. I know people who have a hundred million dollars, and even for them, it's never not a struggle. Sure, they have different issues than people who don't know how they are going to make the mortgage payment month to month. But, believe me, everyone has *stuff*. The sooner you embrace this truth, the sooner you can leave behind the bitterness of what you don't have and start trying to get what you want.

The Fight is a way to *do* something about your *stuff*. Whether it's leveling the playing field or beating the competition, there is nothing better for overcoming hopelessness than digging in and getting to work.

Every day, everyone's fighting to survive and be more—and it's not negative. It's not a fistfight because you're angry. It's not a punch in the face. It's doing whatever is necessary, no matter the outcome. It's a sharpening, a constant and wonderful struggle, much like my boxing classes, where if I don't prove I want it enough, I'm not even allowed in the ring! According to my trainer, I have to work out at a level high enough for the privilege of getting into the ring for more punishment. Does that make sense? I have to show up, kill myself conditioning for forty-five minutes, and *if* I've worked hard enough, I'm permitted in the ring for the chance to vomit my guts out. If that sounds like a win to you, then you understand the Fight.

THE FIGHT IS . . .

What words do you use to describe the Fight? Here are some of mine:

STRUGGLE

WORK

REFLECTION

PASSION

HOPE

ADVANTAGE

CHALLENGE

VICTORY

FAILURE

ACCOMPLISHMENT

2

WHAT ARE YOU FIGHTING FOR?

*If people keep saying no and you keep wanting it,
that's the definition of Fight-worthy.*

A friend of mine—a successful executive—decided that since her two kids were off to college and out of the house, she finally had a little time to pursue something she had always wanted to do: painting. Not house painting, but the kind you put a lovely frame around.

This is a lady who I have no doubt could pretty much do whatever she set her mind to. Well, being a lover of the arts, she decided she wanted to paint pictures. So, she bought paint-brushes, paints, canvas, and an easel—and put the whole setup in the most beautiful sunroom you can imagine, with the most perfect lighting and all manner of artistic inspiration. She even hired an art teacher to come to her house once a week to give her some instruction.

Problem was she never painted. Ever.

When, at a business meeting in her office, I asked her how her painting was going, she answered in her typically blunt style. "I never do it," she said.

Despite having vast resources at her disposal and talking about taking up the hobby for years and years, she explained that the paintbrushes and canvas just sat there untouched. She felt guilty every time she walked by them—so much so that what had once been her favorite room in the house had turned into a place she hated. After creeping around her extra room for a couple of months, she finally faced the simple fact that "if I really wanted to do it, I'd do it."

She is absolutely right. Now, this example might seem kind of trivial, but it gets to the heart of a major stumbling block in fighting for what you want—and that's figuring out what you want.

People tend to romanticize their goals. Whether it's learning to paint or making a lot of money, at times we think we want things that down deep, we really don't want. Goals can seem important because of our parents or sexy because of the people we follow on Instagram. Did you always want to be a dentist, or are you in dental school because that's what your dad does? (I'm not talking to you, Dr. Cutbirth. I know dentistry is your calling, because you are a genius. Can I have that rebate now?) Do you really want that huge house with more dormers than Dracula's castle? Or is it just that everyone in your town wants a McMansion of his own? (Those huge lawns are murder to maintain. I know because I've been fined at least thirty times by my homeowner association, and I'm never even home to enjoy my house.) It can be hard to separate yourself. Everyone gets sucked into false goals, me included.

My I-don't-really-want-this goal was to play the piano. I didn't expect to become Jerry Lee Lewis (I laugh out loud as I write that analogy because I could have used John Legend, Alicia Keys, or even Elton John, but nope, I immediately went with a guy from the days of black-and-white TV who also married his cousin), but I wanted to become decent enough to perform on-stage. I tried. I took lessons and practiced . . . for a while. Soon, however, I was blowing off both. Everything new is challenging at the beginning, and as I said, I typically love a challenge. But with piano it was different. As soon as it got frustrating, I told myself, "I'm no good." And I quit.

But I'm usually not put off by sucking at something. Sucking at something has never kept me from going after it, never when it's a real priority. My actions—or lack of action—proved that piano wasn't a true goal. Despite what I told myself, it turned out I didn't really want to play like Jerry Lee or marry my cousin.

Unfortunately, we can only prioritize so much. It's impossible to do eleven different things at once—at least not at a high level. That's because time is limited. (Unless you're stoned, or so I'm told. Still waiting to try that. If I ever do, which I probably won't, I'll definitely go the edible route. Do they make weed Werther's Original? That'd be crazy.)

Figuring out what's truly important to you (and not to your mother, first cousin, significant other, or dog) is the first step to the Fight. And it's worth spending a little time up front on sorting through your true motivations and fantasies in order to keep you from wasting a whole lot of it later.

FIGHT = TIME + WORK

WHAT'S WORTH FIGHTING
FOR—AND WHAT'S NOT

Do I really want this?

That's not an easy question to answer. Painting and playing the piano can be seen as superficial examples. When my executive friend and I gave up on our "passion projects," they had very little bearing on our lives. Some decisions—like getting married, having children, or pursuing a particular career—carry a ton of weight. But the questions you need to ask yourself are the same, whether you're choosing to play tennis or quit your job.

For me, figuring out the career part of my life has always been straightforward. There has never *not* been a time in my life that I didn't have a clear vision of my dream job. It has always been a national morning radio show and a TV talk show like my hero David Letterman. Every step I make—from comedy to music to writing—is a step in the direction of that goal. That doesn't mean I've always gotten what I've wanted or even known *how* to get it, but I've always known *what* I want—and as I said, that's the first step to this whole Fight thing.

My personal life? Well, that's a whole other story. Despite all the wonderful women I've dated and all the therapy I've had, I still don't know what I want. The way I grew up—with a mom whose addictions were so bad I was adopted by my grandmother—created conflicts that are hard to get over (yup, I've had *a lot* of therapy). In some ways, I recognize that my drive, when it comes to work, is a function of the fact that I can't figure out how to get and give love like a normal person, so escaping into work is a defense mechanism at times.

I perform every day, whether it's on a microphone or onstage. Why the maniacal need to sing, dance, act like a fool for others, all the time? When it comes down to it (I mean really down to it, like therapy down to it), I'm just looking for the love of others. We *all* are—in our own ways. Although no one has cornered the market on the proper way to find and reciprocate love, some people undoubtedly have healthier methods than others. I have a friend who is overly kind. Is that even a thing, you may be asking yourself? Yes. One hundred percent. He's the guy who's trying to buy everybody's meal at every dinner, in a way that is so over the top that you don't even want to go out with him. Or he's late to his kid's recital because he was at his friend's kid's recital. He's so nice that he actually makes his own life worse. "You're not doing good," I've said in a frank talk with him. "You're doing harm—to yourself."

I think love is why everybody does everything. But you must figure out if your Fight is for *what* you love or what you're *doing for* love. That's an important distinction. As human beings, our A-number-one instinct is to find love, but that's different than having a purpose and a plan. It's not easy to completely untangle this (uh, that's why therapy costs so much and takes so long). But you can ask yourself one important and clear question: Is my Fight good for me?

To find the true answer, nothing beats some deep-down soul-searching. (I'm talking to you, millennials—pick your head up from Instagram to finish this sentence . . . but only after you follow me @MrBobbyBones.) There is no substitute for reflecting on your actions and feelings—and how the two interact.

THE POWER OF NO: A SHORTCUT TO FIGURING OUT WHAT YOU WANT

If you're twentysomething and rolling your eyes right now, just know that I also rolled my eyes when I heard older people tell me the exact same thing about the importance of reflection and experience in finding your path. And now here I am repeating it. It's the natural cycle of things.

But, fine, if you want a simple life hack, here you go:

If you keep being told no, and you continue to keep trying for it, that's how you know that you really want what you think you want. Put another way, if someone saying no to you doesn't make you want your goal any less, then you are following the right goal.

Even in an industry—show business—known for rejection, I've been turned down an absurd amount of times. I'd say twenty-five nos to one yes is an accurate average for me. Those stats are brutal. And yet, I've never thought about quitting.

It's kind of like a Masochism Meter. When people repeatedly say no and I keep going, I think, "Okay, I must really want this. Otherwise, why would I put myself through so much abuse?" You can ask yourself the very same question.

You don't need to have a Ph.D. to know if you're going for something that's "good" or "cool" but doesn't feel right. If you're pursuing what you want and you're not getting any satisfaction (or even worse, you feel awful), you have to step back for a second.

It won't be comfortable to question your motivations, but it won't kill you, either.

This process of deliberation is especially necessary when you're heading into murky areas of your life. For me, as I said, that's relationships. While I totally know my mind about business, with women my head isn't always screwed on right. I've pursued girlfriends who were fun, pretty, smart, nice, and successful—but that doesn't mean they were right for me (or me for them, as I'm sure they'd attest to). What's perfect on paper isn't what's perfect in real life. That's not only true for matters of the heart but for careers, friendships, even what you want to eat for lunch!

Unfortunately, to figure it out, you gotta go through a lot of making the wrong decisions for the wrong reasons. That's the learning process of growing up. It'd be great if you'd known what you needed to do back before you needed to start doing it—but unless you have a time-traveling DeLorean (old reference that you youngsters won't get; move along. From my contemporaries, let me get that fist bump. Shout-out, Michael J. Fox!), it ain't gonna happen. Sometimes you have to go through a lot of relationships to find the right one or try a lot of jobs until you find what you are passionate about.

FIGHTER IN THE SPOTLIGHT: AMY BROWN

More than five years ago, my cohost Amy was on a mission trip to Haiti, where she visited an orphanage and fell in love with a little boy, whom she couldn't stop thinking about when she returned home to Nashville. Amy and her husband—who were having trouble conceiving—returned to Port-au-Prince to meet the two-year-old boy again, whom they immediately decided to adopt, along with a five-year-old girl.

Well, they might have started the process immediately, but there's nothing immediate about the process. Amy spent years doing paperwork, paying tens of thousands of dollars, completing lots of home visits, background checks, and other security reviews, and becoming their legal parent—and still she had trouble getting her kids home! It was heartbreaking for everyone. Her kids suffered, but so did Amy. There were times when she broke down, but there were many more when she should've broken down and she didn't. Instead of getting depressed, Amy constantly corresponded with government agencies, cheered her kids up over FaceTime, and visited Haiti, where the show and our listeners have supported the children's orphanage and also created a bakery that offers both food and jobs for lots of folks in need.

How Amy functioned every single day, refusing to give up no matter how frustrating things got, well, that's a Fight. She never thought this process would take as long as it did; still, she wouldn't stop fighting. "Even if it had taken ten years, we would never give up on them," Amy said. "Two little humans were depending on us. When things seemed hopeless, I prayed for more faith in the process. How could we ever walk away and give up on something we had asked for?"

Amy relied on her husband, family, friends, and faith to get through the hard times. She also hung pictures of her kids as a constant reminder to never lose hope. "I had their sweet faces up in our hallway over a year before they actually got here," she said, "because eventually this would be their home, too."

Finally, roughly five years after she found the children, she was able to bring them home. "They are truly a gift, one that we had to work hard for but a gift nonetheless, and I thank Jesus for them every day," Amy said. "Even though it's like I was pregnant for sixty months instead of nine months, it all worked out."

WHAT'S YOUR FIGHT?

What do you want to NOT suck at? What are you willing to fail at so much that you embarrass yourself? What will you do anything for? Here are some questions and exercises to get you thinking about your Fight—and whether it's really the right one for you. These are questions you can return to over and over whenever you're having doubts.

If you're still searching for your Fight:

- *What moments in the past have made you the happiest?* They can be small or big ones—or even certain periods of time. Don't overthink this, just see what comes to mind.

- *What was it about that time that made you happy?* Is the essence of that time something you can re-create now? For example, if the happiest time in your life was summers working outdoors as a kid but now you have a desk job that's killing you, maybe try volunteering at a local park or outdoor recreational area to see if you can recapture that feeling. Volunteering or a part-time job is a great way to make incremental change without upending your whole life.

- *What are you passionate about doing?* Be honest. Even if it's eating in restaurants, that might be a big clue to a job you'd be passionate about.
- *What percentage of your day/week/month do you spend devoted to your passions?* Is that enough for you? If not, how could you increase it?
- *What areas of your life need a lot of work?* Relationships with family members, dating, losing weight— those are classic ones. What specifically relates to you? How much control do you have over the situation, and what, if anything, could you do, no matter how difficult, to improve?

If you have a Fight but want to do a gut check on it:
- *When you think about doing the thing you're fighting for, what do you feel?* Does your stomach knot up? Or do you just want to put this book down and get back to it?
- *If you are a procrastinator or are scared to put yourself out there to achieve your dreams, what is holding you back?* Is it fear of failure, or something less intuitive—fear of success?
- *Where do your dreams and goals come from?* If they are yours, when did you first conjure them up? Does anyone else you know have the same Fight? If so, why?

- *If you succeed at your goal, where will it take you in five years?* How about ten years? What's the pinnacle of that path? Picture yourself there and see if you like it.

MY BIGGEST FAILURE: CHRIS STAPLETON

Chris Stapleton, who has written hit songs for everyone from Adele to Luke Bryan and has won multiple Grammy and CMA Awards as an artist, has been coming to my radio show since long before he became seriously famous. He's not only a cool guy but someone I've developed a personal relationship with over the years.

"The day that my dad passed away, I was in South Carolina, taking my kids to the beach with their other grandparents. I got the call—my brother called. So I took a little walk, kinda soaked that in. You know, I had seen my dad two days prior. We had played a show near where he lived, and he had told me good-bye or whatever. I could have stayed over. I could have figured something out. But I used some lame excuse, like 'I gotta get on the bus 'cause it's leaving.' That was a failure. I don't have many regrets, but I do regret those two missed days. For some reason those two days magically mean more than all the other days I could have been there saying hello, or doing something with my dad. That was a failure as a son, I guess. You can't get those things back, but you can learn to try not to let the professional outweigh the personal or steer it more than it should. That, for me, was the lesson."

3

FIND SOMEONE WHO TELLS YOU THAT YOU SUCK

You read that right. I want you to actually go out and seek people who'll say to your face, "You're not good."

Now, I don't mean someone on Facebook or Twitter. (People on the Internet already think you suck. Go ahead. Ask them.) I'm describing what some call "constructive criticism." Or what I like to think of as your coach in the corner of the ring as you Fight. Someone looking out for you from all angles.

The best example of this in my life is in my comedy gigs. I just wrapped up a weekend doing stand-up in Modesto and Monterey, California. As a matter of fact, I've been on the road most of my weekends this year doing stand-up. Slowly growing as a comedian from super mediocre to somewhat stomachable.

Let me back up. I've loved comedy ever since I was a kid, watching my hero David Letterman on TV. *Late Night with*

David Letterman (also known later as the *Late Show*) was the one thing that I looked forward to every single night. It was a constant for me. Now that I do comedy myself, I love it even more. I love the pressure to bring others joy. I love the torture of it. Think about walking up on a stage, alone, with the goal of entertaining a crowd with words and movements alone. And by the way, they didn't get in for free, so you'd better be pretty freaking funny. I love all of it. The blinding lights, the expectation, the challenge, and simply making people feel good.

Comedy is something I'll never be great at. Or even good at. But that's what's awesome about it. I love the chase of a successful joke. Especially when the odds are that you aren't going to nail it.

Let me tell you a bit of my story of comedy tragedy and triumph—and how this can relate to whatever the Fight is in your life.

I don't think anyone thought I was serious when I said I wanted to pursue a legit career as a comedian. I wasn't talking doing little spots here and there like I've done for years, but headlining. People listened to me on the radio, or watched me online, or came to watch my band . . . but the odds of them paying fifty bucks a ticket to watch me stand alone and tell jokes weren't good.

My journey in proving those odds wrong or die (onstage) trying started at the end of 2016. In my management's office, surrounded by my team, we were in a meeting to plan my 2017 schedule and goals.

(By the way, I've always felt that it's pretty pretentious to talk about your "team," a.k.a. your agents and managers and lawyers. But now that I live in that bubble, they are absolute. Let me sidestep for a second from my tale of comedic glory and explain how my life works with all these random people, whom I nicknamed "the Percentages." I call them that because each one of these fine professionals gets a percentage of what I earn. I'll introduce you to them:

My manager: she manages all aspects of my career and for that gets 15 percent of everything I make. Straight up. Before taxes.

My agent: he finds jobs for me and gets 10 percent of what I make.

My business manager: she handles all my money and gets 2.5 percent of my earnings.

If you do the math, that's 27.5 percent of my money that comes right off the top to pay for my team. Take out taxes, and for every dollar I "make," I'm really getting about forty cents. That's how it works in showbiz, folks.)

In the office where all my Percentages were gathered, I made an announcement.

"Listen up, everybody," I said. "I want to headline a stand-up comedy tour."

There. I had said it. That's always one of the first steps of the Fight for me: saying it out loud (more on making your goals concrete in chapter 6).

I could tell by the way their mouths hung open (and the one guy who shook his head) that they thought I was nuts. Not because I don't say dumb things from time to time, or take big chances all the time. The people who work with me are totally used to that. But to headline a stand-up comedy tour of one-thousand-to-two-thousand-seat theaters across America is insane for an unproven comedian. Especially for me. Theaters aren't cheap to rent, which is why tickets aren't cheap.

"You've never done over twenty-five minutes of stand-up at

once," one of them said. "You can't go out on the road unless you have an hour."

"I know I'm not great, but I will get better," I said, thinking of my Raging Idiots model of growing into your audience. "I can definitely get a solid hour together."

I had trouble convincing some of them, but that's always been the case for me. If ever one of my ideas is universally loved, I automatically feel that it's too safe. Something that makes "a lot of sense" usually means it's safe. I hate safe.

My philosophy is that if I'm not afraid of the worst-case scenario—failing—why should anyone else be? What do I have to lose by losing? Embarrassment? What I dread more than bombing big time is not taking the shot. You've heard the idea: you don't regret failing as much as you do not trying. As clichéd as that sounds, here's the thing about clichés—they exist for a reason.

Right now, think of all the things you wish you'd done when you were in college. Or a career you wish you'd tried before you started doing what you do now. Those are real regrets. Now think of a time you made a wrong decision. Those are much easier to digest, because at least you gave it the ol' Brady Bunch effort—and it was a learning experience. I don't regret anything I've screwed up (except being fined one million dollars by the FCC. That one stung). My only regrets are not trying.

Not knowing if I have the chops to succeed at comedy doesn't work for me. At least being terrible is closure. At least asking the girl out at the bar, even if she answers, "No, I'm not into skinny guys who look like Harry Potter," is better than just wondering what if.

So the Percentages and I mapped the Funny and Alone comedy tour, over thirty cities all around the country. We put the tickets up for sale all at once. There was a lot of pressure in this all-or-nothing approach. If the tour sold terribly, I might have just canceled the entire thing, blaming it on "vocal issues" or an "anus replacement." But if it sold really well, I better be freaking funny, because people are paying upward of sixty dollars a ticket for me to make them laugh.

The day of reckoning arrived. ON-SALE DAY. Holy crap, I don't know when I felt worse—before or after. The tickets sold (I'd give it a solid 7.5 out of 10 on a scale of first-day satisfaction). Now there was no turning back. I had *a lot* of work to do. The last thing I wanted to do was disappoint anyone willing to part with their hard-earned money to see *me*. So I set out to write a longer and funnier set as fast as I possibly could.

First I needed material. I always need material—I host a radio show every day, which is why I'm always taking notes. But I ratcheted up my usual practice by scheduling in hours of writing right after I finished my show. (Always put things in a schedule. There will be a terrible case of guilt if you don't get it done and a cool feeling of accomplishment if you complete it. Draw a line in the sand with yourself.)

Just in case I forgot or wanted to forget my new imperative, I made my lock screen my new goal: "Pay attention, be perceptive, and always write it down." See it. See it. See it. Achieve it.

Then I booked small shows in tiny places around Nashville— even multiple small shows a night at a tiny venue—in order to try out the stuff I was writing down. I used the folks inside as guinea pigs for my new material.

Most important, though, was my mental state. I decided I was going to give this tour everything I had. For the months leading up to the start of my national tour, comedy was my life.

I was 100 percent committed after my radio show was over each morning.

Despite all of that, to those who came out to my first head-lining show in Virginia Beach, I just have one thing to say: I'm sorry.

First of all, when I took the stage, the theater looked humongous. There were people as far as I could see. In reality, it was about eighteen hundred, which in terms of venues isn't all that huge. But when the blood is pounding in your ears and your stomach is doing flips, everything is so much bigger and moving so much faster than in reality.

I wasn't good. I like nerves, but I let myself get TOO nervous. I focused on audience members who got up from their seats. When people talked to each other I imagined they were saying, "What a waste of money." I'm not sure if anybody really talked or got up, by the way. The whole hour was a blur, so nothing I'm reporting has any factual validity. Those might have just been the voices in my head saying, "This guy blows."

I wish I could blame the whole fiasco on nerves, but I have to be honest with myself. I also had pretty weak material. The weird thing about comedy is that you can't figure out how good your jokes are without an audience. It's not like musicians, who can practice songs, licks, and scales over and over alone in a room until they've developed the technique and muscle memory to carry them through the jitters of a live performance. As a comedian, you must take your practice to the people. You're only skilled when you can answer yes to the question "Did they laugh?" Early in my tour, the answer was "Not as much as I had hoped."

When jokes don't hit and you've got a room full of folks just staring at you, it's worse than getting kicked in the nuts by my dog when I'm sleeping. Much worse. In bed, it's one quick, brutal blow to the nads, and then I fall back asleep. Bombing a comedy gig is a sweaty, silent death that will still go on for another forty-seven minutes.

But I had committed. Not only to the tour but to getting better as well. As soon as I got off the stage in Virginia, I didn't talk to anyone or take a moment to feel sorry for myself. Instead, I took my set list of jokes and started marking them up. One-third were gone completely. Cut for total lack of hilarity. Another third got to remain with a big "needs work" caveat. Then the last third I deemed pretty good.

In one night, I went from a solid hour of material to a shaky twenty minutes. That's not the end of the world. There's an old saying that all writing is rewriting. The only problem was that I had another hour to do . . . THE NEXT NIGHT!

That's why caffeine was invented. I didn't sleep much that night as we made our way to Roanoke, Virginia. Instead, I stayed awake in the van crossing out a lot more than writing. It was 10 A.M. before I stopped scribbling and started having a slight panic attack. By the way, I don't have to drive in a van all through the night and stay at crappy hotels. I'm doing pretty well. But I loved chasing this dream so much that the sacrifice of time and quality of life didn't even register. So load up the van and the trail mix with far too many raisins and not enough chocolate, and let's go grind it out! That was another reason I knew I had to keep going with comedy: I didn't hate the worst part of it.

After sleeping for a few hours (thanks, generic version of Xanax), I headed over to the venue early. In the theater, I walked around the stage, sat in the audience's seats, and did everything I could think of to get myself comfortable in this new environment. More important, though, I had to get myself comfortable in my own body.

I believe that a controlled heart rate is a large key to success, whether it's going into a job interview or giving a speech at a wedding. This isn't some New Age hippy-dippy talk. Think of it this way: imagine all the times your heart was beating out of your chest. You probably didn't make the wisest decisions or say the smartest things in that moment. When your body is screaming "I'm freaking out!", it's hard for your brain to ignore that.

MAKING NERVES WORK FOR YOU

You are going to get nervous sometimes. It's natural. Everybody gets nervous. I always say nerves are a sign that whatever is happening—good or bad—matters. Usually the adrenaline gets pumping at a crucial moment, such as asking someone for a raise or out on a date. It's a moment of performance where you have to step up. You're a fighter getting into the ring. Your heart should be beating a little faster than usual and your senses heightened. Those hormones are running through your body to give you laserlike focus.

But if the adrenaline floods your system and your chest starts banging around like an old radiator in winter, well, you're probably not going to be effective. You aren't balanced. And balance is what you need to speak effectively.

When nerves turn into anxiety or even full-blown fear, your brain can't settle down enough to think about your words, your crazy twitching eye, your body language, and anything else you need to put yourself in the best position to succeed.

I don't know about you, but I don't work well with my heart pounding through my neck. When I'm anxious, I don't do anything right. I don't think right. I don't speak right. I don't look right.

I have a trick, though, when my nerves-o-meter starts to veer into the red: take the part of your body wherever it's hitting you the hardest physically and spread it from that point throughout the rest of your body. Here's my routine:

1. I find a quiet, calm place where I can be alone (a bathroom stall works fine) and close my eyes. Even if you can't be alone, take a few seconds wherever you are and just block the world out. Sometimes I just focus on something I really care about that makes me happy. Like my dog. Or Kate Beckinsale (*boom*, got my second shout-out in two books).

2. First I ask myself, "Is it a good thing that I'm nervous?" Usually it is (unless it's a pregnancy scare, but it's been a long time since I've had one of those). Most of us get nervous in the face of opportunities that we're worried we're going to screw up.

3. I remind myself that opportunities are awesome. Being nervous at this moment is a by-product of something great.

4. Then I turn the liability of anxiety into the advantage of adrenaline by spreading my nerves from that particular spot throughout my entire body. I don't put pressure on myself to get rid of the nerves completely. That's not realistic. But I can spread them out.

Everyone gets hit hardest with nerves in one spot: stomach, chest, throat, legs. For me, it's my neck. When I'm freaking out, I feel like my neck is bulging. I visualize the ball of energy in my neck and stay there for a second, just experiencing it and allowing it to pulse and constrict. Then I send it down and all around my body. I imagine that anxious feeling going from my neck down into my chest, through my arms and legs, and all the way to my fingers and toes. I try to get my toes nervous!

You still have the same nerves after this practice, but you dilute their power by spreading them out all over. This approach takes practice. Heck, it doesn't always work for me now. But whether you can make those butterflies move or not, this exercise gives your brain something to focus on—besides being nervous. You are literally focusing on something else for that moment, whereas before you were only focused on not having a panic attack. And also, if you screw up, no one really cares anyway. We'll talk more about that later, but the truth is we feel like everyone is always watching and judging us. Nope. People just care about themselves. You've likely seen someone really botch a presentation or be really nervous speaking in public and never given it a second thought once it was done. Return the favor to yourself.

If you know anything about me, you know that being on time and being prepared are two things I excel at. Talent is not a big ingredient of my success; it's showing up, over and over again (even when nobody wants me there) and being better prepared each time.

That night, as I waited to take the stage in Roanoke for the second performance of what now felt like a very long comedy tour, I knew I might bomb again—but I was as prepared as I could be in that moment. I had stayed up all night rewriting my material based on "feedback" from my first show. I had covered every part of the theater physically and mentally. And before the show, I did my visualization exercise so that my jitters didn't kill whatever kernel of humor I had left in me. And then I got dressed.

I'm very into patterns. I love routines. I think they build brain muscle memory and foster a feeling of familiarity, which provides comfort for most of us. I have different rituals for different occasions, but when it comes to my stand-up shows, I get dressed the same exact way every time. As a matter of fact, I wear the exact same "uniform" for every show. For my tour last year, I always wore a short-sleeved button-up shirt with a tie, black pants, red socks, and red shoes. (Recently, I embarked on matching all my red socks, which is probably about two hundred pairs. I dumped them all onto the couch and after two hours only made thirty matches. Boy, was that dumb.)

I actually named my tour this year the Red Hoodie Comedy Tour because I wanted to wear a red hoodie to every show. If my routine or options are limited, so is the chance for me to mess it up. And it's one less thing I have to worry about when I pack to travel to shows. When I do finally put on my "artist armor," it feels like it's time to go to work. Getting dressed is a routine I put in place to make me feel a certain way. Here's how I do it each time:

socks always first
then black pants
then shoes
then shirt
then the hair
then the tie
and finally: the glasses

This may seem absolutely insane to you, but my routines and superstitions keep me from thinking about anything else but comedy. When it comes to my clothes, I already know, and like Biggie said, "If you don't know, now you know . . ." (Writing my routine down, I'm aware of how insane I sound. Insane but efficient.)

After straightening my glasses, I took the stage in Roanoke . . .

And I killed!

Just kidding. I didn't. But I did better. Baby steps.

I can remember every moment of that show in Roanoke as if I'm onstage right now. I was so drilled down into my set that I felt each laugh and silence in the room as if they were happening in my own body. I registered my hits and my misses, but when my timing was off or a joke didn't make sense, I didn't freeze or freak out. When the audience didn't like some of my material (and it was clear when they didn't), it wasn't something happening *to* me. I didn't feel like a passive victim. Instead, while I was still at the mic, I thought, "Oh, that didn't work, but next time

I think *this* will." It was amazing what trying to improve did for my comfort level—and I couldn't have done that if the audience didn't allow me to see clearly exactly where I sucked.

And here we are, at the main point of this whole chapter: why you need to have someone in your life who'll let you know when you suck.

The crowd at a comedy show laughs hard at the start of every set. They want to like what they've just paid money to see. The first time they don't laugh, you know they are now dialed in and expecting true entertainment. When that crowd doesn't laugh, it's really on. Instead of getting angry or annoyed that they aren't throwing me freebies anymore, I think: *It's about to get awesome.* When I tell a joke and they *don't* laugh, that's what excites me, because I know I now have to earn every single laugh. And so, every laugh that comes after the first miss is an honest-to-goodness piece of greatness. I earned it. The question here is whether you accept being told you suck. Or will you just stand there with the attitude "Oh, they just don't get me"?

The same is true with friends. While it's important to have champions, those folks who tell you that you're great, it's equally important but a lot harder to find an honest critic who also wants you to succeed. Lots of people will fluff you up (particularly if you start to do well). You need someone you trust in your life who will always give their real opinion. If a person can tell you, "That wasn't good," you'll really believe it when he or she says, "Hey, that was great." If you find a friend or colleague like this—one whose compliments mean more because their criticism is real—hold on tight to them, because they are rare and valuable.

It's hard to be told things we don't want to hear. Who wants to know that what we're doing isn't perfect, or even any good?

But if we/you/I really want to improve, you have to be willing to be coached by hearing about what's not working. Again, it's not easy or comfortable. For real, it feels like crap. But if you can intellectualize the idea that criticism is awesome because it will lead to actually being awesome, you can move past hurt feelings and into true hope. AND THE COMPLIMENTS ARE THAT MUCH MORE AWESOME when they do come, because you know they are real.

Let me put it another way: people's praise makes you no better at whatever it is you want to do. So, do you want to get better? If so, then nut up and understand that being told YOU SUCK is great! I get a lot of YOU SUCK from the Internet, people calling my radio show, the audience at my live comedy shows, and I appreciate the honesty of it. It makes the laughs that much sweeter.

The audience in Virginia Beach made me better for Roanoke, which made me better going into the next weekend of this massive undertaking. Standing under the lights of venues that my comedic heroes like George Carlin, Ricky Gervais, and Chris Rock had played, I wouldn't have been able to speak a syllable if I didn't accept that it was okay for me to not be amazing—as long as I was moving forward. In fact, I took a lot of pressure off myself by believing I didn't have to get funnier to feel like I was getting better.

I have to admit, though, that no matter how much I pride myself in taking constructive criticism, sometimes even I am slow on the take. Case in point, my *Beauty and the Beast* bestiality joke. Here goes:

"Why is everyone going so crazy about the new live-action *Beauty and the Beast* movie? Frankly, I'm weirded out by it. The premise is great: hot girl gives ugly guy a shot; he proves his heart is amazing; and they are together forever. But I saw the trailer, and I can't get past the fact that it looks like the Harry Potter girl is having intercourse with a large, angry donkey. And if I wanted to see a female and an animal get it on, I'd look at [pointing to guy in the front row] this guy's phone."

On tour, I tried that joke twenty ways. Nothing. Crickets. As I'm writing this I still can't figure out why people didn't find it funny. Maybe the structure was no good. Or maybe there isn't a large market for animal-and-human sex jokes. Whatever the reason, I scrapped it from the act. But not before running it into the ground. That time, the feedback just took a long time to sink in.

Going back to my John Mayer talk mentioned earlier in the book, he said something that resonated with me. "The things that we think are the absolute most creative, amazing parts of our minds really don't resonate with the masses as much as we'd like them to," he said. "It's mostly that stuff right in the middle where we're like, 'This is just pretty good' that hits the people in the best way." He was probably talking about some super-genius guitar playing or musical masterpiece that he had written that hadn't made it to the top of the charts. For me, it was a joke about humping a donkey.

Anyway . . . back to my original point: the moral of my failure at bestiality humor is that when a joke doesn't land, you don't quit comedy. You work on that joke, or just move on to a different one. Don't throw the baby out the window if you don't like the temperature of the bathwater. Or whatever that saying is.

I have no problem admitting that I've said a thousand dumb things on the radio and written many bad jokes. And I'm glad I look back on those moments and cringe (and I'm NOT including my *Beauty and the Beast* joke in that list; that one was funny, no matter what everybody else thinks). If I'm not ashamed of whatever product I put out eighteen months ago—at least a little bit—then I've stopped growing, or stopped caring about growing. I'm into thinking that my old work was bad. I'm good with that.

I used to hate my self-hatred. That's why I would never listen to or look at anything that I had done in the past. If I heard a few minutes from one of my old radio shows, I was filled with embarrassment—for me that I put out such a dumb show, for my bosses who were dumb enough to pay me to do it, and for the poor people who had to listen to it while they drove to work.

But now I take a much more positive view of that negative feeling so many of us get when we look back on past performance, professional or personal. My new mantra is: constant dissatisfaction is the way that I stay satisfied. Just like I turn my nerves from a debilitating condition into my rocket fuel, so I take my angst with myself and turn it into a marker of how far I've come. I now listen back on shows from two years ago and think, Man, I wasn't very good then. But if I didn't feel that way, if I thought those shows were awesome, that would be a terrible sign. It would mean I was the same! In my world, if you aren't moving forward, you are moving backward.

It doesn't matter if you're telling jokes or working a spreadsheet: never be satisfied with where you are, and always find a new way to engage in the Fight. Enjoy being embarrassed tomorrow by what you are doing today.

I guess what I'm saying is, who better to tell you that you suck—than *you*!

Quiz: Do You Need to Find Someone to Tell You That You Suck?

1. *When your food arrives cold in a restaurant, you:*
   a. Eat it
   b. Eat it but complain the entire time
   c. Respectfully ask the waiter person to heat it up
   d. Throw your plate against the wall

2. *If your boss asks you to redo a work project, you:*
   a. Cry
   b. Quit
   c. Ask a lot of questions and do your best to meet his or her expectations
   d. Play *Plants vs. Zombies* for twenty minutes on your phone, wait to be asked by your boss again, and then scramble to redo it

3. *You look in the mirror:*
   a. Rarely
   b. Often
   c. Whenever necessary
   d. Just to watch yourself dance so you can see your sweet dance moves

4. *A perfect Sunday for you includes:*
   a. Going to church and seeing family
   b. Working out and then brunch with friends
   c. Catching up on your reading and correspondence, then cooking healthy food for the upcoming week
   d. Playing *World of Warcraft* and having your mom drop off lasagna

5. *Which word best describes you?*

    a. Compassionate

    b. Independent

    c. Go-getter

    d. Fun

6. *Your idea of hell is:*

    a. Going on a corporate retreat where you have to do a lot of trust exercises and tell people what you really think about them in front of a moderator

    b. Getting the middle seat on an airplane, between a chatty grandma and a mom with a baby

    c. A boss who undermines your efforts

    d. Volunteering

7. *If you could get any car, it would be:*

    a. A 2017 Chevrolet Volt because of its safety and fuel efficiency ratings

    b. A Mini Cooper. What else?

    c. A Toyota Highlander

    d. A Dodge Ram

8. *You would never:*

    a. Cut the line

    b. Pay full price

    c. Do a job that goes against your values

    d. Work on the weekends

9. *Your best friend is:*

    a. Your mom

    b. Your best friend

    c. You can't choose a "best" among your friends

    d. Who makes up these questions anyway?

10. *You're reading this book because:*

   a. You would like to become more assertive in going after your goals

   b. You hope to become famous

   c. There's always room for improvement as far as you're concerned

   d. You love that dude Lunchbox so figured you'd give his boss a chance

ANSWER KEY

If you answered mostly As:

You probably need someone to lift you up more than you need a critic. I'm worried that hearing that you suck will only send you deeper into your shell, when what you need to do is come on out! You seem like a very nice and responsible person. Don't worry so much. Make a whole bunch of mistakes and then we'll talk.

If you answered mostly Bs:

You gotta lot of life in you. That's mainly a good thing, but sometimes you could rein it in a little. (Like your need to tell everyone at work what they're doing wrong. Or leaving those mean notes on the office fridge, telling people when you don't like how their lunch smells.) On the other hand, you sure are the life of the office Christmas party. Anyway, you definitely need someone to tell you that you suck and it's going to have to be someone with a backbone of steel, 'cause you don't take criticism lightly. It's gonna suck for them, but be great for you! Search out those who are willing to take you on and try to be (a little) nice.

If you answered mostly Cs:

You're the star student and you know it. You work harder than everyone else; you're more generous than everyone else; you floss more than everyone else. It's kind of bordering on ridiculous. You, too, need someone to tell you that you suck, because yes, even A+ students suck sometimes. Get over it and stop constantly trying for perfection. If you are always acing the test, it means you're not challenging yourself! Your suck-monitor will let you know where you have to push yourself.

If you answered mostly Ds:

This is just a wild guess, but you probably have *a lot* of people who tell you that you suck. But you don't listen to any of them, because you think they suck even worse. What you need is someone who you respect *and* tells you that you suck. You're honest and fun, but you've got a lot of potential you're wasting. A little nudge is all you need to take it to the next level.

4

NOT EVERYONE IS
GOING TO LIKE YOU

Last night was crazy. So crazy that I had to include it in this book. And I know I've been writing a lot about things happening to me during comedy shows, but I mostly write this on weekends, so suck it up and listen to another story, please.

It started out as a normal weekend day—which, for me, means out on the road. I had just finished a really fun show at the Wilbur Theater in Boston. On the drive to the next tour stop in Northampton, Massachusetts, I was in an especially good mood and ready to celebrate—which, for me, means food.

After doing my sound check and meeting about a hundred fans, I left the theater in Northampton and walked over to a place called Local Burger so I could eat. Normally, I'd go with a turkey burger or salad, since I try to eat light and tight. But there was something on the menu that I just couldn't ignore.

Just in case you don't believe the awesomeness on the menu, here is visual proof . . . freaking Cap'n Crunch chicken. Man. It was delicious.

Cap'n Crunch Chix Tenders.

Fried chicken in Cap'n Crunch cereal! What's next, Froot Loops hot dogs? (I'd totally try that, too.)

I crushed these pieces of amazing cereal-covered chicken. They brought me a lot of joy for a couple of reasons. First of all, as a kid I could never have afforded Cap'n Crunch (we settled for Sgt. Crunchy, in the bag on the bottom shelf of the cereal aisle. It was kind of like Cap'n Crunch but cheaper and without the toy in it), much less those sweet, sweet tenders—and that thought, a reminder of how far I've come, always brings me a moment of happiness. But also, normally I eat like a monk abstaining from all pleasures of the flesh. (I eat the same thing for lunch every day. It might not be delicious, but it maintains my girlish figure. I don't have built-in "cheat days," like most people who eat very healthy, mainly because I think the concept is weak. Change your lifestyle slowly. No one goes from 0 to 100 in a day, week, or even month.

You will have setbacks, and that's fine. But to call it "cheating" makes it seem like you are doing something wrong. And then to sanction doing something wrong? What if you continued that logic beyond food and into the rest of your life, and set aside once a week as a "cheat day" at school, at work, in a relationship . . . nope. Not my style.)

A little heavier than usual but a lot happier, I returned to the theater to get ready for my 8 P.M. show. Around 9 P.M., after my first two opening acts finished, I walked out on the stage to the White Stripes's "Seven Nation Army" and could tell immediately it was a good crowd by the clapping in unison to the walk-out music. That doesn't happen at every show. There were fourteen hundred people, most of whom were pretty drunk and were clearly ready to enjoy my shenanigans.

A half hour into my act, I was in the middle of a joke about a car ride I had taken that day when I noticed some scuffling in the lower right side of the theater.

"I'm going to shoot you!" someone yelled from the audience.

I heard it as clear as day—and so did everyone else in the venue, which was now filled with screaming. I stopped the show and sat down on the stage. Of course, the rare time I needed to use my athletic prowess and dart-like speed was the first time I had eaten Cap'n Crunch chicken tenders and felt as heavy as a waterlogged brick. I didn't leave, because I felt like I was down low enough on the stage that if the audience member was hoping to shoot me, I'd be a really tough target. (Not to mention the fact that if I left, the promoter could say I didn't fulfill my contractual time and not pay me. I gotta eat, after all—hopefully more meat dipped in Cap'n Crunch.) I couldn't really tell what was going on, except that eventually the cops arrived and I assumed the troublemaker was escorted out, because the screaming stopped. I stood back up, and although I had lost most of the crowd, the show must go on. I told a few more jokes, juggled a bit, and played a few funny songs. I did the best I could do to get back an audience that had just heard a man yell he was going to shoot someone. I'm not sure even Chappelle could do that. (Actually, he probably could. That guy seems pretty unflappable.)

After the show I was debriefed on what had actually happened. Turns out, someone *really* didn't like my jokes. It started with a bit that rolled my issues with mustaches and a recent experience with an Uber driver into a song called "Mr. Uber Driver," which goes like this:

Mr. Uber Driver, I'm standing on the curb
your mustache makes you look like a perv.
I don't want to judge you by the hair that's on your face
but I've got 911 on my phone ready just in case.

A guy in the audience (perhaps a mustachioed Uber driver) heckled me, because he didn't like the song. Then a lady who apparently enjoyed my comedy stylings told him to shut up, which made him so angry, he threated to "shoot the chick." Cops came and, bam, it was my first show with an intermission in the middle of a set.

I've spent a lot of years wondering how to get the most people to like what I do. I mean, I'm in entertainment, and the entire mission is to be popular. And yet, despite all the work I put into being liked, there was a man out there in the audience so offended by me that he was willing to threaten murder. (The joke wasn't that great, a solid B at best, but *shoot someone?*)

Okay, I can imagine what you're thinking right now. *That's* your best example for why it's foolish to try to win over the world? Look, I don't have a normal life. So I've got another one for you, and it involves the favorite medium of haters: Facebook. Hurtful posts—now, that's something every single person can relate to.

I'd like to share just one of the many, *many* Facebook posts on how much I suck. This one came from another radio guy. One who I don't know if I've ever met.

In the post, my radio "colleague" goes to great lengths to discuss how much I suck, how I funded a smear campaign against myself, how I fooled my staff with fake death threats and needs of bodyguards, and that my successes caused thousands like him to lose their jobs. He also called me a "narcissistic, self-centered buffoon."

I'm the first one to say how much I suck. But despite him BOLDING the word "truth" in his actual post so you know what he's writing must be real, this post irritated me because it was literally a bunch of lies. If you want to complain about me being a loser, have the courtesy at least to stick to the facts. There are plenty of 'em.

If it isn't readily apparent, let me break down the jerkiness of this Facebook post:

- **Fake death threats**: Here are the facts. I've never faked a death threat. On every occasion where something crazy has happened (like someone trying to stab me on my way into work, or the correspondence I've received, more than once, where the sender professes wanting to kill me), I've called the REAL cops because it was a REAL threat.

- *The story about how I spent money to reverse-engineer a billboard campaign against myself*: Well, I guess that "inside source" he got that from was me, because I told that story in my last book before anyone else got their hands on it!
- *"Narcissistic, self-centered buffoon"*: In fairness, he did get a few things right.

I only went through this painful and not all that productive exercise of analyzing a hater's post because in this age of Facebook, Twitter, Snapchat, and the rest, pretty much every single human being on earth has had someone he or she probably doesn't know come at them with baseless and just plain mean accusations. Unfortunately, in the Internet age, it is just too easy to take people down. You are safe and hidden behind the computer screen—which means most of the online haters are nothing but cowards. It still hurts, though, when folks don't like you, and there is nothing you can do about it.

Repeat: sometimes people aren't going to like you, and you can't do anything about it.

Nobody is saying that accepting that fact is easy. Because life is essentially just a search for love, it is probably the hardest thing I'll ask you to do in this book. Everyone wants to be liked—even a constantly irritated guy like myself. That instinct is so strong that whenever we are *not* liked, we have to find reasons the person who doesn't like us is wrong . . . or simply stop caring. And the act of not caring, ironically, makes you more likable! Whether it's dating, your career, or making new friends—a lot of people find others more attractive when they are aloof. Unfortunately, caring can be misread as desperation or neediness.

There's a weird phenomenon where once you say "Screw it," others find you more attractive. It's not unlike the cool kids in high school or college; the most popular kids were always the ones who acted like they didn't care (or were rich). And I wasn't either one of them—because I did care.

My technique of flipping unlikability on its head started out as a defense mechanism. When I was young, popularity wasn't even on my radar. I would have settled for just finding a place or group where I fit. For me, though, fitting in has never been straightforward. It started early. I was so poor, I had to be Raggedy Andy for three years in a row on Halloween. That was my costume! Literally, my costume was to dress up as a poor kid.

The theme continued through the early part of my career, when, as an alternative and pop radio DJ, I was deemed too country. And yet, when I moved over to country music, I didn't fit in there, either, because people said I was too pop.

I think I wear people down more than I win them over. I'd compare myself to a web-TV series like *Ozark*, where Jason Bateman plays a forlorn money launderer banished to a resort town in Missouri. At first, I thought that show was terrible. The pilot was so slow. But those rednecks on the show are basically . . . me. So, I stuck with it, and by the third episode I was hooked. The show is fantastic! That's who I am. A slow burner. An acquired taste.

My presence has never made sense anywhere I've been (or at least any place I've wanted to be). And since I've never been a member of the cool club from the start, of course I'd come up with a philosophy that centers around how not being popular is pretty cool in itself.

So, yeah, my belief that chasing acceptance is a waste of time is definitely a defense mechanism. But it's a good one, because it's kept me honest. Anything I've ever embraced because "everyone's doing it" has never worked out for me, to the point where it's better for me to trust my instincts going into any job, relationship, or outfit. In the short term, people might think I'm crazy, but my experience has proven it worth the long-term investment.

Never fitting in anywhere has forced me to learn how to survive and THRIVE everywhere because of the lessons I can learn.

POPULAR MATH

This is a pretty simple equation that I've seen written many times in many ways. Basically, you can have 50 percent of people hate you and 50 percent love you. Or 100 percent have no passion for you whatsoever. And as much as it sucks to have people not like you, you can't control that if you are trying to make an impact. I can't control how everyone is going to respond to me. Sometimes there might be a guy like the one in Massachusetts, who didn't like one of my jokes and therefore wanted to shoot someone. But a lot of people that night *did* like my joke. And that's better than no one hearing or reacting to my joke at all. (The very best thing is that no one was shot.)

The answer to how to be the most likable person is to be so real with yourself that it just doesn't matter to you.

DON'T LOOK FOR
THE NEGATIVE NEEDLE

Hate can often feel louder than love. I'm not just doing my best impression of a yoga instructor or preacher here. That sentence might sound like a cheesy platitude, but it's true. Love can be silent, but hate is noisy and obnoxious.

Think about it this way. Rarely do people call or e-mail an airline to pay a compliment for a wonderful flight. But you can guarantee that if something is amiss—from lost luggage to the flight attendant running out of Sun Chips—Southwest Airlines is going to get an e-mail, a tweet, a Facebook message, and possibly a turd by FedEx.

Because we don't outwardly react when things are positive (choosing instead to appreciate silently) and get so vocal when things are negative, it's easy to become overwhelmed by the sounds of fury. And because we live in a time when there are so many outlets for that anger (see above: Twitter et al.), the noise is that much more amplified. When you are on the receiving end of the hate, it can feel awful—no matter how great your life is.

Major musicians and other big-time artists suffer from this phenomenon all the time. The one who comes to my mind, because the level of criticism he receives is in inverse proportion to his popularity, is Sam Hunt. He's currently the biggest thing in country music, which is a minor miracle considering how progressive he is at times in a format not known to be open to progressive sounds. The country format rightfully takes great pride in its roots, but at times adherence to those roots can be counterproductive to making great music. Anything with a different sound is often fought tooth and nail by the purists of the format. The term "that's not country" is used too often as a definition, when really it's just one person's opinion. The irony is that many of the extremely successful artists I've talked to about this idea were told they weren't "country" either. Garth Brooks is an example. He told me he was tagged with the "that's not country" label many times after he moved to Nashville. Now we look at Garth as a staple of the format. Also, he's the highest-selling American solo artist of all time. Not just in country, but in all formats. Bigger than Elvis. Look it up!

These days, if you listen to any of the very vocal traditionalists, you'd think people actually hated Sam Hunt and his sound, which is rooted in country but with a significant R & B influence. He didn't win any of the major awards for his song "Body Like a Back Road," which was arguably the biggest hit of the last five years. He sells out amphitheaters in minutes. It's nuts how unembraced he is by a small decision-making section of Nashville. Yet Sam continues to create and is absolutely loved by the mostly silent majority. I guess not getting the big awards is okay when you sell out everything you touch and every song you put out turns to gold. (Update: This was written before the April Academy of Country Music Awards, in which Sam finally won an award!) In a recent talk I had with Kip Moore (check out his episode of my podcast. It's great. He gets up and pees right in the middle of it. Kip DGAF), another country artist and now a friend, we spent at least half an hour discussing how hard it is to ignore the one or two people having a bad time at a show. There can be ten thousand dancing and singing, but once you see that negative needle, it throws you. I learned from Steve Martin, who said, "Look only at their foreheads."

Performers can be at the top of their game, and still a harsh review from a critic or a nasty meme about them making the Internet rounds can ruin their day. (Of course, they can console themselves with a four-hand massage at the Ritz-Carlton or a shopping spree.) Seriously, though, insults affect everyone personally. The only reason celebrities don't acknowledge them more, publicly, is because there's a rule of stardom that you're never supposed to "punch down." Even if the biggest Internet troll is biting at your toes in the most terrible way, you don't react. Engaging in an insult match with anyone about why you don't suck is not a good look.

As you can see if you read the beginning of this chapter, I absolutely do not follow this rule myself and have no problems punching down, no matter how stupid and petty it makes me appear. I'm willing to rip apart a Facebook post about how I'm a liar in a *book,* something that sticks around a lot longer than sounding off in your feed. But when has good taste ever stopped me before? Never, that's when. No matter how successful I become, there's a part of me that will always be that kid who cares a little too much. I know it's not winning me any points, so since this is a self-help book, let me give you a piece of advice: don't follow my example on this one.

My desire to shut down anyone who hates on me is not only ultimately bad for my image—it's also futile. The scenario of being punished for your success is no different than back in elementary school when bullies beat on the kids with good grades because they don't feel good about themselves. (I'm not excusing giving anyone a black eye as an ego-boosting mechanism—I'm just saying, it's a thing.) This is the law of nature, like gravity or the gene in men that makes it impossible for us to put the toilet seat down. If you are doing well, you are going to get the bad from others who aren't doing so well. It doesn't matter if they don't have talent or haven't put in the work, people are always upset at others getting stuff they don't. I get upset! But I try to use my jealousy as fuel for my Fight and not to take down others. (Note the word "try.")

When others turn themselves into emotional stumbling blocks on the path toward your goal, the right thing to do is wish them the best, keep your face forward, and continue to Fight. Take the good with the bad.

But we're humans, not saints. Turning the other cheek is great, but not if it gives you an ulcer and totally erodes your self-confidence. Knowing that having one's ability questioned bothers *everyone*—even the rich, famous, and talented—is a good first step in putting negativity in its place. You're not in it alone. Nobody likes it.

There's another important strategy I use to stay strong in the face of any amount of criticism. Don't search for the negative needle in the haystack, because no matter how huge the stack, you'll find the needle. Here's what I mean by that: if ten people give you a compliment, and one says that you suck, "you suck" are probably the two words you're going to remember the most.

Break the habit. You never truly will, but at least be conscious of your tendency to do this. In a recent episode of my podcast, *The BobbyCast*, I talked with Cole Swindell about this very issue. As I write this, he has seven number-one songs as a performer, ten as a writer. And he talked about seeing only the bad comments that poke out like a cold sore! (Instead of my cold sore metaphor, which I recognize is pretty weird, I was going to say "sticks out like a sore thumb." But I realized that's probably dated, and I've never actually noticed someone's sore thumb. I always notice when someone has a cold sore, though. Maybe I'll make that saying a thing. Just a little insight into my process.)

Learning to accept that you did a great job, or were a great friend or a great spouse, instead of constantly searching for the thing you did wrong, isn't just a feel-good policy. And it has nothing to do with taking constructive criticism. They are two separate planets revolving around the sun that is you. Negativity hunting doesn't lead to self-improvement or personal growth.

I know what I'm talking about, mainly because I'm the worst when it comes to looking for the negative needle. I'll pore through thousands of positive fan comments with all the concentration of a researcher combing through rare manuscripts in order to find the two comments that completely destroy me. The. Worst. Me.

I spent a lot of wasted time torturing myself in this exercise, not even aware of what I was doing. It wasn't until I saw the trait in others that I recognized it in myself.

If you have a few minutes, search for *The BobbyCast* on iTunes and listen to that episode with Cole Swindell. He has it all. Young guy, success, talent, money. But still, those little jabs that don't matter were mattering to him! It opened my eyes.

"Why are you paying attention to this?" I asked. "It's a totally worthless, throwaway opinion."

No sooner had the words come out of my mouth than I realized: Crap, I do this, too! Once I was able to acknowledge in myself something I hadn't been smart enough to notice before, I began to see it everywhere. I watch people in a wide array of fields who are great at what they do be waterboarding-level tortured by one or two offhand remarks. I know an amazing chef who had to get blind drunk after reading a negative comment (too offensive to repeat in my book) that someone wrote with pen on the bathroom wall of his restaurant! It didn't matter that his food has been written up in magazines as some of the best in the South or that you can't get into his place on a Saturday night. Nope, some Sharpie scrawl in the john sent him over the edge.

Why would you let anyone, particularly someone with no knowledge of your story, take apart all that you've accomplished? Part of the Fight is resisting that natural reflex to look for the negative needle. Things aren't often going to go right in your Fight, so when they do, however you define that for *yourself*, just enjoy it. And when you catch yourself not enjoying it, be conscious of it. Maybe next time you will. Small steps.

OH, AND DON'T BE A HATER

Just for good measure, don't be a hater, either. We all do it. Even if we don't mean to. Or if we mean to but think we're justified because, of course, the thing or person or place we're hating on deserves it.

Once you accept that we all have hater tendencies, you can get to the business of establishing some boundaries. You are getting absolutely nothing accomplished by aiming negative thoughts or words at someone else's action. And you're wasting your own time when you could be accomplishing something that someone else could be hating on. Why spend time and energy doing something counterproductive to what's good for you? There is no answer other than it makes us feel good in the short term. Long term, though, we usually feel worse than before we started because we're embarrassed by our own shortcomings (the reason for the hating in the first place) and how we handled it (the act of hating).

We can make more money, friends, kids. But the only thing we can't create more of is time. We get what we get—and everything in life takes time. I bring up this precious commodity in terms of helping you to figure out what your Fight is all about. Time is also a major factor in the equation of negativity.

You can spend your time making fun of a work colleague or putting down someone's looks, because you're really jealous. Or you can spend that time still feeling that way but instead of acting on it, acknowledge it and then question *why* you feel that way. Instead of going off on Facebook, take an honest glimpse inside and ask yourself, "Do I feel like this because I'm not doing as well as I want to?"

If the answer is yes, you know what you gotta do: stop looking at others, put your head down, and get back to your Fight.

It's okay that not everyone likes you. And you don't have to like everyone, either. But use your time and energy to build things instead of tearing them down.

Nothing ever came from being critical of the accomplishments of others—unless you have a job as a critic, and I'm not sure how well those are paying these days.

MY BIGGEST FAILURE: CHARLAMAGNE THA GOD

This is the guy I call whenever I need someone to lean on or make sure I'm not crazy. He's always got my back, and I always have his. Maybe that's because this radio and TV personality came up the hard way, like I did—and has never forgotten it.

"My biggest failure was not listening to my father, mother,

grandmother, and every other elder who was trying to tell me to change my lifestyle at an early age. I had a hard head, and as they say in the country, a hard head makes a soft ass. My father always told me if I kept running the streets the way I was I would end up in jail, dead, or broke sitting under the tree. Two of those things absolutely happened for brief moments in my life (clearly death wasn't one of them), but that failure to listen led me to jail and sitting under the tree broke. That failure to listen also led me to be who I am today, because it made me START listening. Smart people learn from their own mistakes; wise people learn from the mistakes of others. Sometimes we have to bump our own heads in order to learn. Well, that's exactly what I did, and now I'm here, all praises due to God!!!"

FIGHT IN REVIEW

BOBBY WORKS: THE SERVER EDITION

I've had just about every job there is under the sun. And just as I've learned from the people I've worked with over the years, I've learned something important from every single job I've done. The principles I've gathered from my experiences still apply to my life and career today, so I figured I'd share a few of them with you.

If waiting tables isn't a fight, I don't know what is. For a couple of years, I was a proud member of the service industry—a.k.a. a busboy and then a waiter. In that time, the biggest shock to my system came with how dependent I was on the generosity of others. As a waiter, you can crush it and do a fantastic job, and still get nothing. Or you can do a terrible job, and a kind stranger will take pity (or just to show off in front of their date) and tip you big.

The upshot was that my entire existence, from rent to food to gas, depended on people tipping me. I didn't have car insurance money unless my customers hooked it up. That meant being as helpful and positive as I could in my interactions with everyone, no matter how incredibly rude they could be. (And if you've never been a waiter, you have no idea just how hateful people can get.) I will never forget what it felt like to deal with folks who are ugly and mean for no real reason at all except for a superiority complex. Perhaps that's the greatest gift I got from waiting tables: the desire to never, ever be an ugly, mean person to someone waiting on me.

I'd like to take a moment and do a PSA on how to treat wait-staff, so bear with me. Here goes:

Next time you are in a restaurant, do these things for me . . .

1. *DON'T BE AN AWFUL PERSON.*
2. *Understand that this waiter has to deal with people being UGLY and MEAN for absolutely no reason all the time.* And they have to smile through the experience, because they have to buy toothpaste and tampons.
3. *Your servers are people, too.* Working hard. They go home to their lives just like you do from your job.
4. *Servers also control your food, and they control your food when you don't see your food.* And they can do whatever they want to your food in the kitchen. So don't be a jerk, because it's not nice and you may compel them to fart on or spit in your food.
5. *Tip like your bill payments depend on it, because theirs do.*

And if something happens at a restaurant that's not right, remember there could be many reasons. Your server is only the face or front line of the whole operation. In my experience, the kitchen messed up a lot of the things I was asked to provide— and I got blamed. And you know what I had to do? Take it! I said I was sorry and then tried to fix the problem by adding a little something extra.

You are paying for a meal *and* the service, so it should be pretty right on. But if it's not, don't freak. Once I dropped an entire tray of drinks (probably eight in total) all over a table. One man bore the brunt of most of the liquid. I was mortified as I ran to get him towels, a lot of towels. He didn't yell, and the table continued their dinner. I felt terrible. At the end of the night, he left me a hundred-dollar tip on a bill of $120, with a note that read, "It happens to the best of us. It's not the mistakes we make, but how we handle it afterward. Thanks for hanging in there."

I was blown away. The gesture was so kind I wanted to cry. If I could find that man, here's what I would say:

"Mr. Gentleman in your late forties from seventeen years ago in the gray suit who had a tray of liquids spilled on him in the Hot Springs Village . . . I appreciate you. I still remember you *to this day.* That moment we shared many years ago in the DeSoto Club made me a better person." I use that situation constantly to remind myself of the power of "extending grace." Doing good things stands the test of time.

For the record, I'm the greatest tipper known to man, excluding those rich celebrities who drop ten thousand dollars because they hear that the server's great-grandma needs a new eye, a fact randomly mentioned during the meal.

I always wonder about those huge tips that celebs leave. How many times did the waiter have to bring that story up for someone to finally give in?

And do they just use the I'm-an-in-need-waiter story for famous people? The rich-looking people in the nice clothes eating lobster? All the people? My guess would be that they try to shoehorn their sob story in as much as possible just in case . . . and every once in a while, as my grandma would say, even a blind squirrel finds a nut. I would be in absolute shock if a one-time mention turned into a nine-thousand-dollar tip on a forty-two-dollar dinner bill, but what do I know. By the way, I'm not hating. Nothing illegal is happening. Nobody is getting hurt. And total transparency, when I was working in an older (people) part of town, I didn't stop the ladies from pinching my butt on occasion.

When you're in the Fight, you do whatever it takes.

Part 2

GRIND

5

IT'S AS BAD AS IT SOUNDS

Imagine this: you're not a morning person. Not at all. In fact, you're the kind of person who likes to stay up to watch all the late-night comedy shows every single night—and then sleep late. Then imagine that in order to do your job (and I don't mean do your job well, but just to do the bare minimum, like showing up on time), you have to wake up every weekday morning at 3 A.M. Sound like a living hell? Yup. This has been my life for more than fifteen years.

I can't tell you how terrible it is to hate mornings so much and have to experience them so fully. There is no amount of caffeine that can make the crack of dawn okay for me. There's a range of torture, and it goes from soul crushing to just plain awful. Every single time my alarm goes off so that I can make it to the studio to wake everybody else up with my radio show—it's a struggle. And by my calculations, I've had to hit that stupid phone alarm at an ungodly hour about four thousand times since my career began.

This is the Grind. It's the dirty work.

If you're reading this book in order, you're ready for the Fight. You've figured out a goal or vision for yourself, analyzed your motivations, and now you've got the fire in your belly.

Maybe your Fight is getting your kids to do their homework every night. Maybe your Fight is keeping the warehouse you manage running at top level. Whatever it is that you're looking to succeed at doing—from being a good parent to opening a restaurant to doing a radio show—you're going to have to Grind. You're going to have to execute all those tiny, everyday, ordinary tasks that put you in the position to make the big things happen. Also, let me say beforehand that I'm going to use the word "grind" a lot in this section. In the context of Fight, Grind, Repeat, I feel as if it represents the grinding of a material. However, it is also the term I use at times to describe my dancing to songs like Ginuwine's "Pony." It will not be used in the dancing context at all this section. So, friends, get your mind out of the freak-dancing gutter.

Each of us makes so many decisions every day that they can come off as insignificant. But I argue that these decisions create the structure for your dreams, sort of like the bricks that create a home.

I have options, now, when it comes to my morning radio show. I could go to bed later, sleep in longer, and have one of my producers do the work of gathering the daily content that I do the night before every show by reading the news, watching television shows, taking notes, writing bits. I mean, maybe if I got more sleep I wouldn't hate mornings so much. (But to be honest, a late night for me is staying awake past 9 P.M.) I don't have producers creating large amounts of material for my show, even if it would make my life easier, because I don't think the end product would be as authentic or, frankly, as good. (The thing is, I'm probably wrong. I bet my producers would crush it.)

The Grind is relentless. As I wrote in the introduction, it means taking the Fight and doing it again. And again. And again. Going back to my boxing classes analogy, look at it this way: anyone can fight for short amounts of time. That's why boxing matches consist of three-minute rounds. It's three short minutes, over and over. You might be able to get through three minutes of punches, but to keep going back for more? The repetition is the killer. As my football coach back in Mountain Pine, Vic Gandolph, used to say, "If it was easy, everybody would be doing it."

This is the step where a lot of folks lose their way. Partly that's because the Grind is not exciting or glamorous. But it is also because it's not straightforward. If the Fight is about the idea, then the Grind is the actions you need to take—and those are never straightforward.

Once you've figured out what's important to you in the big picture, you've got to start filling in all the small details. This is where failure comes in, because, really, none of us knows what the heck we're doing here. You have to do a whole lot of trying to figure out what actually works before you land on the right actions. Like me and my TV show ideas: I keep throwing them out there (some of which I'm sure are going to be winners), but so far nothing's stuck. I've done this Fight, Grind, Repeat thing long enough to know that eventually I'll get it right.

> The Grind is everything that's not going to get you whatever piece of glory you're looking for. But it gets you closer to *maybe* having a shot at the piece of glory you're looking for.

Finding your success is like dealing with your health. Everybody's body is different. There are some things that most successful people have in common to make them successful, but there is no one-size-fits-all. A doctor can diagnose you with whatever she thinks the problem is, but she doesn't know for sure. Everybody has a different makeup. Essentially, I'm saying that Viagra didn't work for me like it did the other guys.

Fight, Grind, Repeat is a process—and one of the most important elements I've learned from it is that if you're ever going to stick with something long enough to be in the position to succeed, you've got to burrow a tunnel in your mind that ends with your goal. It's not unlike how horses wear blinders so they can only see in front of them. There can be no distractions (especially what other horses are doing) as they race to their goal. But unfortunately, our paths aren't as neat as a racetrack.

When you start down your tunnel or path, you'll find it forks into smaller paths that are often dead ends. Then you have to turn around and seek out bigger, smoother paths.

Your lifeboat during the Grind is consistency. It's consistently doing the small things. And doing them all the time. Developing a pattern is absolute, because if you aren't doing the little things right, you *definitely* won't do the big things right.

My Grind of waking up early every morning is at once the easiest and hardest thing for me to do. I mean, all I have to do is get my butt out of my warm, soft bed when the alarm goes off. (My mattress is very nice, one of those Sleep Number jobs that predicts your movements. Fancy.) But no matter how many years go by of this pattern, every morning the little evil voice in my head tells me to hit the snooze button. I don't listen, though. After the initial discomfort passes, I know that I am going to get up, go to the job I love, work as hard as I can that day, pay attention to the little details, and crush it. That's why, literally,* I have never hit my snooze button.

TECH TOOLS FOR THE GRIND

I'm a big believer in using your smartphone as a tool in Fight, Grind, Repeat. You're looking at the stupid thing all day anyway, so you might as well put it to a better use than checking out your ex-husband's Instagram feed. I use my phone in all sorts of ways (see more about goals in chapter 6), but one app that I've found helpful for the

---

* I'd like to say something about using the word "literally." Please use it only in its accurate sense. I'm fine if you say, "My head exploded when my boss handed me this assignment." I get it. You probably had a lot going on mentally. You can even say, "My head exploded, figuratively, when my boss handed me this assignment." Not the route I would take, but it's accurate. But don't say, "Literally, my head exploded when my boss handed me this assignment." Because you are lying. It didn't. We get what you're saying without using a word that means you are describing something exactly as it happened. I know this has nothing to do with the concept of this book, but do me a solid: stop saying things are literal when they aren't. Just stop it. You lose nothing. Thanks.

Grind is Streaks, "the to-do list that helps you form good habits."

Now, I'm sure there are about a bazillion of this kind of habit-tracking app on the market, and I'm not getting paid for this (although Streaks, if you want to send a check, please make it out to Bobby Estell . . . or Venmo is fine, since we are talking apps). This just happens to be the one I use and like, but feel free to go ahead and find a better one.

Streaks works this way: you get to choose up to twelve tasks you want to turn into daily habits. (The limited number of habits is purposeful, since it forces you to decide what things are truly important to you and concentrate on those.) You come up with them yourself, so they can be anything from drinking eight glasses of water to writing in your journal to wrestling an aardvark. Every time you complete the task, you tap this big button on the screen and—boom!—you got another day in your streak. If you skip one day, however, you go back to zero. (You can set the app for habits that aren't meant for every day without breaking your streak—like getting to work on time can be Monday through Friday.)

The reason the app works is that (1) it's really simple, (2) there's nothing more satisfying than hitting that big ol' button, and (3) there's nothing worse than breaking your streak once you get going.

Streaks creator Quentin Zervaas told raywenderlich. com, a site for programmers, the core idea behind his app: "To become successful is really just a matter of persistence: you keep trying things, many will fail, eventually, some things succeed. These things won't last forever either, then it's on to the next thing."

Sounds like a Grinder to me. (Not to be confused with the tasty sandwich. Or with Grindr, another app. Equally effective but for totally different purposes.)

SWEAT THE SMALL STUFF

"I'm best under pressure."

"Wait until I get on the big stage, then I'll really turn it on."

"When I'm the boss, I'm going to show them how it's done."

Ever heard anyone express these sentiments? Ever said something like this yourself?

Thinking like this keeps you stuck. If you don't perfect the small things, you won't even have a shot at doing the big stuff where it counts. And if for some crazy reason you do get a lucky break (like your uncle owns the company or the song you wrote and performed yourself goes viral), if you haven't perfected the art of yourself, you are going to flame out faster than Chumbawamba. (If you don't remember Chumbawamba, YouTube it real quick. They had that song "Tubthumping." It was one of the biggest one-hit wonders I've ever experienced. "I get knocked down, and I get up again . . ." Remember it now? Yeah. It was the jam. But what happened to them? I hope they didn't all die! Just googled it. They didn't die, literally. But figuratively they are dead. Sing it with me, "pissing the night away, pissing the night away . . ." They don't make songs like they used to, kids.)

When I look for people to hire, promote, or partner with, it's fantastic if they have big accomplishments. But some folks have impressive achievements because of factors that don't show up on their résumé. That's why I look at the small details, which I've found to be a much better indicator of future success than fancy titles.

I'll get more into the nitty-gritty of this in chapter 7, but what I'm talking about is commonsense stuff, things like: Does this person show up to work late? Does he send out mass e-mails with tons of typos? Does she regularly hand in assignments late? These are the small factors that don't seem to mean much in the moment, but add up quickly to become a real problem.

The details don't just matter in professional settings. In fact, they probably mean even more in personal ones. Sending hand-written thank-you cards, checking in with someone who hasn't shown up to exercise class in a while even though she isn't a great friend, just telling a kid when he did a good job—these are the small acts that often have a lot more impact than the grand gestures.

I like to watch how people treat others when it doesn't matter or they don't think anyone is looking. Picking up litter at a gas station, so somebody who works there doesn't have to, or not getting angry at the waiter when he delivers the wrong meal: they can be real insights into character.

It's returning the shopping cart to the store after you've put all your groceries in the car. I know what you're thinking: there are people starving all over this planet, and you're worried about grocery carts? Yes! You can look at it as not having any effect in the grand scheme of things, or just the opposite. If everyone did one small act of kindness every day, the effect would be huge. That's the shopping cart conundrum.

"I'm going to roll this grocery cart and put it back, so the person working here has one less cart to fetch in the parking lot" vs. "I have my groceries in the trunk. Time to get home as fast as I can, unload them, turn on *This Is Us*, and eat ice cream!"

Sure, we are all worried that our ice cream is going to melt, but the folks who resist that instinct, because they understand the consequences beyond their own personal reality, prove there's more than one layer to their thought process and that they think of people outside of themselves.

I have given this shopping cart idea a lot of thought. I freaking worked at Hobby Lobby and had to gather all these carts. I know the shopping cart struggle on a very personal level. I can guarantee that people who care about the little things will definitely get it right when it comes to the big ones.

> ## THE GRIND IS . . .
> EVERY DAY
> SMALL DETAILS
> CONSISTENCY
> TUNNEL VISION
> ESTABLISHING GOOD HABITS
> DISCIPLINE
> DETERMINATION

THE GRIND TO END ALL GRINDS

For lots of folks—myself included—eating right is the ultimate Grind. The Fight is losing weight or just being healthy, but the Grind is the regimen of not shoveling doughnuts, pizza, and Cap'n Crunch chicken tenders into your face every day.

The classic scenario goes something like this: you hear about a new diet (Paleo, keto, SpaghettiO—I personally enjoy the third one the most) and you're super psyched to get started. The beginning of any new self-improvement project is an optimistic moment. But then you get to the doing, or, in the case of diets, the sticking to it after a few weeks. That's when it gets hard. At times, for me, it seems impossible.

With the penchant for addiction running strong in my genes, I have to remove temptation completely. I know if I put a cake in my refrigerator, I'm going to eat that cake in the refrigerator. The entire cake. In one sitting. Therefore, I don't put the cake in the refrigerator.

. . . Or Werther's Originals in my kitchen. I know what you're thinking: "You're way too hip and cool to eat an old person's candy." Let me tell you a story before you get on your Jolly Rancher high horse.

As my grandfather was saying good-bye to us to move on to heaven, he reached his hand out and said, "Bobby, take this." It was three Werther's Originals. I looked at them probably the same way you do every single time you see them at Walgreens next to the adult pee pads. Not good, but I crammed them into my pocket. After my grandfather passed I decided to eat one. And it was amazing! That hard caramel taste invigorated my taste buds. I felt like a new candy man. I saved the other two for posterity, but ever since then, I've had a particular affinity for those hard candies. By the way, that entire story is made up. I never even knew either one of my biological grandfathers, but I do love me my Werther's. Anytime there's a bag of them in my house, I will eat the *whole* thing. And let me tell you, that's a lot of Werther's. I've even resorted to having friends hide the candies throughout my bedroom and only tell me every few days where they are tucked away.

Jokes aside, weight loss is like many other issues people struggle with, such as quitting drinking or coping with anxiety; it can be so hard that it feels near impossible. While I have my own host of problems, weight isn't one of them. I've never been obese or gone through a tough weight-loss experience, so I don't pretend to know what that's like. But my approach to how I eat is a really good example of what the Grind is all about. I took a hard reset with my body starting in 2012. Since then I have adhered to the same practice, which is, for the most part, not to let cake or any other fattening foods in my refrigerator or anywhere else near me. I don't even let myself have options, because I'm bad with options. I know myself; if I have them, I'll just make mistakes. So, I eat the same food every day for breakfast and lunch—and usually dinner, too. (Sometimes I have to do work events, and for some reason they don't like you to bring your own food from home for those kinds of things.) Literally (that's right), the same exact meal. Then every few weeks, I change it up. For example, right now, lunch is roasted cauliflower with grilled chicken and vegan almond cheese. That's basically the Steve Jobs turtleneck of foods for me right now.

I'm not telling everybody to limit their options this way.

This isn't a diet advice book. What I think is that people should know themselves. I have friends that can sit in front of cherry pie, ice cream, and a bowl of chocolates—and eat a scoop of ice cream and leave the rest without giving it a second thought. That's them. That's definitely not me.

I credit a big part of my success to putting myself in the best situation to succeed (part of the preparation described in the Fight section). Sometimes the act of putting yourself in those situations is in itself hard. When it comes to sticking to my diet, that means keeping junk food out of my refrigerator and eating the same thing every day. (And in case you're wondering, no, vegan cheese tastes nothing like regular cheese.)

6

THE BEAUTY OF BABY STEPS

Another true cliché: we are our own worst enemies.

I wrote earlier about rejection and the role other people play in your Fight. But ask any psychologist or self-help expert, or any of my bosses—more than *anyone else,* we undermine ourselves.

Sometimes it's through bad behavior (cue the beer or cake in the refrigerator). Other times, we simply psych ourselves out. Folks have trouble trying their hardest, giving something their all. That block stems from the common fear of failure. It's scary to fail, for everyone.

There are no two ways about it: failing sucks, man. As much as I talk about how great it is to fail, let's be real. Failing invites a whole lot of heartache. You can't help but think, Maybe I'm not good enough. Trying to avoid those kinds of feelings can keep you from taking on a challenge. We've all been there—in school, career, or relationships. That's how it may *feel*, but failure is the only path to success. We have to retrain our brains and hearts to think this way, so that when we bomb, we don't instantly go to the negative place. Instead, we need to be able to say, "No, I'm still good enough. Let me go again. And again and again." I often set psychological markers for myself before I get into something challenging. This book is a good example. Before it has even come out, I am convinced no one will care about the content.

"Who would want to read a self-help book by a radio personality?" one negative voice in my head says.

"Is it any good?" another one asks.

Those are normal thoughts to have in the middle of a new endeavor that really means something. As those voices piped up in the process of writing this book, I had to remind myself that they were also present when I did my last book. And that one turned out pretty well! (Thanks to my people!!!) It was a four-week *New York Times* bestseller. Had you asked me prior to its release how I felt, I would have said the exact same things currently running through my head about this one. Thanks to experience, awareness, and ability to diagnose my mindset, I can set those negative emotions aside—sort of.

THE FREAK-OUT MONSTER

A lot of my friends in business who hate doing presentations will plan out every word, click, and breath. That's great, since being prepared is always the first step to feeling more confident. But no matter how well prepared my friends are, as the presentation gets closer, the Freak-Out Monster creeps up. "This isn't good enough," it sneers. "You should be very, very nervous." You can arm yourself against the Freak-Out Monster by knowing that it's going to attack you regardless of how much prep work you've done. It's like the predictive text feature on your phone. But instead of inserting an emoji, it's inserting the wherewithal to know you are going to freak out regardless. Predict your craziness. You know your habits and how nuts you are. By telling the Freak-Out Monster, "Welcome, I was expecting you," you take away its power.

Another unfortunate mind game many of us play is overwhelming ourselves before we've even begun. Think of the Fight as a very long, very steep ladder that you have to climb down. If you look down, the climb is pretty scary. But if you focus on just the next step, it's manageable. All of those rungs of the ladder, each one necessary to keep you from falling on your butt, they are the Grind.

Don't let the big prize get in the way of the necessary steps you need to take in order to get it—either because you've scared yourself *or* impatience tempts you to try to skip a few rungs of the ladder.

That last one has burned me more than a few times. I've tried to cut out steps that ultimately proved vital to the process in pursuit of something I wanted. As you can imagine, doing this has only pushed the goal farther away from me. When I used to date on the apps, instead of taking the time to have a little back and forth, I would just say, "Let's meet." That was a disaster on many different levels. You can't rush success. My most recent example of this is buying Bitcoin. When I learned about the digital currency, I was all in. I was going to be a Winklevoss twin. Woo-hoo! Cut to me losing 30 percent of my original investment (and still counting down), not to mention feeling like by getting involved in crypto currency, the Russians have somehow hacked me!

Taking baby steps also helps you to alleviate anxiety and avoid mistakes. But it also makes the Grind go by a lot easier. If you're concentrating on the doing, you don't get so caught up in *how* you're doing or how far your doings have taken you.

For a while my exercise of choice was running. (I know, you're sick of me writing about exercise by now, but stick with me.) I wasn't a good runner because I didn't have the mental strength to do the exact same motion over and over. That's a real skill. I've already said how much I hate exercising—in every form—but running is the worst. Talk about a Grind! Even though I think running is a voluntary form of torture, I ended up running ten-mile stretches by tricking myself into it. My method was to find little landmarks, such as trees or signposts, every thirty yards and run from one to another without ever stopping. That's what I did the whole time, because as soon as I started thinking, I have another fifty-six minutes to run, I was exhausted immediately. But if I told myself, I've got about thirty-two steps to that tree, that was a piece of cake. Ten miles is impossible, but putting one foot in front of another? That's not so hard.

That's how I work, too. It's hour by hour, show by show, week by week, quarter by quarter, year by year. Sometimes I even break my goals down into fifteen minutes! I'm not kidding (see the next section). The smaller you break down the activity or time it takes to do something, the more manageable it becomes. You can also see success quicker in your small goals, which is quite encouraging! Going "tree by tree" in all things has allowed me to overcome my insecurities and achieve a lot, little by little.

MY BIGGEST FAILURE: BROOKLYN DECKER

Brooklyn—who has two kids with husband Andy Roddick—is used to being in the spotlight. The model-actress was on the cover of the *Sports Illustrated* Swimsuit Issue and appeared in major movies and TV shows. That doesn't mean she's always felt like a star.

"I actively went after my 'big break' as an actor and tried to ride that wave. I did it way too early. What I should have done is studied my ass off and gotten significantly better at my actual job before seeking any sort of employment. What ended up happening was I got a few opportunities before I was ready. I wasn't worthy or skilled enough, and I ended up making all my rookie mistakes on a massive stage (in my case, massive films). It almost ruined my career. I had to claw my way back to any sort of credibility. No one took me seriously. It's still a challenge today. I wish I had taken the time to lay the foundation of a career. I wish I had made all those mistakes on a smaller, more forgiving stage. I wish I hadn't sought out opportunity and success, and instead worked to make sure that I was 100 percent ready when the opportunity actually did come my way. We're moving away from this as a culture, but there's a lot of power in delayed gratification. I wish I had known that before."

MAKE YOUR WORDS COUNT

The very first thing I do when I make a new goal is to say it out loud. This is an important step, because I'm labeling what I want to achieve for myself. Then I put it out into the world.

At times, I will make huge public statements, knowing full well they are not true (yet). In a recent interview with *Rolling Stone*, I proclaimed that behind Howard Stern I am the best interviewer in all of radio. Now, let's be honest for a second. I don't actually think so highly of myself. (Not to mention the fact that there's a serious leap in logic here, since I haven't listened to every interviewer who has ever been on the radio.) But I put it out there. In a national magazine.

If I put a statement about being the best interviewer into the universe, I must now live up to it, or at least be held accountable for it. Either way, I'm going to work that much harder. Every freaking interview that I now conduct, I hear these words screaming at me: "Don't suck, because you said you don't."

You don't need a national platform to make your goals public. The example of my life is extreme in every way (remember, I eat vegan cheese every day for lunch). You can achieve the same result by telling your family, friends, or just one particularly judgmental and nosy person. The point is to take your ideas from the theoretical to the practical.

Words work. Words turn into thoughts. Thoughts turn into action. It's math. Sort of. It's at least logic.

THE POWER OF WORDS

Dr. Ellen Langer—a social psychologist at Harvard University and author of eleven books—has been called the "mother of mindfulness." She focuses her research on the idea of mindfulness as "stressing process over outcome," or basically not just doing the same dumb thing over and over for the same result. A lot of her experiments have had to do with the idea that the words we use to describe or explain an action fundamentally affect our experience and outcome of the act. Get this: she did an experiment with forty-four hotel maids who were out of shape. These women said they didn't have time to exercise. But when they were told their work scrubbing and cleaning was actually the same as a serious workout at the gym and asked to think of their jobs as "exercise" as opposed to "work," they all lost weight! After a month, the forty-four maids lost an average of two pounds each, as well as greatly improved their blood pressure and other vitals. These women didn't change a single thing other than how they *thought* about their work—and it was enough to change their bodies!

I like to keep my goals in my periphery at all times. Remember, the Grind is All. The. Time.

I create layers of reminders, so that I have no excuse to stop Grinding. My phone is my first tier, a whiteboard in my room is the second, and Amy, my cohost, is often my third (when it comes to anything regarding the radio show). That's *my* ranking system of reminders, but you should create your own (because Amy is a very busy lady). I recommend that you make one of them physical and visual (like the whiteboard) and one of them human (like Amy). And *everyone* should use their phone as the first line of defense, because let's be honest, most of us live through our phones these days. We might as well use those things to make ourselves better humans, instead of wasting time on Candy Crush.

I look at my phone more than I look into the eyes of other people, so there is no better place to remind myself of my goals. My phone is basically my constant, traveling whiteboard, since I look at it five hundred times a day. If there's something that I really want to make a focus, I take the document app, write a note on it, and save it as the wallpaper of my lock screen. It could be doing more romantic stuff for my girlfriend (at the time of writing this, I had one. At its publishing, I did not. Quite possibly because I stared at my phone too much!) or eating less fried food. (Food, sleep, and exercise are the most frequent subjects of my lock screen.) Whatever I want to be at the top of my mind and need the most support in doing goes there, so that every time I hit my iPhone button to unlock my screen, there it is! The problem is, I only have one phone. That's not really a problem; that's called being a normal person. But I need ten phones when I have ten things I want to do.

SAMPLE LOCK SCREEN MESSAGES I'VE WRITTEN TO MYSELF

Hey, don't eat sugar for 3 days

Write 1000 words today, even if you don't feel like it

For every episode of a show you watch, you have to read a
    chapter of a book
Stop saying the word "like" so much
Give sincere compliments
Pay attention to your email tone

When I was in college, guys and girls would cut out images from magazines of people they wanted to look like—ripped weight lifters or bikini models—and put them up on their refrigerators or bulletin boards. I'm suggesting a modern, more productive approach to that idea, except it's in your face a whole lot more.

Sometimes my goals are for one day only. When I recently hosted and performed at a corporate event for Dollar General, I didn't get to sleep until midnight and I knew I was going to be toast the next morning for my radio show. Except I can't afford to sleepwalk through a single show. So before I went to sleep that night, I changed my lock screen to: "You are tired this morning. You must crush the next 5 hours. If you don't, someone else will." I probably check my phone ten times while doing my show, so I saw that message ten times that morning, and you know what? It worked. I'm not saying it was the best show, but it wasn't terrible.

Again: words work. Put them in front of you.

Never chase money. Chase confidence.

I told you that when I speak to groups, the question I am asked most often is "How do you become successful?" That's number one. The second-most-asked question is some version of "How do I make a bunch of money?" (And let's be honest, for a lot of folks, success = money.)

I have a unique formula for the relationship to success and money, and I'll share it with anyone who'll listen.

Finding something you love to do + working hard at it (simply out of love for it) = success + money.

You're just playing the odds. The more you love something, the harder you are going to work at it. And the harder you work, the more likely you are to be successful at it—and that's when the money comes! This is life, however, and not an equation; the reality isn't quite as neat. The payout also depends, for the most part, on the field you enter. For example, I have a friend who works in child-protective services, and she's crazy fulfilled by her profession. But she ain't ever going to get rich off saving society's most vulnerable children. Teaching, hospice care, clergy: these aren't jobs known for big paychecks, but the reward comes in a different form. If I had chased money, I would never have gotten into radio and comedy—because there was *no* money in it. And for the longest time, I had no money. I was broke forever but never unhappy as long as I progressed in my career.

Sometimes success has nothing to do with money and is just being able to do what you love to do. When I was in high school, my mom married my stepdad Keith, who worked at the local mill. I guess he was lucky to have a job, but he hated it. *Hated* it. I remember wondering what it must be like knowing that every day, for the rest of your life, you were going to hate your job. Work is such a big part of who we are because we spend so much time doing it. It shapes our identity.

I do believe you have more chance at success if you love what you do for a living. But there's also this: if you don't wind up making a lot of money following your passion, you're at least still doing what you love. I like to present worst-case scenarios, because that's usually what we feel happens to us.

We as people-ish creatures tend to see "what we could have had" more than "what we have." How many times have you looked at a car that was awesome and compared it to yours, which probably isn't that awesome if you're comparing it? The same is true for jobs. We tend to romanticize other jobs and look down on our own. There is the possibility that your circumstances could be far better, but there is also the same chance they could be way worse. What we tend to focus on is what we *don't* have instead of what we *do*.

The people I've met who've pursued careers for money alone tend to be the unhappiest folks I know. What I've noticed from watching others chase money is that there's usually a short burst when they do pretty well. After the initial fun of making bank fades (everything fades after a while), they wind up miserable. And because they're miserable selling real estate or investment banking, they end up not putting in the work required and really sucking at it—and then not doing well financially any longer.

There's also the truth that if your life is measured by money, then you can never have enough. I'm not talking about financial security. Having grown up poor, I know how terrible it feels to have *no* money. But if your only aim is to be rich, you'll wind up feeling poor. That's because there is someone out there who is likely better at everything you do. There is someone funnier, smarter, more magnetic. If you can acknowledge that, you become more comfortable at being you, which is the ultimate success.

I acknowledge that "I'm the best me" is a pretty lame thing to say—particularly from a guy who admittedly has done pretty well doing what he loves. It doesn't matter how much money I have in my bank account—the only way that I really feel successful is feeling that I'm really good at being me. Any other comparison will only invite eventual heartache.

"When you ask kids today what they want to be when they grow up, the most common answer is, 'Rich and famous.' And that's not a job." —Lauren Greenfield, director of the documentary *Generation Wealth*

A QUICK EXERCISE TO IMPROVE YOUR DAY

I love breaking my bigger goals into micro (read: achievable) ones. To get into the practice, do this simple exercise. Don't sweat it; just see what comes to mind and then see it through.

- Take ninety seconds to evaluate the biggest challenge facing you tomorrow. Think about what makes you nervous about it or why it's important. Imagine the scenario playing out.
- Take ninety seconds to think about one thing you can do to prepare for the challenge. It can be anything from preparing two ideas to say at a work meeting to mentally

picking out your outfit for a blind date to preparing your lunch so you stick to your diet.

- Write it down.

MY BIGGEST FAILURE: CHARLES ESTEN

The *Nashville* star is a mighty talented actor. He's appeared on *Big Love, The Office, ER,* and a ton of other shows. He was once a Klingon on *Star Trek: The Next Generation.* (He's not a bad musician, either.) But he didn't just saunter onto the set of the starship *Enterprise;* he had to earn it.

"Many people know that I was fortunate enough to be a recurring cast member on the longtime hit improv show *Whose Line Is It Anyway?* Some are aware that my participation in that show goes all the way back to the original British version in the early nineties. Very few have any idea that, at one point, I actually lost my spot on that show, failing my way out of one of my first and favorite jobs. Looking back today, it's one of my biggest, and favorite, failures.

"Although it would later find American exposure, running on Comedy Central and then YouTube, at the time I auditioned, the show was only on in England. Looking back, it was the idea that 'no one I know will ever see this,' along with the safety of a steady job I already had playing Buddy Holly on the West End stage, that somehow made me immune to the nervousness that might be expected of a young guy making his television debut— with nothing more than the next thing that popped into my head! I was improvising live on tape, in front of a British studio audience, with some of the most intelligent, hilarious, and yes, experienced improvisers in the world, and I wasn't even nervous. Until I was.

"The reality of my situation began to occur to me. My role as Buddy behind me, I had grown to really love the show and knew very well what a great job it was. I also knew something else about *Whose Line Is It Anyway?* Every appearance was, in a real sense, an audition for your next one. With plenty of incredible talent waiting to sit in that limited number of chairs, one bad show could mean the end of it all.

"By the time I appeared on the show in England again, my only thoughts were ones of nervousness and outright fear, all condensed into the worst comedy mantra ever: whatever you do, BE FUNNY!

"Of course, I wasn't—I was terrified, and promptly lost my spot on the show. They just stopped calling, leaving me to deal not just with unemployment, but with the knowledge that I had done this all to myself. In hindsight it was obvious that there was no muscle I could flex to 'be funny.' All I could ever really do is just try to relax and do my best. I had done the opposite, freaking myself out and folding under the pressure.

"Not too long after, when the U.S version of *Whose Line Is It Anyway?* began airing on ABC, it included many familiar faces from the British show, most notably my incredibly talented friends Ryan Stiles and Colin Mochrie. Painfully, I was not among them. It wasn't until the second season that I was told that I would be able to audition all over again. I was sincerely happy to get that audition, and went prepared not only with more improv experience, but with a brand-new thought in my head: not 'be funny' but 'have fun.' As obvious as it sounds, that simple twist I had learned the hard way changed everything. I relaxed, performed well, and got back on the show, and went on to appear many, many times thereafter. Still today, whenever I find myself in an extremely intimidating situation (and it happens all the time), I remember that favorite failure and the valuable lesson I took from it. And I have fun."

7

DRILLING DOWN

I'm so into boxing that I'm thinking about getting into the gym business. (I told you, once I'm in, I'm all in.) When meeting with potential partners, I enjoy going out to lunch and glad-handing. (Actually, not so much. I love to work, but I hate to schmooze. And you know I don't like to vary my lunch menu.) My real litmus test, however, isn't the quality of the steakhouse they pick for our meeting, but rather what's going on with the trash cans in their existing gyms. That's right—the trash cans.

Here's the deal: I look at the trash cans in their gyms to see if they are empty or overflowing. Sure, sometimes trash cans get full (the person who is usually in charge of trash pickup is out sick). But most of the time, full trash cans signify a lack of attention to the small details. And remember: the small details are the essence of big dividends.

As I've said, these details are the essence of the Grind, and most of us aren't looking for them. They're like microbes—they're all over the place and we couldn't exist without them, but we don't see them. The little things that grow into a career, lifestyle, hit record, or new set of friends seem invisible because they are so incremental. They aren't the headline-making changes that come from long periods of the Grind.

The Grind is only apparent when it's you doing it—or someone you're very close to, such as a spouse, family member, or very good friend. Covering the music scene pretty closely, I see a lot of people Grinding away. As glamorous as the Country Music Awards or the Grammys are, the life of a musician—hitting the road, promoting their music through any and all media, and making more music—is hard work. You get off that treadmill for one second? Someone else will take your spot. And I'm talking about the folks who've already made it!

I have a musical artist friend who's on the road more than anybody else I know. She also practices more than anybody I know. In her downtime, she's in radio stations talking to program directors or doing promotional appearances anywhere they'll have her. Not that you'd know it—unless you know her. Because these aren't the kind of things you put on your Instagram feed. She's investing all this time and energy so that, hopefully, someone will eventually say, "Hey, we have this great thing for you." The Grind is never about the actual opportunity. It is about being ready for opportunity when it comes.

Usually, you are the only one who knows the full details of your moment-by-moment focus. And that's the way it should be. I've mentioned my decades-long struggle to wake up early. However, that's just the tip of the iceberg. Morning, noon, and night, I have an obsession with being on time. Just the thought of being late stresses me out. The reason I feel like I'm successful is that I show up. But even that isn't good enough for me. I have to show up *on time*.

Here is my struggle with being on time: I leave *way* early for EVERYTHING. This is no exaggeration. I'm like the grandpa who makes you get to the airport two hours early for a domestic flight. (You miss your plane, you are screwed—and ain't nobody gonna let you cut the security line no matter how soon your plane is boarding. The airport is cutthroat.) I give myself enough time when I go to work in the morning that if I got a flat tire I could change it and still get there on time. I end up arriving for most meetings or appointments upward of thirty minutes early. I end up just sitting in the parking lot. The fear of being late results in me sitting in my car for half an hour, listening to the radio. And that's okay. Sitting and waiting is far less stressful than checking my phone wondering if I'm going to make it in time.

When people are late it drives me crazy. It's insulting to the person kept waiting. I have friends who are late all the time. I don't get why they can't move their lives up fifteen or twenty minutes so they don't waste other people's time. If you are chronically late, why not make that obvious tweak and leave earlier? I know it's not as simple as that. (When chronically late folks give themselves fifteen minutes extra time, they just fill it with another task—because they think, I have all this time!)

I also know it's not a simple thing because of how much effort I put into my calendar. The other day I had a meeting with reps from a car company, a big client that advertises on my radio show. Well, there was zero chance I was going to be late for something as important as that. But I also had a lot of other important things

I needed to get done that day: a meeting about a two-day charity event for St. Jude Children's Research Hospital, a cause that is very close to my heart; a production meeting for a TV show I was working on; and interviews with three candidates for a job answering phones for my morning show. If that was all going to happen, I had to put even more time than usual into scheduling my day.

My big trick for carving out more time in your day and space in your brain when you have something important coming up is to be pre-disciplined. What I mean is, get all the little everyday tasks out of the way that you can so that you "keep making the main thing the main thing," as Deion Sanders, a friend of mine, says. For me, that means gassing up the car, preparing my food to the point of grab-and-go-container meals, and laying out my clothes. It might sound silly, but you'd be amazed at how much easier a difficult meeting or challenging schedule becomes when you're not worried about ordering pet food for your dog. It's kind of like how I treat my radio show. I prepare enough that as soon as I sit down in the studio, all I have to do is execute it. Believe it or not, being on air is the easy part!

It was worth it, though. I got to the very important meeting with the car company reps thirty minutes early. (Yes, I sat in the parking lot and did a conference call in my car.) If something is important to you, you'll get it done. If you don't get it done, it wasn't as important to you as you thought. And nothing gets done without working at it.

Remember how I said there is no key to success? I lied. Here it is, the key to success, and it's not even the end of the book! Get places, and Get to them on time. That's right, I used a capital G. The more you show you can consistently be trusted with just being there, the more opportunities you are going to get to create your value. There you go. You can shut the book now if you want. I have more to say, but that's the key. Always be ready and willing. And always be on time.

DEVELOPING DISCIPLINE

Being on time, a core value of mine, takes constant work on my calendar. But I have developed a discipline as it relates to my scheduling, because as you have probably figured out by now, I see it as one of my strengths.

Everything comes back to discipline. You want to lose weight? You need to develop discipline when it comes to food and exercise. Make friends or date more? Meeting-new-people discipline. Switch careers? Job-hunt discipline. The path to any desired goal is made up of a disciplined approach toward said goal. That's why from time to time I'll take on a challenge for the express purpose of developing my ability to maintain personal discipline.

Try to break a habit or create a new one! It's tough, but there's a lot of satisfaction that comes from working on yourself. The easier disciplines also get you in shape for the harder ones. Smaller changes, such as cutting down on chocolate, are like baby steps to the bigger hurdles, such as being a better friend.

Being a better friend has been a real goal of mine. I don't have a circle of friends like the kind you see on TV. I love and appreciate all those I call friends because, man, you have to be a pretty awesome human being to tolerate someone like me. As much as I care about and need these folks in my life, I'm horrible at keeping in touch. I know I'm not alone in this. (Dudes are particularly bad at doing stuff like picking up the phone just to say hi.) Still, I'm reeeeally bad. I am also bad at small talk and hanging out. You're in the hospital and need to find a kidney or your house burns down and you need to rebuild? I'm your man. I'll be the first one to pitch in and lead the effort. But you'll never get a text from me on your birthday. I will never post a happy birthday message on your Facebook wall.

Okay, I need to take a beat to talk about Fake Facebook Birthday Wishes. For a while I changed my birthday on Facebook to weed out all the people that just log on to write "Happy birthday." My birthday is April 2, but I changed it on my profile to April 6. So when April 6 came along and everyone posted "Happy birthday Bobby," I knew they didn't mean it. Or they might have meant their post, but their posts had little meaning. I'm only being slightly hyperbolic here: people who write "Happy birthday" on your Facebook wall are absolutely not friends of yours. Fake friends use prompts like the little red dot on top of Facebook that marks a birthday to send generic symbols of closeness that are, in reality, totally meaningless. Real friends know it's your birthday whether they are on social media or not. Or they don't. But it doesn't matter anyway, because you communicate meaningfully on a regular basis about other aspects of your life. I'm way too passionate about this subject. Check out my next book, *Facebook Friends Are Not Real Friends*.

Back to the story of my trying to be a better friend of the non-Facebook variety. One weekend, after I'd been traveling for months during the weekends (after doing the radio show all week), I found myself at home—and by myself. I wanted to call someone to hang out, but I was paralyzed by guilt. Who wants to last-minute hang out with the jerk who drops off the face of the earth only to reappear whenever it suits him?

So, I did whatever I do whenever I want to work on an aspect of myself: I came up with a little Grind that spoke to the bigger goal. In this case, I wanted to cultivate my friendships by reaching out more consistently. I came up with a goal: send ten texts that have nothing to do with work, every day.

It was no different than reading at least a chapter of a book a day or drinking the proper amount of water. I took out my whiteboard and wrote down, "10 texts a day!" It didn't matter what I wrote—I needed to find real-life messages to send to other humans. When I saw on Instagram that a friend had adopted a new puppy, I texted him congrats and my favorite dog food brand. After I finally got around to watching *The Walking Dead,* I texted someone I know who's a huge fan just to say I was thinking of her because I was also freaked out by the scene—**spoiler alert**—in which Negan took his baseball bat to Glenn's head. Holy moly. Did that episode have to be so gory? I guess if it hadn't, I wouldn't have sent the text or written about it here. But jeez, man, let's move the camera angle a bit upon impact.

The texts didn't take a lot of effort, and they didn't result in anything. At least not immediately. Sending texts was like planting seeds, and it worked. My communications became easier as they grew more frequent. I suddenly had friends shooting me messages on a random Tuesday night: "Hey, we're going bowling. Come!" Or on a Thursday morning: "Bbq at my house tonight." Most of the time I couldn't take them up on their invites, but there have been the rare occasions when I could. Every now and then, someone will ask if I want to go to a yoga class on a Sunday afternoon or a movie on a Saturday night, and because I happen to be in town, I do. It's great and would never have been an option if I hadn't asked myself, "What's something small I can do every single day to make my friendships better over the long term?"

With every Grind, you are basically breaking a habit or trying to create a new one, which, if you've ever tried to do either of those things, you know is a lot harder than it sounds.

Recently, I decided I didn't want to curse at all anymore. Zero. Not because I think cursing is wrong. I don't have a moral opinion on this; they are just words and sounds to me. On the radio or doing stand-up, I have always worked completely clean. But as soon as I wasn't in front of a microphone, I used to curse like crazy.

I started to notice my cursing was becoming a mental crutch around the time I was looking for a new way to challenge myself. It had felt like a while since I had stretched myself. I needed something new to focus on, so I stopped cursing. It seems random, and in a way it was.

While de-cursing, I had to completely retrain how I talked. For me, that meant catching myself—and, at times, punishing myself. That sounds like *Fifty Shades of Grey*, but what I do to myself in my own bedroom is my business. I concocted small but irritating penalties for cursing, like waking up even earlier in the morning, working out longer, or not getting to eat my favorite meal if I slipped. I was acting as a parent to myself, grounding *myself* for bad behavior. It sounds like loony-bin stuff, but that's what works for me. I'm disciplined enough to hold myself accountable to my own rules. And I come up with punishments I want to avoid enough that they motivate me to follow through with my original goal. That's just me, though. This definitely isn't everyone's jam.

I was watching one of those hour-long news shows (the kind that I used to call "old-people shows" but now find myself loving—I guess 'cause I'm old) that included an entire piece about the best way to motivate weight loss. The reporting centered on an experiment in which one group of dieters was offered money to lose weight, while the second group was threatened with naked pictures posted online if they *didn't*. Then the groups were switched so that the first received the punishment method and the second, the reward. In this examination of positive reinforcement vs. negative reinforcement I was fascinated by how people responded to one or the other, but not both. For example, those who were motivated by money could not shed pounds no matter how embarrassed they were of the naked photo set to circulate on the Internet.

I find nothing enticing about a reward. On the other hand, I'll do anything to run from punishment. The only reward I care about is achieving my goal. When I eliminated cursing from my life, it allowed me to go into a different place mentally. At first it was uncomfortable saying things I would normally say with more color. I had to find the other roads to take. Almost like Lois and Clark! Or even Lewis and Clark! Both the nineties *Superman* remake and the great explorers! The process constantly kept me on my toes.

You'll have to do your own study and experiment (and likely get it wrong a few times) to figure out what motivates you. In addition to the reward-punishment question, you should also consider the role of other people in your Grind. I have lots of friends who look to others to hold them accountable when they set a goal. Some people like to reach for goals with a buddy. (One woman I know wanted to meditate regularly but couldn't seem to get it done, so she found a friend to check in with every day to make sure they both stuck to it.) Me? I don't need anybody in my business. Nobody needs to tell me what I'm doing or how I'm doing it. All I need is my whiteboard or a cell phone screen.

Whatever works for you—whiteboard, accountability community, truffles, or corporal punishment—once you find it, be consistent!

EXERCISE: CREATE A HABIT

If you are just starting out or know that you have trouble keeping resolutions, begin with a very small and doable action. Stay away from enormous and amorphous goals, like "I want to be more positive." You can't just switch something as internal and massive as your level of negativity by whipping out a Sharpie and writing it down. Instead, you have to work backward and figure out the smaller steps required before you can take on that larger Fight. (For instance, a good step toward "being more positive" might be to write down five positive thoughts every day.)

Because the point of this exercise is disciplining yourself to do something over and over (the essence of a habit), it doesn't need to be hard. A big part of training is just remembering! Putting something into your daily routine—and making sure it happens regardless of rain, snow, sleet, or a new Netflix series—is the first, most important, and only step of this exercise.

So pick something small. It can even be something that doesn't make sense to do, such as keeping a quarter on the corner of your night table and flipping it over once every day. (I've never done the quarter exercise. I just happen to be looking at a quarter on my table right now. But if I were to make that my latest discipline, I would drive myself crazy making sure I remembered to flip that freaking quarter over.) All you're doing is training yourself that the one little thing, repeated every day, is important—because it's the start to many other achievements by giving you confidence to try other, bigger tasks.

GRIND SPOTLIGHT: MIKE DEESTRO

It's so hard to change our routines, even for positive reasons (especially for positive reasons). We know what the right thing is to do. Yet we continue to make bad decisions. Being disciplined or following your training is a life-long challenge.

That's what makes my producer/writer Mike Deestro's radical weight loss all the more amazing. Although Mike lost 120 pounds, he didn't set out to do that. He didn't wake up one morning and say, "I'm a different person today. I'm going to lose half my body weight now." Nobody does that. No, he disciplined himself—and slowly made all the little changes that added up to, well, 120 pounds!

In case you don't know Mike, he's now a true scrapper. He started out as an intern on the radio show after contacting me on . . . Myspace. Hoping to do a podcast of his own, Mike reached out for advice. My advice was "Just come up and watch." He showed up to *The Bobby*

Bones Show and basically never left. Seriously, after his internship, he just hung around and kept working (for free) until he finally got a weekend gig at the station. The rest is history.

Back to Mike's bod: at his heaviest, the five-foot-seven Waxahachie, Texas, native weighed 280 pounds. As he put it, the initial impetus to lose weight was fashion. "I just wanted to wear cool clothes," he said, "and they weren't in my size." (Now, let's be clear, Mike's idea of "cool" is skater/Goth. The whole *Twilight* look. We can disagree about his taste in clothes, but not his work ethic.) Shopping for shirts in 2XL and pants in size 40, Mike says, "I didn't like the way I looked or felt anymore."

Mike didn't buy a ten-pack of SoulCycle classes or begin a diet exclusively consisting of hot water, lemon, and cayenne. A mellow guy who quietly goes after what he wants, he kept it simple: eating a little better, laying off the soda, and running. Mike explains that he began jogging because "it was the easiest thing for me to do . . . just go outside and run." (The fact that it was free meant a lot, because, let's be honest, radio doesn't pay all that great when you are starting out.)

Things could have gone very differently for Mike had he decided from the get-go to run three miles a day or some other unrealistic goal out of the gate. His feet would have been bloody, his muscles would have been beyond sore, and he would have quit. Unrealistic expectations lead to such negative outcomes, you never want to try the thing that made you feel that way again. It's a tough balance because we want to achieve our goals, but the best way isn't always the fastest way. Sometimes you have to grind it out over a long period of time. That's the absolute most effective long-term solution.

Mike started out nice and slow and lost his first thirty pounds by making those small changes—jogging and not drinking soda. "Once I lost thirty pounds, I was like, This is something I can do," he said. "That was all the motivation I needed."

In one year, Mike lost one hundred pounds!

"No crazy diet. No surgery. No pills," he said. "I just put in the work."

A big part of that work remained running. Mike went from being unable to run one mile in 2014 to running more than thirteen on a regular basis. In 2017, he ran the Nashville Marathon. "It's crazy to me because I never set out to run a marathon," he said. "I started running a few years ago as a way to get healthy and lose weight. My goal was to be able to run a mile without stopping."

The longest Mike had ever run before marathon day was twenty miles, and during the race he kept up a pace of a 7.5-minute mile for the first twenty miles, but the last six miles were really rough. He described feeling as if he were running in place. "Mentally I started to break down," he said.

But the dude kept pushing, and he finished the marathon.

Even more impressive, Mike, who is now 160 pounds, has kept off the weight.

"I've got the entire vampire wardrobe now," he says, laughing.

MIKE D'S TOP FIVE TIPS TO LOSING WEIGHT

1. Don't Keep Sweets in the House
Remove temptation! If it's not in the house, you can't eat it. My first big step was throwing away a half-gallon of mint chocolate chip ice cream, which was really hard for me to do!

2. Don't Sweat Your Workout "Buddy"
Working out with a friend sounds like a good idea in the beginning. Problem is . . . it usually doesn't last! You can't afford to drop off just because your buddy can't make it to a workout.

3. Don't Eat Before Bed
Eating dinner right before bed is one of the worst things you can do. Your body doesn't have enough time to process the food, and that's how you put on weight. I always try to eat at least two or three hours before bedtime.

4. Drink Enough Water
I used to be bad about not drinking enough water. I realized a lot of the time when I thought I was hungry . . . I was just thirsty! I make it a point to stay hydrated and drink a glass of water before every meal.

5. Watch What You Put in Your Coffee
I love coffee. It's my one vice. Coffee itself isn't terrible for you. The problem is all the stuff we add to it (sugar, creamer, whipped cream). So I had to stop all that. Every now and then I will add a little cinnamon, but no sugar!

8

THE ART OF SUCKING IT UP

It pays to suck it up and fight through the pain. Most of the time.

My high school football coach Vic Gandolph used to ask me, when I was lying on the field in pain, "Are you hurt, or are you injured?" There is a difference. Hurt, you can go back in. You can get back to work. Injured, you can't. If you are injured and you return to the game, you're going to make whatever is wrong with you worse and maybe even lose the game for the team.

For all those times you are *hurt*, metaphorically or otherwise, I encourage you to get back in there and push on. But the extra effort to keep up your routine when you're hurting will not bring instant gratification. Just the opposite; you will feel pretty terrible while you're muscling through your shift, the last six miles of a marathon, Thanksgiving with the family, whatever.

Here's the first reason it pays off, though. When you do finally break down, get sick, emotionally lose it—people will actually believe you. "If Carrie isn't at work, it must be serious, because she always sucks it up." That's the reputation you want to have. I don't miss work. I'm not late. If I ever were, my producer would send a search party out for me. When you're dependable, everyone knows it. Including your bosses.

Reputation is important, but I wouldn't say that's the most important reason for sucking it up. There's the mental toughness that develops and keeps you nailing your goals even as obstacles pop up. When the pain is nothing more than a memory, you'll be so happy you fought through it. Proud, even. You may also have a cool story to tell about how tough you are!

Here's one of mine.

JANUARY 9, 2017

RYMAN AUDITORIUM, NASHVILLE

My band, The Raging Idiots, was hosting our second Million Dollar Show, which raises money for St. Jude Children's Research Hospital. The show had sold out the venue's 2,362 seats in about three minutes. I was psyched but not surprised.

This is because we had an amazing lineup of major artists who were going to make cameos throughout the night. I called on friends like Brothers Osborne, Rascal Flatts, Thomas Rhett, The Band Perry, and others to jump in and play some songs with us. Sam Hunt came up with the song he wanted to play—Travis Tritt's "It's a Great Day to Be Alive"—while sitting on the beach and celebrating his recent engagement to his longtime girlfriend.

The public knew some of the talent performing, but we kept some of the acts a surprise. They were gonna go crazy. For the big finale, my favorite artist, Garth Brooks, planned to present a check for two hundred thousand dollars to St. Jude.

It was going to be an amazing night. Except for one thing . . .

The morning of the show, I lost my voice. And I was puking everywhere.

I missed rehearsal. I missed sound check. I missed seeing straight. I was so sick that even I—Mr. Fight himself—didn't think I'd be able to make it. But I always have faith in me. The night of the show, as I continued to vomit everywhere, I was convinced it would pass. It had no other option but to pass!

Two hours before showtime, my manager, Mary Forest, took me to the doctor.

"Stop the car!" I yelled from the passenger seat of her white SUV. Mary Forest slammed on the brakes in the parking lot of a shopping center in Nashville, where we found a MinuteClinic-type place. I tossed the door open and puked all over the parking lot, probably catching a bit on the side of her truck as well. Then I got out to puke after that. It was an amazing sight. If I were watching me, I'd have sworn I was the drunkest guy to vomit all over West Nashville. I'd have probably Snapchatted it (or insert whatever the cool recording social media is when you read this) and had a million views. It was violent vomiting. That's probably what I would have titled my YouTube video: "Dude Violent-Vomits Near the Dollar General."

With ninety minutes until the start of the show, the doctor checked me out. Mary Forest had to do most of the talking for me, because I was, you know, vomiting. But I got a few sentiments in:

"I'm Chris Stapleton, and I need all the drugs you can give me to get me through the night."

Sadly, the doctor, a Stapleton fan, didn't fall for it. Also, my real name was on his chart.

"Okay, how's this? I'm about to perform in the biggest show of my life. GARTH BROOKS is going to be there. And GARTH BROOKS is going to have one of those BIG OL' CHECKS you see on TV when people win Publishers Clearing House. I love BIG CHECKS! For a good cause!"

The doctor was older, so I knew he'd get my "Publishers Clearing House" reference. Always play to your audience!

It worked. The doctor shot me up. Steroids. IV fluids for de-hydration. Enough ibuprofen for a giant. He even let me use the clinic's penis pump. Okay, there was no penis pump (despite my request), but the doc did all the things I needed for that night. Bam bam bam bam. I got fake-healthy for the night in the fastest way possible. I wasn't, under any circumstances, going to miss that show.

Back in Mary Forest's car it was boom-time vomit again. Walking through the back alley behind Ryman Auditorium, I did something I never did before: said no to a fan who asked for a picture. I didn't actually say the word "no," because I was afraid if I opened my mouth, I would vomit on her. So, I just walked and waved, trying to get to the Ryman dressing room . . . where I vomited again.

While I changed into a barf-free T-shirt and jeans, I could feel some of the drugs kicking in. I heard someone calling me to come out onstage to say something about St. Jude to kick off the show. I have no idea what I said. I don't remember walking onto the stage to sing any songs. There's a lot I don't remember about that night. I do recall singing a song with Thomas Rhett where I went a little too hard and had to swallow my own puke back down my throat. That's gross—and burns. The sensation must have shown in my expression, because Thomas looked at me wide-eyed in the middle of a song and said, "Are you okay?" I was and replied, "Let's roll."

I wasn't injured, only hurt.

When Sam Hunt and I sang "It's a Great Day to Be Alive," I mimed my part, not wanting to risk throwing up on the famous Ryman stage. The crowd—which got louder and more pumped with each act crushing it more than the last—kept me going. (The drugs didn't hurt, either.)

As I played "Life Is a Highway" with Rascal Flatts, I looked to the wings and, in a leather jacket and ball cap, there stood Garth Brooks. He was up next.

Any illness left my body. He had the touch of a magical country music angel (and he didn't even have to touch me).

He walked onto the stage and had that big check with him. Except it wasn't for two hundred thousand dollars. It was for two million dollars! That's right. Garth brought a check for St. Jude in the amount of two million U.S. dollars. It was crazy. Then it got even crazier.

Garth didn't come out onto the stage with a guitar, because he hadn't planned to perform. He donated two million dollars, every single penny of profit from over a month's worth of his album sales! Wasn't that enough? Nothing is ever enough for me. I had Garth Brooks onstage at the Ryman. The crowd was eating it up, and I knew if I asked him to sing one with the band he for sure would. He didn't have a choice! He's Garth Brooks! He gives the people what they want! That's why he's the greatest of all time. (Just restating a fun fact here: he is the highest-selling solo artist of all time. Not just country. All genres. Look it up, I say! That guy.)

"Hey, Garth," I said in front of two thousand screaming fans. "Let's do a song."

His expression said he knew it was coming. The band started the first lick of "Friends in Low Places." The crowd went nuts. I went nuts.

There I was, singing the most famous Garth Brooks song with freaking Garth Brooks! In a dream come true, I held nothing back. I didn't care if I vomited all over the front row; I sang so hard. I watched the master at work. Garth, playing to the very last row, made the person with the worst seat in the house feel like he was the biggest part of the show.

I keep a picture in my house of Garth and me singing into the same microphone. It's funny to look at it now, because Garth was doing his thing, crushing it, without a clue that I was dying of the bird flu and probably passing it on to him. He hugged me at the end of the song and walked off. Out of respect, I think the crowd stood and cheered for six more hours. Rumor has it, they were still there the next day cheering. I've been to a lot of concerts and never seen anything like it. There is video of the concert somewhere online. Find it if you can.

After the show, I thanked the crowd, went to my dressing room, and vomited everywhere. In the sink and the toilet and maybe even the shower. But it was awesome. That was awesome vomit. It tasted like victory and a job well done.

That's not only my best story of playing *hurt*, it's also indicative of how I live my life. Success isn't just about showing up all the time; it's about showing up ALL THE TIME. I don't stop unless I'm truly injured. If I'm only hurt, I'm going back in the game. Again and again.

My bosses know that if I call in sick to the radio show, I'm close to seeing the light at the end of the heavenly tunnel. I will run to the bathroom during every song if I have to. But I will not miss. Winners win because they play. I'm always in the game.

Be the example of someone who refuses to quit. Create a reputation for yourself of complete reliability. With good people, that stuff is contagious. Soon, you'll have an entire team willing to play hurt.

GRIND PLAYLIST

You've got to psych yourself up sometimes. Music is a great way to put yourself in a positive mindset, no matter what's happening. For the last nine months, I've *always* listened to the same three-song playlist right before I walk out onstage to perform. Nobody can interrupt me and nothing can happen in the ten minutes these three songs play in the same order. Am I so superstitious as to think they make good things happen? No. But good things have happened when they played in the past. So why not keep them around? The worst that happens is that I listen to music that I like (which isn't only country, by the way. I do listen to country a lot, but I don't MOSTLY listen to any format. I don't even consider music to be made in formats, which is just a corporate construct). The best that happens is that these songs put me in a positive place, which will probably garner better results. Because if I'm feeling better, I'm performing better.

1. "Rich" by Maren Morris

I figured out the first song on my playlist the same way I do a lot of other things in my life; it worked for me once, randomly, so now I do it all the time. In this case, Maren Morris's album Hero *had just come out when I was in Washington, D.C., on a stop during my comedy tour. I was kind of edgy from a less-than-awesome set the weekend before, so I decided to listen to Maren's new record. I like Maren's sound—soulful, pissed off at times, and honest. "Rich" played right before I walked onstage and crushed my set with maximum hilariousness. I made a mental note: "That's it. I will listen to 'Rich' until I go out and absolutely suck."*

2. "Seven Nation Army" by the White Stripes

I bring up this song a lot on my radio show. People call in a lot wanting to know a good song to listen to when they're feeling anxious, and I always recommend "Seven Nation Army." There's something in the slow boom, boom, boom of this rock tune that builds to a large place, which I find soothing. I was really nervous before doing a "home show" in Nashville. I knew the entire industry would be in the audience, waiting to see if I was any good, so I listened to "Rich" for its positive associations and then added "Seven Nation Army" to bring my heart rate down. It worked, so I kept it.

3. "The Next Episode" by Dr. Dre and Snoop Dogg

I love nineties hip-hop. I was about to go out in Boston and I knew the crowd was going to be hype. Or, as the kids would say, HYPE AF. As such, I wanted to get myself there a bit mentally. Those Boston crowds are always ridiculous. If you bring it, they will reward you. On the flip side: if you don't, they may wait for you after the show to beat you up. My type of people! Love you, Boston.

HOT YOGA = REAL LIFE (OR WHY YOU SHOULDN'T BE EMBARRASSED TO LOOK STUPID)

Remember how I said I've tried every exercise? I wasn't kidding. In addition to Tae Bo and Jazzercize, I have also tried my hand at hot yoga. If you don't know what that is, here's the Mayo Clinic's definition: "Hot yoga is a vigorous form of yoga performed in a studio that is heated to 105° F (40° C) and has a humidity of 40 percent."

It's not up everyone's alley, but I kept hearing about how great this hot yoga was for creating lean muscle mass. And I'd like to have muscles, especially lean ones, so I decided to give it a try.

I was pretty clueless, except for what I had looked up on YouTube and the Wiki article I read on yoga etiquette—and with that I drove to my first yoga class. I went by myself, because I decided that if was going to look stupid, I'd rather it be with complete strangers.

I began to regret that decision, however, as I walked down the hallway to the class with a group entirely made up of women. You'd think that being the only guy in a female class would be an appealing prospect. But when you have no confidence in your abilities, it's the opposite. I'd rather look stupid in front of a bunch of dudes any day (even ones I know).

A blast of heat greeted me when the door opened to the yoga studio. My glasses instantly fogged up. I know: pretty smooth. Especially because you aren't supposed to wear glasses in class. I rolled out the new mat I had bought and looked around. Some of the ladies were drinking water. (I had brought none; it wasn't on the YouTube video.) Some were doing poses that I also hadn't seen online. A few others were lying on their backs in shavasana. That's dead man's pose. I knew that one from the video. I decided to play dead, since it seemed like the easiest thing to mimic.

The very earthy (see: armpit hair, but somehow it worked for her) teacher walked in and asked if anyone was new to yoga. I would never raise my hand to that question. You might as well stand up and scream, "If you want to get a good laugh, please watch me for the next sixty minutes."

And with that, we began. Them first. Me about a half step behind. Yeah, only a half step slower! Especially at first, because I actually knew the early moves. I didn't feel too out of place at first, only slightly. But as the class progressed, the moves became more and more foreign to what I thought bodies are supposed to do. There were poses like "crow" or "triangle." My favorite was called "milking your cow." (Okay, that's not a real group pose but mostly something I do alone.)

Halfway through the class, I was absolutely lost and becoming very self-conscious. The woman next to me was, for sure, watching how dumb I looked and definitely going to group text all her friends about it immediately after class. The teacher was absolutely eyeballing me and going to share on the group message board about how this nerdy, pasty dude came in and looked "as confused as a cub bear with his peter in his hand" (as my grandma used to say). I could feel the whole room staring a hole in me. (Not staring at my "a-hole." That's totally different, but could have happened, too, given all the weird positions.) After four days, the class finished. (Okay, it was only sixty minutes. It just felt like four days.) I gathered my belongings and walked out to my car. Embarrassed, covered in sweat, and still wearing foggy glasses.

Despite that I was sitting in a pool of my own fluids, when I got into my car I was happy, because I had tried something new. It didn't matter that I had probably only accomplished one-third of the "practice." By the way, yoga is always "practice." If I'm going to practice, I want to play the game. I can't find any pick-up yoga games around town, though.

Back at home, I chalked up the class as my one shot at yoga. I tried; it didn't go so well; I was ready to move on. That's what I thought until I saw the receipt from the yoga studio in my e-mail. I had completed one of my three-class pack. Oh no! I had accidentally bought three classes. Now I had to go back! The classes were twenty bucks apiece, and there was no way I was going to waste forty bucks. People who grow up broke don't throw money away like that!

So I returned for round two of hot yoga, and it was a little better. I knew what to expect this time around: how to put my mat on the floor; not to wear glasses; what fidgety things to do before class to look like I belonged; even to bring water! I was already way ahead of the game compared to last time. I didn't know all the moves yet, but I caught on to a few that I hadn't the time before. And I didn't feel like the entire class was staring at me. At least not as much.

After my third time doing hot yoga, I pretty much dominated (see: barely functional) and decided to buy another pack of classes. It took a few more sessions until I finally got into the groove. During that time, I saw new people come in and could tell they had the same preshow jitters that I did. Once class started, though, I turned my focus inward to do my best "practice." I never watched anyone else. I didn't care what they did or how bad they were at pigeon pose.

That's when I realized that no one was ever watching me be bad at yoga or giving me more than a single thought. While I worried that the ladies in the class were making detailed mental notes of all the ways to make fun of my form, they were concentrating on themselves. No group texts. No message boards. No one cares about anything other than their own practice!

My big takeaway from yoga isn't my rad downward dog but that nobody really cares what you're doing. So don't waste any emotional energy about worrying if you look stupid. This isn't just in yoga but in life.

Fired from your job? Sucks for you. But you can dig your way out. Embarrassed? Sure. But here's the thing; no one outside of your super immediate circle cares. They are all too busy worrying about their own jobs.

Want to audition for community theater in your town, but don't want to get made fun of by your friends at work? Do it. Who cares? They don't.

The understanding that most people are too self-absorbed or worried about looking foolish themselves to notice what you're up to should free you to try new things or recover from stumbles without concern about looking foolish.

We create these unbelievably harsh narratives in our heads about what others are thinking and saying about us. I was convinced there was going to be a headline about me on the cover of

Yoga Illustrated: "Nashville Dork Desecrates Ancient Tradition of Yoga." It didn't occur to me that everyone in that class was once in the exact same place as I was—the newbie on the mat. I was too busy imagining their post-yoga social (that they didn't invite me to) where they reenacted my worst poses.

I hope the idea that nobody cares what you're doing gives you permission to do whatever you want. Go do whatever you want to even if you suck at it. Try yoga. I'm still going to classes.

GRIND IN REVIEW

BOBBY WORKS:
THE HIGH-MAINTENANCE EDITION

The job most instrumental to creating my understanding of Grind was working maintenance at a golf course.

Mowing greens: that's what I did every morning. As soon as enough of the sun had risen for me to see in front of my face, I was out there with a green mower, mowing those dumb massive lawns before golfers started hitting their overpriced golf balls. That might sound like an easy, if tedious, job. Oh, no. Wrong! For golf course greens, you have to mow in straight lines that alternate between lighter and darker shades, depending on which direction the mower goes. That requires making an exact turn with your mower, which is a lot harder than it sounds.

First, you have to eyeball the edge of the short part of the green, because God forbid you mow the fringe! (That's the grass around the putting green that's usually cut higher than the green, but lower than the fairway.) As your mower approaches the fringe, you lean your elite grass cutter backward and spin it just as it mows the very last putting service but before it lands on the grass that's an eighth-inch taller right outside of it. It was brutal, but I was like a surgeon with that thing. Walk, push, flip, repeat.

Every day, post-mow, my fellow lawn care specialists and I were judged harshly on our straight lines, edge position, mowing speed. My lesson from mowing greens is that while you might never achieve it, you should always strive for the ever-elusive perfect green. It's the hole in one, the full-court buzzer beater, the ninth-inning walk-off grand slam of Green Mowing. I never nailed it. Few have. But I knew it could be done, so I chased it. I wanted my superintendent to stop work for the day and make everyone come look at my perfect green. That didn't happen, but I'm proud of the fact that I didn't stop trying.

The real lesson that "the work never stops" came from the sand traps. Holy crap, the sand traps. The sand-trap hustle, as I used to call it, requires you to rake every stinking patch of sand on the course so that it's as smooth and uniform as a Japanese Zen garden. When you got done with your Buddhist monk penance of endless raking, the whole thing had to be raked again, because it rained or some men in khakis trampled through the traps like a herd of rich old elephants.

One day away from the traps might as well have been a two-week vacation on a luxury cruise. It was the most repetitive work I've ever done in my life, and at the time I really hated it. Raking the traps was akin to psychological torture. It screws with your head to do something with the knowledge that it's just going to get messed up again in the next fifteen minutes. Although it was such a big part of course maintenance, there was zero glory to getting it right. That's because if they weren't done right, it was readily apparent, but if they were done right, nobody noticed. But that was the job—and if I wanted to get a promotion, which I did, I had to continue to rake the traps, over and over and over again.

THE GRIND IN A FEW STEPS

The Grind is relentless. It's taking the Fight and doing it over and over again. There is real struggle here, but just knowing that makes it easier.

The most important aspect of success is to develop a practice. It almost doesn't matter what it is as long as you show determination, discipline, and consistency.

Break your big goals down into smaller, achievable ones. They can be goals for the next year, next day, or next fifteen minutes.

Speaking your goals out loud has power. Tell yourself, tell other people, shout it from the rooftops. Whatever it takes to hold yourself accountable. Shame is a great motivator for some (see: me).

Create layers of reminders for your goals, so that you have no excuse to stop. Smartphones have lots of ways to keep your goals front and center.

Every Grind is about breaking a habit or creating a new one.

Execute all those tiny, everyday, ordinary details with as much care as you would if you were giving a presentation to the boss or performing in front of thousands. The little elements done right again and again are what make the big things happen.

Suck it up, no matter how much it sucks. Your reputation and never-quit attitude will be your reward.

When going after your goals or trying out new things,
never worry about looking stupid—because nobody is
looking!

Part 3

REPEAT

9

STARTING FROM SQUARE ONE—
AND LEARNING TO LOVE IT

Repeat is the most annoying of the three steps. It's the most fruitless *and* the most rewarding. It's a contradiction wrapped up in self-doubt, frustration, and a whole lot of expended energy. Man, so much freaking energy.

If the Fight is knowing your mind and what it is you want to do; if the Grind is getting up every day, keeping your goals front and center, and executing all the little details; then Repeat is doing the first two steps completely right, not getting the results you wanted (if you get any results at all), and then starting the whole process over—never knowing where any of this will lead.

Having fun yet?

Well, we've gotta bring up the F-word again.

Failure.

Remember at the start of the book when you were reading

about all those amazing, famous, smart, successful people who failed and failed and failed until they didn't? Remember how cool and obvious you thought that was when thinking about Walt Disney or Steve Jobs? Not quite as cool when it's you doing the failing, is it?

Well, listen to me: don't give up! First off, failure is so subjective that sometimes it's hard to define. Is failure not getting what you wanted? But what if you get something better (even if you don't realize it at the time)? Or is it getting nothing, not a positive or negative response but radio silence?

Repeating can feel like you didn't succeed, but think about hammering a nail into a piece of wood. The first time you hit the nail, it doesn't go in all the way. Even twice will not get the results you want. You have to keep hitting the nail, which doesn't mean you are failing at hammering. As long as you don't miss the nail altogether or bend it sideways, you are making progress. It just takes a bunch of shots to get that sucker in. And if you do bend it sideways, get another freaking nail! Don't stop building the house!

In the Repeat process, initially there's a kind of recoil. I've said it before and I'll say it again: nobody loves to fail. It's simply a fact of life, like gravity, taxes, and *Friends* making me laugh. (The one episode that gets me every time is when Joey goes on a game show, *Pyramid*. The second time he yells, "A ghost!" I still laugh out loud. Go google "joey on pyramid." Sorry, back to my inspirational stories now.) The instinctive reaction to retreat is good, because you should say, "Whoa. Let me take a moment to think about what just happened." This crucial period of evaluation after a failure sometimes comes quickly and sometimes doesn't. (I have failed a lot, so I've grown accustomed to it. It still sucks, but like anything else, the more you do it, the quicker and easier the process is.) After you've reflected, the final piece is to strategically use the knowledge you gained to decide how to do the same thing better or, at least, differently. There's that famous quote, supposedly from Einstein, that goes, "The definition of insanity is doing the same thing over and over again and expecting different results." So, to avoid insanity and to keep learning, you need to keep mixing things up. Even trying the same thing but with different people is a form of doing things differently. It's not insane if you keep adding a twist, which can be anything from the "who" to the "when" to the "where."

The Repeat step does require a lot of resilience. Don't worry, though: much like discipline, being able to bounce back is a quality you can build up. If you are going to Fight, Grind, Repeat, you have to callus up. Wait for it . . . another boxing metaphor! When I first started boxing, my hands hurt crazy bad after each session. My hands were so soft, the guys at the gym called me Gummy Bear until my fifth professional match. (The nickname and pro bouts are lies, but you get the point.) I push buttons and sit in the AC for a living. If I wanted to keep boxing, I had to bandage up my bleeding knuckles . . . until one day, just like that, I didn't. My calluses were a revelation.

Rejection is great, because it's building up your calluses! I should know because I've been dismissed so much in my life, I'm basically one big callus. Case in point: people tell me I'm not funny *all* the time. Even as my radio show continues to grow, I get told how awful it is on a regular basis. People have been telling me how much I suck for forever. From my first shows on the radio to my shows today, from my first time on a stand-up stage for twelve people to doing shows for crowds of two thousand, I've been told,

"You just aren't that good." Or, my favorite, "I don't get it." The only thing that has changed is the size of the platforms of those who think I suck. Ten years ago, I would have had a minor panic attack if the *Arkansas Democrat-Gazette* gave me a bad review. Now, Anderson Cooper could go on CNN to proclaim me the unfunniest man in America, and my first thought would be, Join the club. (My second: Why is Anderson Cooper reporting on the unfunniest man in America?)

Part of the process is that the process is going to be tough for a good long while. If you know that from the get-go, it's not such a punch to the gut when you're proven upsettingly right. And if it does happen to go well, then congratulations. Pin a rose on your nose! (*Full House* reference.) For the most part, however, you'll save yourself a lot of heartache if your expectations are in line with reality. You may walk into a new job and get a free cupcake, but probably not the corner office.

NO ONE IS TALLYING YOUR FAILURES (BESIDES YOU)

I once had an intern who kept submitting segments for the show—something I always encourage. I always want everyone on my staff to pitch ideas, but I also tell them that they probably won't make it on the air. The more you fire, however, the better odds you have at hitting the target. And this guy fired away. Every day for about three weeks this intern would write four or five segment ideas. And every day they'd get beaten by other segments. When you are competing with seven other people (and mostly me) who have been doing this work for a long time, it's tough. I checked in with him every couple of days, during which he expressed his frustration at never making the cut. I encouraged him to stick with it and keep to his own voice but, at the same time, to study the segments that made it to the air so he could figure out the type of material that fit with the tone of the show. He never did get a bit on the air, but that's not the saddest part of the story. The saddest part is that the intern quit because he thought he didn't have "what it takes."

A week after he quit, I remembered a bit of his that I had saved. It filled a hole I needed, so I used it on air. I e-mailed him to say the segment had turned out great and I wished he hadn't bailed so quickly. When he officially left the show, we had to hire someone else immediately to replace him. He replied that he left because he felt like he was letting everyone else down by not contributing. *What?* No one thought twice about the fact that he wasn't getting segments on except *him.* He was only an intern, after all. He walked himself right into failure by quitting. It had nothing to do with talent. (I occasionally still see that ex-intern, who's now in real estate, and still give him a hard time about quitting. He didn't want it bad enough. He admits that now.)

We create a lot of rejection for ourselves where, really, there is none. Because our missteps feel way worse to us than anyone else, we make them into bigger moments than they deserve to be. Just as it was a waste to worry about looking stupid in hot yoga class, it's just as much of a waste to get hung up about the round of high fives in the boardroom, or whatever glory you've dreamed up for yourself. For the most part, people aren't cruel when you don't succeed. I'm not saying everyone is going to love all your ideas. But chances are, they will just disagree and move on to something else, like lunch. Don't hold on to that moment, because I can promise they aren't. They're too busy holding on to the lunch menu.

WINNING . . . AND REPEATING ANYWAY

Repeat isn't just about redoing a process after a failure. You can win and Repeat. If you have a great job or relationship, you don't just switch to autopilot. Or, at least, you shouldn't, because if you do I can guarantee the winning streak won't last for long. Winning and Repeating means taking your skills to the next level.

I can't think of a time when I've tried to mimic my success. Even if I'm really pumped with the result, I always say to myself, "Man, wait till next time. If that worked, next time is going to be crazy!" Constantly seeking out new challenges, even in arenas where you're doing well, is also a way of keeping life interesting.

My attitude toward my radio show is a prime example of this. *The Bobby Bones Show* means doing five hours in a chair every day. That's a lot of day-in-day-out material. Still, I never want the other show members to have any kind of preplanned grid for the broadcast. I don't want them to know what's coming. I need every day to feel different. I need every day to feel fresh. I need every day to feel real. I could create a formula for colleagues to easily fall into, and it could work very well. But there's no adventure in that for me. So, I change it up a lot, every single day. Each morning, I have different goals, whether breaking an artist or coming up with an interesting take on something everyone's talking about. There's obviously risk to an ever-evolving format. And I'll admit that some of my experiments work better than others. Like when I sent one of my cohosts, Lunchbox, out to do his street segment where he interviews random people outside or does some kind of gag in public. Despite my typical control-freak tendencies, the way the timing worked out, I wasn't able to listen to his bit before it went on the air. "Is this one funny?" I asked before playing it.

"Yes," he said. (Lunchbox is a man of few words.)

Well, it wasn't. His segment, called "Honk for Hillary or Toot for Trump," was nothing more than people honking their horns for their favorite political candidate. And in case it's not obvious, you can't tell the difference between a "honk" and a "toot." That's when I decided I was always going to listen to the first minute of any segment brought in from the streets before I aired it. Live and learn.

Success doesn't make doing the same thing over and over any less boring. I love what I do, but I still have to work to stay motivated and create excitement for myself. Anything you love can get old if you let it. Take pizza and sex: two things that pretty much almost everybody likes. Still, if you had the same kind all the time, you'd get sick of pizza and sex, too. That being said, of the two, I've only personally ever gotten sick of pizza. And that's probably because I actually get to eat pizza. Just sayin'.

REPEAT IN A FEW WORDS

REPEAT IS . . .
FAILURE
SUCCESS
PERSPECTIVE
RESILIENCE
LEARNING
IMPROVING

10

BUILDING RESILIENCE

I apologize up front that I don't have many "relatable stories" (that's what my editor calls them). The only thing about me that's normal is my dog. (My editor also said something like, "You should say some things about your dog so you don't seem so weird.") Okay, I love my dog. I've had him fourteen years. He's been sick during most of my time writing this book. Odds are, he probably won't be around when this thing is published. It makes me sad to write that. See, I do have feelings! Other than that, I'm a freak. No close family. No chores. No poker nights with the guys.

Remember how I had to give myself a goal of sending texts to friends? Well, get this. I'm writing from a hotel in Hawaii, where I'm spending Christmas by myself. Before I left, my therapist told me to create a list of things to do and to do at least two of them every single day—in an effort to get me to leave my room during my vacation, and not just work and sleep (or, as I call it, "reenergize for more work"). That should tell you everything you need to know about me.

So, forget my dog. Here's how you can make the story below relatable: insert your own big-time disappointment into the narrative. Is it not getting enough financial aid to go to the college of your dreams? Or did the girl you thought you'd marry just break up with you? Maybe you've been out of work for six months and just got what seems like the millionth rejection from an employer.

Now back to me—in my epic Fight, Grind, Repeat cycle to get my own TV show, the death of my reality show about a married couple in country music was a real flick to the nads. Not gonna lie. By the time the network said no, I had been working on it nonstop for seven months. There went all the time and creative energy we had invested in making the pilot episode, not to mention the money! Pilots aren't cheap.

There's no worse investment in time and money than making a TV show (well, maybe making a movie is worse). That's because the likelihood of anything actually getting on air (or in front of the public) is pretty low—no matter how many people tell you how great your idea is. I knew what I was getting myself into, but still, when the television executives pulled the plug, I was hurt. I had to give myself one of the ol' Coach Gandolph talks. After losses, my high school coach would tell us, "The sun is going to come up tomorrow either way." So I might as well be up with it. It was only the end if I made it the end.

And—*boom*—the next week, another pilot I had produced *was* picked up! This was an even better one, my own talk show on a cable network! We went ahead and shot that pilot. How could two shows good enough to make pilots get canceled within the same week? What were the odds? Pretty good, it turns out. The execs behind the talk show were let go by the company. It had nothing to do with me, but still . . . show dismissed.

Fight, Grind, Repeat. Except the flick to the nads the second time was more like a fist. But the sun was going to come up the next day—with me or without me. What's funny is that the more times I fail at achieving my dream, the less anxious I am. I've had three shows go to full pilot at this point (the other was an ABC daytime talk show). That's kind of a big deal because of the cost required for a full pilot, which is when they shoot the first episode (sets, costumes, and all) and edit it in hopes that the final product will prove an entire season is worth making. Each of my pilots took up almost a year of my time and attention. Each failed for different reasons. The sun still came up after every loss. As I write this, I'm talking to *American Idol* about being a mentor in its first season back on ABC. Meanwhile I'm also talking to CBS about a show they have starting in 2019. I'm even talking about doing . . . Well, I can't reveal that yet. This book comes out before I'm legally allowed to say. (Not to mention a "good news" show I'm writing and producing myself.) And the thing is, odds are that none of these will work out. But I believe eventually one of these suckers is going to hit. And until then, the sun will still come up.

As much as I pride myself on pushing through rejection, it would be unhealthy if I had said to myself after any of these letdowns, "I'm not hurt." Part of changing your reality is accepting it.

Still, too much wallowing isn't productive, either. If my goal is to repeat this whole thing again (and again, for who knows how many cycles), I can let my disappointment hold me down for a while. But then, at some point, I've got to pick myself back up.

When I received the news about my canceled talk show, it was a Thursday evening. I made the conscious decision to give myself three suns (Friday, Saturday, and Sunday) to be upset. But I couldn't let it affect my radio show and the rest of the work I had to do Friday. So, it didn't. The knowledge that I'd have plenty of time for feeling down later was enough to get me through the workday just fine.

Whether wallowing or celebrating, I go through the same process of allotting specific amounts of time to actively focus on how I feel. It may be recognizing an accomplishment I'm really proud of by feeling great, or being bummed out because I goofed big time. Either way, I set my own limits on how long I will let myself stay in either state.

The time periods—from as short as fifteen minutes to as long as a couple of days—vary depending on how devastating a blow or great an accomplishment it is. If I get a week's worth of great ratings, I'm not going to spend two days celebrating it. Instead, I might actually go and have a nice lunch. (To be honest, I probably wouldn't even do that. I might spend a few minutes being happy before I start hyperfocusing on the next week.) I'm the last person to feel good about me, even though I realize that I have to sometimes because everyone should. I don't recommend being full of self-loathing, either. I've done that, too. It just ends up detrimental or expensive. Or both.

My system of emotional time-outs stemmed from the fact that I have trouble enjoying my successes. It's not my natural state. My instinct is to immediately move on to the next thing. It's hard for me to enjoy success, since I worry it will be very short-lived. That's because I don't really have a single thing that sets me apart from anyone else. I'm kinda funny. I'm decent looking. I'm sort of smart. Because of that, I move quickly to the next hurdle. In his recent Netflix special, Dave Chappelle says that comedy is easy for him. He writes random punch lines and puts them in a bowl, draws one, and then writes the joke after that! Recently I was talking with Dave Haywood of Lady Antebellum (they've won lots of Grammys), and he explained how music just came easy to him when he was a kid. So easy that he didn't understand that he had a talent. It simply existed in him. That's what I want! To be Dave Chappelle in a Grammy Award–winning trio! Instead, I'm a dude who has to hustle.

Always chasing the next goal is a recipe for burnout, so I had to create a goal (yes, I wrote it on my phone's lock screen) of appreciating my wins. Taking the baby steps approach, I started with fifteen minutes of patting myself on the back, which could be simply enjoying a small snack, lying in bed with my dog, or putting on a record and thinking about nothing other than my achievement. I sat on the stage at the Paramount Theatre in Austin after my first sold-out show (ever) in my favorite (ever) theater. I just sat on the stage with the one light they run while locking up after the show's over and took it in. Someone took a picture of me, and I have it on my bedroom wall.

I found, however, that the same method is productive for bouncing back from failures. By restricting the period of time I spend high or low, I'm released from any guilt I have over feeling that way—because I know it's finite. And when it ends, I refocus my energy on the next steps.

COMMON REPEAT TRAPS

Comparing yourself to others is the biggest trap in the world—and one that people fall into all the time. The guy in the cubicle next to you is promoted and all you can think is, "He's better at this job than me." Meanwhile, what you didn't know is that because he'd asked for a raise and been rejected three times in a row, he spent the last year working overtime at home without pay to get recognized. Or a fellow nursing school student seems to ace every test without effort. Little did you know, she failed the class last semester and is giving it her all this time around. Or maybe the person at work who doesn't seem to deserve his position has a cousin who's a high-ranking executive at the company. There's nothing you can do about that. You can only do you. Anything else is wasted time and energy.

Rejection, failure, struggle—these are all just facts of life. Those who don't experience any of these are outliers (or single inhabitants of their parents' basement who spend their days playing Xbox). Not that you'd know it from the media. All we see are the successes, the big winners. The nineteen-year-old who becomes a professional baseball player is such big news precisely because he's the anomaly. Everyone loves the story about the college dropout who becomes a billionaire with his business idea. Or what about those Victoria's Secret models whose images are everywhere? They aren't like most women, are they? They are genetic anomalies, honestly. What's funny is how these anomalies end up becoming our unrealistic standards of normal. Even if we know becoming a Victoria's Secret model is even rarer than a nineteen-year-old making the Major Leagues, we think to ourselves, Well, I don't look anything like that, so I hate myself.

Perspective is the only way out of that trap, and it's something most of us learn only through experience. Your first reaction to any kind of negative outcome from your Fight is understandably going to be a bad feeling—one of "I'm not good enough." But if you can (and I know it's hard to do), pull yourself up and go eagle eye down on your situation. See how many people are way ahead of you; see how many people are way behind. Remember there are many, many variables in every single situation. From way up in the macro plane, you can see how many factors are at play and know that it's not always about you.

JOB INTERVIEW BLUES

That perspective I learned? Well, I learned it the hard way—rejections from thirty-two (I've counted again since the start of this book) different radio stations.

The only way I could survive that much rejection was to shift the narrative away from me ("I'm no good") and onto the folks doing the hiring ("What is the person on the other side of the desk going through?"). Instead of making it personal, I began to put myself in the shoes of a station manager, who probably received more than two hundred air check tapes from radio hopefuls all over the country in response to a job posting. Maybe they didn't like the sound of my voice or my accent, or maybe they never even heard my tape. When I looked at the hiring process from the other side I began to see how many factors were involved. Maybe it didn't work out in my favor because the manager was in a bad mood when he heard my audition. Or it could be that she wasn't really looking for someone, because she already had a different DJ in mind.

The harsh truth is that generally most positions are filled before they get posted. This is true for all types of work. A boss may not have hired someone, but she probably already has someone in mind for the job. In my experience, I've seen very few blank-slate interviews that result in gainful employment. I've never gotten a radio job without having at least two or three rounds of meetings—and usually not for the same position. Typically, if I've been lucky enough to land an interview for a job posting, it doesn't work out. But if I've clicked with the manager and kept in touch despite being passed over for the position, when a new job opens up I'm in a much better place, because I already have a relationship with that person and he or she has kept me in mind. (That's why when I am interviewing, even if I already know who I'm going to hire, I interview everyone with the same intensity. If I don't hire someone now, I might later.) That's how the world works. Instead of letting it get you down, you've got to game it.

Your goal in any meeting for a job should be to plant a seed in the interviewer's mind for the *next time* a job comes open (because you probably aren't getting this one). That's what goes through my head when I take a meeting for any kind of opportunity. I'm not truly there for *that* role, deal, or partnership—I'm there for the ones I don't even know exist yet.

WHEN YOU DON'T GET THE JOB . . .

Don't take it personally

Don't get derailed

You haven't failed, but instead invested in your future

The weird thing is that when you do land a job, you probably weren't the first choice anyway. I was just reading a story about how the actor Matt LeBlanc was originally offered the role of Phil Dunphy on *Modern Family*. The main guy! The *Friends* star turned it down, though, because he didn't think the role was right for him. Fast forward to Ty Burrell, who has made millions as the lovably goofy dad on the hit ABC sitcom, not to mention earned two Emmys and became a household face (I'm not sure about household name).

The point is, Ty wasn't the *Modern Family* producers' first choice, but he sure did nail it when the opportunity came along and presented itself. You may not even know how many times you weren't the first (or second or third) choice for jobs you've done—and it doesn't matter. I wasn't even the first choice for the job that eventually turned into my current radio show.

Lore has it that a dude who used to work for the company that employs me now wanted a couple of songwriters and an-other outside DJ to come in and do a new Nashville morning show. The goal was to keep it local on the Big 98. No syndication. No other cities. But having your own show in Nashville alone was a huge deal, because you are in the flagship city of country music. In the genre, there is no place bigger.

According to the stories I've heard, the station management went through a few people to host the local show, but they couldn't agree on who or how to do it.

I was totally ignorant of any of this, because I was too busy Grinding away at my Top 40 stations. Building my own syndication company out of Austin, I was spending money on technology that didn't work; winning (and losing) one station at a time; and getting in trouble for many things, including putting country artists on pop stations. I was a fan, and I thought good music was good music, regardless of formats. (Ironic, now that I get crap for putting pop acts on a country station. In my Top 40 days there were some areas of the country they wouldn't put me on, because I was "too country to be pop." And yet to this day I still get called "the pop DJ who came to country." I guess I've never really fit in anywhere.)

In the middle of all this, I was flown to Nashville by the execs, who ran multiple formats, including the Top 40/Hip-Hop that I was currently on, and asked if I wanted to be the "biggest country music host the format has ever had," because at the time, there was still no morning show on the station in Nashville. Well, yes, I would! And what did it matter if I was fourth in line for the job? It was still the best job ever (which I made even better by getting them to turn the local broadcast into the biggest syndicated daily show in the format).

Who will you accidentally meet for a job already spoken for? What will they remember about you? Who will turn down the opportunity of a lifetime that will, eventually, fall to you? Admittedly, all of that is out of your control. However, I believe in the expression "The harder you work, the luckier you get." The only thing you *can* control is how hard you work—and how often you show up, even after you've been rejected.

LOSS IS NOT A FAILURE: ASA HUTCHINSON

The governor of Arkansas has had plenty of opportunities in his years of public service, but he's also encountered some political disappointment, which taught him that even loss is a learning opportunity. When President Ronald Reagan appointed the Arkansas native a U.S. attorney, he was only thirty-one—the youngest in the country at the time—which was a meteoric rise to national prominence. His path to elected office, however, was a little less meteoric. But Governor Asa Hutchinson, who grew up on a farm, knows something about grit and determination—and didn't give up.

"In 2006, the first time I ran for governor, I'd already lost two statewide races—one for attorney general and one for the United States Senate. In my third statewide campaign, I lost the governor's race to Democrat Mike Beebe. Even though my first two losses and my third loss were two decades apart, and even though I'd been elected to Congress three times, the loss of a third statewide race is hard for any politician to recover from. In all respects, anyone's political judgment would say that my political career was over. There's never going to be another opportunity.

"I don't really look at those losses as failures. Anytime you're pursuing a goal and come up short, that's no different from losing a basketball game for which you've worked hard and given your

11

LIVE AND LEARN (WITH EMPHASIS ON THE LEARN PART)

I had a buddy who, after spending years in construction, decided he wanted to start his own contracting business. He saw all these guys around him with less experience, skill, and brains making serious bank by buying beat-up properties, fixing them up, and selling them for a healthy profit. Sick of taking orders from others, he scraped together the money for an old, mold-infested house on the edge of town. His family pitched in. They went without. But sure enough, by working every day of the week, from the minute there was light until there was none left to see, he got the project done. He sold the house and made enough money to buy the next wreck. Success!

Except that it wasn't. His second project was a lemon. I think the house turned out to be on a sacred graveyard or something.

Either way, he couldn't sell that sucker for anything. This was a bad situation, but he only made it worse. After blowing his stack, blaming everyone else for his mistake, and burning every bridge he had, he gave up. My buddy liked the idea of owning his own business more than he did the reality. He didn't realize how difficult it would be, especially early on. Sure, he messed up by buying a bad house, but there are folks who have messed up way worse and come back stronger than ever. The bank foreclosed on the house and he went into debt, returning to his old job with his tail tucked between his legs. Not a great ending to the story.

To come back from failure, it takes humility, thoughtfulness, and time. I don't go into projects or enter into relationships thinking they are going to implode. But when they inevitably do (which is what this book is all about), I try to squeeze as much out of the lemon as possible. That means learning from mistakes, which can only happen when I've cooled off.

Emotion is the worst when it comes to trying to figure out why something did or didn't work. That's why I never try to analyze what happened and what I could have done differently right away. I don't know about you, but when I'm upset, I don't think clearly. For lack of a better description, I'm thinking with my heart more than my head.

Just like with love, perspective takes time. The further I get away from major setbacks, the easier it is to bounce back from them and assess what your next step should be. In the case of my friend, he reacted out of such anger in the moment that he ruined any chance of saving his business. He might have foreclosed anyway, but maybe he could have found a middle ground where he returned to his job while continuing to build his business on the side. Who knows? Not him, that's for sure.

The key to this whole Fight, Grind, Repeat thing is that you can wait it out, trusting that if you continue to work hard enough it's going to pay off. Here are a few ways to weather the downtimes and make the most out of them.

1. *Put your setback in perspective before it even happens.* When I have a problem or face a tough moment, I tell myself this is just one of *many* times I'm going to fail at my goal. Doing this makes the experience feel a lot less demoralizing when it happens.

2. *Learn from your mistakes while you are making them.* Knowing that whatever I'm doing is likely not going to work out, I try to learn as much during the process as I possibly can.

3. *Pay attention to all the steps you take toward your goal.* In order to learn from your mistakes, you have to remember what you actually did in the process! This sounds kind of obvious, but most of us are so obsessed with the finished product, we completely ignore how we got there. Leave a trail of mental bread crumbs along the path of your endeavor (taking notes or keeping a very short daily journal on your phone helps), so that when the whole thing is over you can trace your path backward to the beginning.

4. *Celebrate your mistakes.* This sounds goofy, I know. But the more you can make friends with these guys, the less you'll be afraid of them. They're gonna come around anyway, so you might as well invite them in.

LEARNING TO LEARN FROM YOUR MISTAKES

I'm a huge fan of lists. I keep a list of my favorite episodes of *The Office*, my favorite websites that make me laugh, and even my favorite John Mayer songs. I also keep a list of my more memorable failures, so that instead of reacting to the latest disappointment when I'm still heated over it, I can go back a few failures and try to work on that one instead.

- Keep a list of your rejections, flameouts, or anything that is tough for you.
- Look three failures back instead of at your last one. Time and space give you more clarity on solutions. The further we're removed from conflicts, the smarter we are about them. Working on failures from the past will help you with those in the present—without your even needing to try. Sometimes we also notice, when looking back, that the failure wasn't as significant as we thought at the time.

SOMETIMES YOU DO STUPID THINGS, AND THE ONLY LESSON IS THAT YOU'RE JUST GOING TO F UP SOMETIMES

Know that you will inevitably do something stupid. And you'll do it again. And you can bounce back from it, no matter how embarrassing the screw-up. Don't believe me? Get a load of this.

About two years ago, a woman called in to the show to say her mom, who had late-stage cancer, had created a bucket list that included going to Hawaii—and seeing me in concert. Well, they'd already been to Hawaii, so her only dying wish that hadn't been fulfilled was meeting me. I was stunned. There was no way I was *not* going to make this happen.

That night my band, The Raging Idiots, played to a packed house in Springfield, Missouri. The woman fighting cancer and her entire family of seven, including the daughter who called the show, were in the thirteen-hundred-person audience. A quarter of the way through the set, I called them onstage while the crowd stood up and roared. Mom and I hugged. Although chemo treatments had left her fragile and without hair, she gave me the biggest smile. I told her through the noise that I was happy, too, that she could come to the show.

"But if I were you, I would have picked a better person to see than me."

Other than the hug, a quick conversation onstage, and a longer one after the show, I didn't really have a plan. But as I stood there with this nice lady beaming at me, a lightbulb went off. I had the genius idea that she and I should dance. We had the full band right here. I cued my guitarist to play the next slow song on the list. Looking at me for an extra second, she gave me a clear are-you-sure expression. Of course I was sure! I was about to give this awesome woman a sweet memory.

She hit the guitar pedal with her foot and cleared her throat as she readied to sing, usually my job. She seemed to be doing it begrudgingly, which I found weird. Until I heard the first words of the song come out of her mouth.

Ain't no sunshine when she's gone
It's not warm when she's away

I was slow dancing to "Ain't No Sunshine" with a woman who had terminal cancer.

And she's always gone too long, anytime she goes away.

Bill Withers's classic love song took on an entirely new meaning as Mom and I moved slowly in a circle onstage.

Oh, nooooooooo, I thought as my band glared at me. I felt worse with every passing chord and prayed that the song would end in a hurry. When my guitarist hit the guitar solo, it seemed as long as the intro to "November Rain."[*]

Finally, mercifully, the song ended. I hugged Mom again. She still looked happy, but who knows? She could have been a professionally trained actress. I was mortified. I was so embarrassed I couldn't look into the crowd for the rest of the show.

Sure, my intentions were good, but the moment sucked big time. I hoped the woman and her daughter didn't hate me. I also hoped the world didn't hate me. I kept checking Twitter to see if people were making it the terrible viral moment it deserved to be in my own head. But the trolls were quiet online. When I met Mom and her family after the show, no one mentioned anything about the dance, either. Other than my bandmates, it seemed nobody thought I was as stupid as I felt.

FLAT TIRE LESSONS

I've made many boneheaded moves, some of which were in my control and some of which weren't. I call these flat tire lessons.

---

[*] For you kids, that's a Guns N' Roses song, which is something like seven hours long. I know 'cause I had it on cassette.

Nobody wants a flat. Nobody plans a flat. But flats happen. The question is, how will you deal with them? Will you freak out and cry? Or get out the jack, tire iron, and spare?

A FLAT TIRE LESSON FROM BOBBY

I met a couple of listeners after a show. Their wish was that I do their baby reveal for them. I was happy they asked, and was more than happy to tell them what the sex of their baby was going to be! They handed me an envelope with the sonogram. Neither one of them had looked into the envelope. But not only was there a picture of the baby in her belly, they had also told me there would be either a pink or blue mark scribbled on the top so there would be no confusion. I said aloud, "What do you want it to be?" How dumb was I to ask that? It was a no-win question. If I had just pulled it out of the envelope, they would have been excited about either option. But oh no, I made them pick their preference publicly. I had never done one of these before and they both yelled out, "We want a boy!" Well, you guessed it . . . "It's a girl!" I said. Everyone clapped. But everyone also knew they wanted a boy. *Awkward*. I caught up with them recently, and, don't worry, they love their little girl to pieces. But man, did I blow that one.

Lesson learned: sometimes you just read the card.

12

PEER PRESSURE

I'm a loner in a lot of ways. It's in my nature. That's part of the reason why I haven't been very successful in romantic relationships. There are other reasons I don't really date. I'm too old for the apps. I've never been on Bumble because I don't want to be the guy who everyone screenshots and says, "Look at granddad here. I bet he's at least 35. What a loser." Then there's my schedule. Going to bed at 8 P.M. rocks a personal life. "Hey, baby, you want to get a 4 P.M. dinner?" doesn't get many ladies hot and bothered. Lots of folks date their work colleagues, and I've dated a few artists or people in the industry because I don't really meet any other kinds of women. I dated a B+ actress for a bit and didn't tell anyone. I'm still holding on to that secret. Next book, for sure.

A lot of time after I'm done with my day, I just want to decompress—and *not* talk or communicate in any way. Not exactly

Prince Charming material. (By the way, is Prince Charming even a thing anymore? While writing this book and my last, I've realized that many of my references won't quite resonate with the majority of people reading them—a.k.a. you young folk. When I talk about *Friends* or Sugar Ray or Prince Charming, I wonder—is that even a thing to some of you? If not, take a minute and listen to some good ol' late-nineties Sugar Ray. Then come back.)

As the loner dude I am, I recognize how important other people are to your Fight, Grind, and Repeat. None of us succeed alone in this world. I discussed in chapter 7 how, by making reaching out to others an active goal, I was able to develop a richer personal life. No habits you develop (good or bad) stay in one place. They all spill out to other areas of your life. That's what happened to my habit of being a better communicator, which has affected my professional relationships as well. I now shoot off a text to a TV producer when I hear she's won an award that has nothing to do with me, or one to the vice president of programming at my company to grab a quick lunch just 'cause—so now an e-mail from me actually asking for something doesn't look so obvious. There's nothing worse than opportunistic e-mails dressed up like a friendly note.

Here's a fake example of the type of e-mail or text you don't want to send:

> Just wanted to say hi! How are the kids? I bet they are so big!!! I'm so sorry we haven't talked in forever. I've been crazed. We should get together soon. . . .
>
> P.S. I hear you're the new regional director of sales. Could you get me a job?!!?

Analysis of the phoniness that everyone on earth can see right through:

- *broad comments that could apply to almost anyone in the universe*
- *lots of exclamation points*
- *throwing in your real request as if that's the afterthought*

Here's a real example of a phony text, the kind that I get all the time from artists:

> Hey Bobby, let's get a beer sometime. We should catch up! Been a while.

First off, I have no idea how this person got my cell number. If it's someone random, he should start with, "Hey Bobby, it's Frank [fake name]. I got your number from Stew [fake name]." It sets a better tone. Just being opportunistic isn't as bad as fake AND opportunistic. To that end, I don't drink. So, when I receive a message with "Let's have a beer" or "Let's get a drink," I know that not only does this guy *not* know me, but he can't even be bothered to do about five minutes of research on the Internet.

Relationships—whether family, career, or romantic—are long-term investments. The key word here is "investment." You need to put in effort to cultivate friendships on all levels so that you have support as you deal with disappointment and try to get better at whatever it is that you do. Ultimately, being nice for no ulterior motive is the most self-serving thing you can do.

Think about it like this: surround yourself with people who you not only get the most out of, but who help get the most out of you. In crafting a culture that allows me to be my best while getting the best from others, I've asked myself a lot of questions about the folks I surround myself with. A strong work ethic is a requirement across the board for me. Other than that, each situation or sector of my life calls for a different personality.

While recording music yesterday for my EP *The Next Episode*, I was cutting a song called "Good Ol' Days" with a new producer. I've recorded with different producers and even friends, but Walker Hayes (yes, the artist) was the first producer to make me feel like I was any good at making music. Throughout the entire process, he kept yelling things like "That's what I'm talking about" and "Yeaaaah baby!" But Walker is also a pro. "Turn that up a bit," he would say, or "Bring it down here," and he was dead right. In the music studio, where I know I'm not strong, I need someone who has that positive spirit and professional ability. The confidence he brought me made me better.

When it comes to my radio show, I don't need a cheerleader. In that realm, where I'm already confident, constructive criticism—even honest, negative feedback—is much more valuable to me. And it saves time. I need the data, not to be hugged and kissed on the way to it. Amy—my cohost and probably my closest friend because I see her for six hours every day—is my truth-telling sounding board. (Although she still gives me awkward hugs along the way.) The fact that I found someone like her (an honest, loving giver of awkward hugs) is a miracle. Amy is the yin to my yang. Everything about her is the opposite of me, which in theory could be very annoying. But in practice I enjoy her, even when we're in complete disagreement or she's showing me the many errors of my ways. One of the things I admire most about Amy is that she's great at not being "on the radio" when she's on the radio. She'll get upset with me when I'm not communicating with her or the rest of the people doing the show in a human way. Or even the audience. She cries at me sometimes. That's usually my barometer.

HIVE MIND

There's nothing like workshopping your problems. Talking out why you're having trouble attracting new clients with other entrepreneurs in your field or ways to instill discipline in your child's life with other parents who have kids the same age—nothing beats it. Open, honest discussions with peers or mentors about what *hasn't* worked is the best thing ever.

The problem is finding those people who'll be honest. I'm in the media, where everyone has got something cooking, but no one shares any details or insights. You never know about people's projects unless they're a done deal, and you *never* hear about their failures or missteps. You don't talk about what you lose. You only talk about what you win.

I have a few friends in the business I trust, and we discuss the things that didn't go right for us. Whenever I need feedback, advice, or a reference, I hit up Charlamagne Tha God, host of the radio show *The Breakfast Club*. We can talk to each other about *anything* business-wise, to the point where we know each other's contracts. We even recommend each other for jobs that we ourselves are trying to get. Sure, there's competition at times, but not ego. Much like with a brother, you want to win but are super happy when he does, too.

I know A-list artists who call each other to talk about such little things as negative Twitter feedback! The rich and famous do the same things the poor and not-famous do: act out of character in emotional situations, drink too much, enter into bad business deals, and get into relationships with bad people. I've seen others screw up a lot, and it makes you think, Oh, it's okay. I'm not the only weirdo around here. I'm not the only one failing. Actually, everyone's failing. And the people doing it a lot are the ones who talk most about winning.

Let's face facts. It's a heck of a lot easier to learn from other people's mistakes than it is your own. Add to that flaws, issues, problems, ways to fix problems . . . I'm the greatest advice giver in the world. I've never met anybody who gives advice as good as mine. Now, I don't take that advice worth a crap at times, but I can give it wonderfully because I can see everything that's wrong with everybody, all the time. Like, I'm *amazing*. And probably annoying beyond belief.

Seriously, though, when we're analyzing our own situation or how we ended up where we are, we tend to jump all over the place. Because we're aware not only of the actions we've taken with the world outside but of our entire interior landscape of emotions, thoughts, and motivations (not to mention all the should-haves, could-haves), we can't keep the narrative straight or logical. When we consider others, we look at their stories on a much more linear and practical plane. The trick is to take that logic and instead of leaving it in the realm of judgment on others, apply it to yourself.

Whenever you identify a flaw or problem behavior in somebody else, pause for a sec and ask yourself, "Have I done something similar?" Especially if you're really hit hard by their issues, it may mean you relate to them. Instead of thinking, *You're* an idiot, you realize, *I'm* the idiot. That's awesome, because it'll help you stop sabotaging yourself (for a brief period of time).

PAY YOUR DEBTS

I just finished watching *Game of Thrones*, which, by the way, is probably the greatest television show of my lifetime. (I didn't say my favorite, but the greatest, yes.) The detail, the storylines, the sweeping scenery: none of that is easy or cheap. But with *GOT* (that's what we cool kids call it), everything is executed flawlessly.

Side note: I have friends who revel in the fact that they've never seen an episode of the greatest TV show of our time. I never understood the whole showing off about how you aren't interested in the stuff the rest of us are. Maybe if there was a better show, or if you watched it and hated it. But to be the person who proclaims, "I am proud to say that I have not seen one episode of that show." Yay. You win the counterculture hippie award. By the way, you just dropped your iPhone, and your Amazon PopSocket fell off, too!

I believe in the rule of the heavy majority when it comes to entertainment. If most like(ish)-minded people believe something is fantastic, they probably aren't wrong. Most people love pizza. Most people loved *Breaking Bad*. I've never seen an episode of *The Sopranos*. I'm not bragging, I just didn't have HBO at the time. Also, the Mob has never interested me. I've never seen *The Godfather* or [insert any "awesome Al Pacino movie" here], even though I'm sure they are all fantastic, just as I am that *The Sopranos* is fantastic.

Anyway, in *Game of Thrones* there is a family called the Lannisters. And their motto is "A Lannister always pays his debts." I wish we non–quasi medieval totally mythical folks adhered to this a bit more. Everybody in credit card trouble, student loan trouble, baby momma trouble.

Dave Ramsey, who hosts a national radio show about money, talks to people all the time about snowballing their debts, which means paying off your smallest debt first. Even if it's just twenty-five dollars at a time, pay it off. If you are throwing money to pay off a big pit of debt (like that Sequoia SUV with the DVD players in the headrests that you needed to have), you're more likely to give up because you don't feel like you're making progress. With one less bill to pay each month, even if it's only a small one, you'll experience real change. You see it changing. You feel it changing. So it changes! His method is genius, because it tackles the head, the essence of everyone's problem with money.

Money is far from the only kind of debt in this world. I also believe in paying my debts to the Big Man upstairs. Insert whoever your bigger-than-you power is. Can be Jesus, Buddha, your cousin Craig, anyone to whom you'd say, "If you let me get away with X, I promise Y." We've all done it.

"God, hey, listen, if you can just hook me up with an A on this paper, I'll study hard the rest of the semester."

A or not, you didn't study hard the rest of the semester, did you?

I remember a deal I once made with God. I was dating a girl

many, many years ago, and we were somewhat serious. But you know me (at least you would if you read my first book . . .). I was afraid to have sex with someone for fear I'd get her pregnant or my wiener would turn green. So we dated for a long time and never had sex. Well, we almost had sex once, and the "almost juice" got on her lady muscle. About three weeks later, she let me know she was very late getting her period. We didn't even have sex, and this is how I'm going to get someone pregnant, I thought to myself, not by not pulling out, but by staying out. I was pissed. I was scared. She was, too. I would be no treat to have a kid with.

"I'm going to get a couple pregnancy tests," she said.

I was white with fear. It was right then and there I made a deal with the Lord.

"Dear Lord, if you can make her *not* pregnant, I will go out tomorrow and . . ."

I'll give you the rest later. Keep reading.

I actually prayed for her to be "not pregnant," which might be one of the dumber things ever to pray for. It also might be one of the worst structured sentences sent up in the form of a prayer.

The girl I was dating got the pregnancy tests, two of them, and we endured the mind-numbingly slow tick-tock, tick-tock until the results appeared. And BAM, not pregnant! My prayers had been answered.

None of me thinks that a higher power made her not pregnant between the time that I asked for it and the time that she got home. But I did make a deal. And the Lannisters and I, we always pay our debts. So I woke up the next morning, didn't tell anyone, got in my car, and drove forty-five minutes to the skydiving center in San Marcos, Texas. Lots of people skydive, but I'm not lots of people. I don't like rooftop parties, much less airplanes, much less jumping out of one. I showed up and walked up to the desk and said the words I never thought would come out of my mouth.

"I'd like to go skydiving, please," I said.

"How many in your party?" the man working there asked.

"Just me."

"Usually we require reservations days in advance," he said, looking at me a little funny, but eventually he threw me in with another group since I was awkwardly alone.

I made a deal with God that I would try something totally out of my comfort zone if he hooked it up with no baby. Skydiving definitely fit the bill. So up I went in a tiny airplane. This is the part where I tell you how awesome and freeing it was to jump and free-fall out of an airplane and that all my lifelong fears instantly disappeared.

Ain't happening.

It sucked. I hated going up. I hated going down. I hated the parachute being pulled, because it yanked my tater tots. I hated all of it. Except the landing, where I put both my palms on the ground and thanked anyone and everyone for being there to witness it. Meanwhile an eleven-year-old girl who landed ten feet away loved every second of the experience. I hated it, but I had done it. I made a promise and I fulfilled it. A Lannister always pays his debts. I could never ask God for another favor if I hadn't fulfilled the previous one.

The same goes with people! You can't go around promising things, saying you'll do something, and not following through. It may not get you the first or second time you neglect someone, but in the end it will always come around to bite you. I'm so serious about this that I suggest keeping a running note in your phone of any verbal promises you make to anyone. And then fulfill them. You will be known far and wide for your honesty and upright character. Okay, maybe not all that. But people are, surprisingly, so full of crap nowadays that when you aren't, folks are truly amazed.

Snowball your debts to people if you have to. Just start paying them down. Be a Lannister. A Lannister always pays his debts.

REPEAT IN REVIEW

BOBBY WORKS: ROCKY WATERS EDITION

I worked at a marina for a while, where the gig was to have every boat lined up along the dock as precisely as those dudes with the big hats who stand outside the queen of England's palace in London. Okay, maybe they were not *that* neat. But I had to put effort into moving those party barges and fishing boats. They didn't exactly rent themselves.

To convince people they needed to rent one of the boats I was in charge of, I'd give them a quick tour with all the elements perfectly in place. For the fishermen, there were big, juicy crickets jumping around in a cooler on the dock. For the dudes away from the wives, I rolled out the ice machine that made ice to keep their drinks cool. I had it down.

On most days, everything would be moving right along smoothly. I would book a few boats, pump gas for the group of girls staying at the cabin a few miles away, and be just about to get the digits of the hottest one. Then Hurricane Garbanzo Bean would come blowing in.

Suddenly, my perfect boats would be bouncing everywhere.

The crickets would flip over and jump away, the ice machine would start rolling, and the girl would disappear.

That's life on the marina: you've prepared, worked hard, and are ready for straight profit when—*boom*—a storm hits. Uncontrollable forces ruin your best-laid plans. Talk about a metaphor for life. Jeez. Well, since I've gone here I might as well continue.

Storms are never good. They are never fun. They are never wanted. But you get used to dealing with them once you've been through a few. The result is, you begin to see that a storm doesn't have to ruin your entire day. And even if it does ruin a day, it doesn't ruin a week.

Some of the real (not metaphorical) storms I experienced at the marina meant we took shelter and drank free slushies for a couple of hours while waiting out the weather. Some of my most fun memories are of hanging out in a little shed with Evan, another marina employee and a great high school friend, listening to Fastball play on KLAZ, all the while thinking the whole place was going to be blown away.

Sometimes we need a storm. There are times in my life when a storm has led me to a better place, given me a reset, shrunk my head. Storms can be great. Maybe not right in the middle of the high winds and pelting rain. But when it all blows over, you really appreciate the view.

REPEAT IN A FEW STEPS

Repeat is when you've Fought with everything you have, Grinded like crazy, and flamed out, only to start the whole process over with no guarantees.

No matter how you feel, Repeating is not failing—it's

getting you closer to your goal. Even if you learned just a little something new, you are still closer to your goal.

The first step of Repeat is to retreat. This is normal. Nobody likes rejection or failure. Give yourself time to mourn. But not too much time.

The next step (hopefully) is reflection. How bad your loss is and how good you are at dealing with disappointment will determine when you get around to this.

The final step is to use what you've learned in the process to figure out what you should do next: how to do the same thing better or, at least, differently.

Learn from your mistakes. The more time you can put between yourself and them, the easier that is to do. In a lot of instances, we don't have enough time to properly reflect. And that's okay. Keeping a list will help you recall them later. It's human to forget things we don't want to remember. Sometimes looking back at a mistake from three mistakes ago helps the current situation.

Repeating takes a lot of resilience, which is a muscle that can be strengthened in anyone—through rejection! The more you fail, the stronger you get at it.

No one is keeping count of your failures or their magnitude—except you.

Don't compare yourself to others. It's not helpful or accurate. You don't know their Fight as well as you think you do.

Repeat isn't just about trying again after you don't achieve your goal. You can win *and* Repeat to take your Fight to the next level.

CONCLUSION

Ambition, grit, and endurance are the most important predictors of success—and anyone can possess those three qualities. If there's anything people take away from this book, I hope it's that we all possess what it takes to succeed.

The brightest names on the marquee were once just randoms staring at the same marquee, saying to themselves, "One day I'm going to be there, too." Everyone is just someone from somewhere with a goal to do something. The question is, how much of yourself are you willing to invest in your dreams?

That's a real question, not just something a middle-school theater teacher might say to make you feel bad that you haven't learned your lines. My philosophy of Fight, Grind, and Repeat is not about guilt. It's about knowing who you are and what you want—then gaining the tools you need to get it.

If you're not willing to invest much in a goal, this is a big neon flashing sign that your current goal is not where your true passion lives. Don't get down or judge yourself; knowing what doesn't move you is very valuable information in finding what does.

I wanted to share my methodology partly because success seems so distant and even romantic to so many, when in reality it's neither—at least if you don't approach it as such. Look, if I—a welfare, food-stamp kid with a mom who wasn't always around and a disappearing dad, from a poorly educated area— can do it, well then, anyone can.

Nothing about my journey has been romantic, which is precisely why I want to help others feel good about the bumps along their own. Success doesn't mean being the CEO right away. It might not even mean being a CEO at all. Success is figuring out what you really want and taking very small steps toward that vision. If you do that, no matter where you end up, you won't be a failure. I'm not saying you won't feel like one from time to time—or a lot of times. But part of the formula is embracing failure not as an identity but as something that happens to all of us and successful individuals use to push them forward.

My secret ingredient to my success has been *discipline discipline discipline*. It's not comfortable most of the time, and when it gets comfortable, that means it's time to level up.

A tool always needs to be sharpened. Fight, Grind, and Repeat is a way of life that requires fresh motivation from time to time. I hope reading this book provided a serious kick in the pants, but once you've put it down, you've got to pick up something else. Here's my to-do list for you:

Read this book again!

Find another book. (And read a chapter every time you watch an
  episode of a Netflix show.)

Watch Ted Talks online.

Watch documentaries on people you admire.

Put things in front of you.

Say your goals out loud.

Give yourself the opportunity to succeed.

But be vulnerable enough to fail.

Find someone to share with who will have empathy for and
  believe in you.

Have empathy for and believe in someone else.

While your own success is important to pursue, our lives
don't mean much if we don't expand them out beyond ourselves.
I encourage you to take the Fight, Grind, Repeat mantra and apply it to helping others succeed as well.

It wasn't until I started to help others that I realized how
insignificant my struggles were. There's nothing like getting involved in things much bigger than yourself to put failure and
disadvantage in perspective.

The more success I've achieved, the more I've been able to
give back. And the more I have volunteered and pitched in, the
more I've learned that I'm not so important, which is incredibly
liberating. See, if you Fight, Grind, and Repeat hard, you run the
risk of becoming so focused on your own wins and losses as to
become self-absorbed. I'll admit that I've definitely fallen into
this trap.

When I walked into a room at a children's hospital to find a six-year-old with incurable cancer *and* the most positive attitude, I couldn't help thinking, And I'm worried that I didn't have a nine share in the ratings this week? Yup, we're all always learning. Or at least, we should be.

You don't need to have a ton of money or time to *not* make it about you for just a minute. Be an example to others who feel like they're fighting a battle alone. Showing people you can come from a negative situation and make it positive, that you can stay in the Fight no matter what, that's a great service. Through all the small decisions we make every day, we can create our opportunity—for ourselves and others.

Get out of your head and into your life.

Fight, Grind, Repeat.

ACKNOWLEDGMENTS

Well, holy crap. I didn't think I'd ever do one book, much less two. So I have a lot of people to thank. To Rebecca Paley, who is the real MVP, not only for seeing the structure of this book, but also for serving as my literary therapist. I have to thank the people who shared their stories with me in the book: Walker Hayes, Chris Stapleton, Amy Brown, Mike Deestro, Governor Asa Hutchinson, Andy Roddick, Brooklyn Decker, Charlamagne Tha God, and Charles Esten. To those who have been there from the start, Rod Phillips, Jay Shannon, and Oscar Meyer (mostly because I ate their hot dogs and bologna a lot early on!). To my management team, Mary Forest Findley (I spelled her name wrong in the last book, oops), and the KING, Coran Capshaw. You too, Tom Lord. To my bosses at iHeartRadio—Bob Pittman, Rich Bressler, and Darren Davis—for letting me have a real job that allows my other passions to see the light of day. To Jennifer Leimgruber, who is awesome and has had my back so many times that I've lost count. Shout-out to my dude Kevin Legrett. Shout-out, Lunchbox. Shout-out, Eddie. And mostly shout-out to people who inspire me creatively, to be a better person, and to work harder like Charlamagne, Walker, Amy, John Mayer, Lindsay, Adam Carolla, Ricky Gervais, Jimmy Kimmel, and my hero, David Letterman. Thanks to Carrie Thornton, who has had to suffer through two books with me now, and the whole team at HarperCollins. What up, Legina???!!!! Same to Kristie and Tyne at Greenroom. And my agent at CAA, Mollie Glick. Worrrrrrd to Rachel Adler and Cat Carson at CAA as well. And to everyone in my life who has to deal with the roller coaster that is me. And most importantly, the #BTeam. None of this happens without you.

I'm not **supposed to** be writing books. But none of us are **supposed to** be doing anything. We create our **"supposed to."** I hope you create yours.

ABOUT THE AUTHOR

Inducted into the National Radio Hall of Fame as the youngest honoree ever, **Bobby Bones** has been dubbed "the most powerful man in country music" by *Forbes*. His nationally syndicated radio show, *The Bobby Bones Show*, reaches millions of listeners weekly on more than one hundred stations and recently garnered its third Academy of Country Music Award for National On-Air Personality of the Year, also earning a 2017 Country Music Association Award for National Broadcast Personality of the Year. When he's not on the air, Bones is performing stand-up comedy for sold-out audiences, sitting down with country's biggest stars for his own podcast, *The BobbyCast*, or hitting the road with his comedy band, Bobby Bones and The Raging Idiots. Additionally, he appeared on ABC's *American Idol* as the mentor to the Top 24 contestants. His memoir, *Bare Bones*, landed at #1 on the *New York Times*, *USA Today*, and *Wall Street Journal* bestseller lists.

SHOUT-OUT TO THE B-TEAM

Guys, Bobby here. Thanks to each and every one of you for being so incredibly supportive of me. I wouldn't be here without you. I'm proud to have all of your names included in my book.

—BB

A IS FOR ACTION
Aarica Dekker
Aaron & Blaine Simpson
Aaron Eldridge
Aaron Jones
Aaron Kinloch
Aaron Samuel Beck
Aaron Tippett Jr.
Abbey Rhea
Abbey Taylor
Abbi Puricelli
Abbie Bergtholdt
Abbie Wells
Abby & Karen Ready
Abby Bradshaw Mattingly
Abby Eisenhart
Abby Hanson
Abby Helper

Abby Phillip
Abby Spencer
Abby Winkeler
Abby Woodruff
Abcdward Family
Abigail & Heroin
  Reynoso
Abigail Cirillo-Testa
Abigail Hernandez
Abigail Pharr
Able Mahaffey
Abraham Nwamkpa
Abygail Thompson
Adalyn Smith
Adam & Katie Nunez
Adam Armstrong
Adam Burt
Adam Cantu

Adam M J Edwards
Adam Miller
Adam Muenks
Adam Salinas
Adil Smajic
Adly Trevino
Adrian & Alicia R.
  Morales
Adriana Guevara-Torres
Adriana Lilley
Adriana Lindsey
Adriane M. Morgan
Adrianna Chard
Adrienne & Anessa
Adrienne Bennett Nash
Adrienne Cortez
Adrienne Fischer
Adrienne J. Bero

Adrienne Kelley
Adrienne Lozano
Adrienne Proctor
Adrienne Wade
Aeddon Buckmann
Agnes Sagina
Aida Alibasic
Aida Westbrook
Aiden Bowden
Aiden C. Roland
Aiden Jacob Inman
Aiden Success Davis
Aimee Aikins
Aimee Brown
Aimee Hensley
Aimee Lambing
Aimee N Washam
AJ Jameel
AK
Alaina Ryan-Hunt
Alan & Reyna Lopez
Alan Griffin
Alan Jay Ritchie
(TheRitchieTV)
Alanna Hubbard
Alanna Sandry
Alayna Budel
Aleah Thadhani
Alei Tygert
Aleisha Breen
Alejandra Zamorano
Alex & Annette Barajas
Alex & Destinee Duff
Alex Berkley
Alex Castañon
Alex Davis Matthews
Alex Dyer
Alex Grandia
Alex Leeder King
Alex Maldonado
Alex Newman
Alex Reith
Alex Waddle-Murphy
Alex Zion
Alexa Oglesby
Alexander Lopez
Alexandra Comeaux
Alexandra Fithen
Alexandra Fulmer
Alexandra Kate Rynard

Alexandra Kirby
Alexandra Rostad
Alexandra S. Johnson
Alexandra S. Carter
Alexandra Williams
Alexandra Yudell
Alexandria Crawford
Alexandria David
Alexandria Perkins
Alexandria Quinn
Alexandria Voignier
Alexis Arnold
Alexis Carter-Tansil
Alexis DiAnn Ramirez
Alexis Eickelschulte
Alexis Kliever
Alexis Wallenburg
Alexis Zeller
Alfredo & Glenda Munoz
Alfredo Garcia
Ali Chersicla
Ali Coffman
Ali Scherrman
Ali Singleton
Ali Williford
Alice Rivera
Alicia A. Blankenship
Alicia Batts
Alicia Brewer
Alicia Cobian
Alicia Cravey Motycka
Alicia de la Garza
Alicia DeCataldo
Alicia E. Gorman
Alicia Grimaldo
Alicia Kay Patrick
Alicia M. Speth
Alicia Mitchell
Alicia O'Quinn
Alicia Poduska
Alicia Sullivan
Alicia Whitehead
Alicia Worth
Alisha Dean
Alisha Zenor
Alishia (Moore) Klocke
Alisia McLendon Ware
Alison Edwards
Alison Kanak
Alison L. Dicksey

Alison Mellon
Alison Takacs
Alisonne Crossingham
Alissa Pace & Kim Godwin
Alivia Pranger
Allen Joseph Smith
Alleshia Fox
Alley Seifert
Alli Hermiller
Allie G
Allie Kaminski
Allie Meador
Allie Starbuck
Allie Vidunas
Allison B. Eaton
Allison Duran
Allison Edwards
Allison F. Barbour
Allison Krumski
Allison Lynch
Allison Nicole Reyes
Allison Ramsey
Allison Stark
Allison Stringer
Allyson "AG" Gelnett
Allyssa Richardson
Alondra Garcia
Alvin Guajardo
Aly Dietz
Aly Kayleigh Ella
Aly Thompsett
Alycia Greenwalt
Alycia M. Ulrich
Alyson Barnstead
Alyson Faye
Alyson McKinley
Alyson Sims
Alyssa Abney
Alyssa Agrella
Alyssa Benjamin
Alyssa Boring
Alyssa Breanne Natal
Alyssa C. Adamson
Alyssa Calton
Alyssa D. Gonzalez
Alyssa D'Arco
Alyssa Da Re
Alyssa Edelbacher
Alyssa Hutto
Alyssa Klimpe

Alyssa Lenius
Alyssa R. DeAngelo
Alyssa Reitz
Alyssa Salmans
Alyssa Schauer
Alyvia Alayna Gonzales
Alyxandria Truman
Amanda & Andrew Kohman
Amanda & Olivia Gilseth
Amanda (Cox) Newton
Amanda Adeline
Amanda Amin
Amanda Andrade
Amanda Armstrong
Amanda B. Trahan
Amanda Baldwin
Amanda Barber
Amanda Beth Ridgway
Amanda Boike
Amanda Brinkofski
Amanda Brown
Amanda Burbank
Amanda Carleton
Amanda Cofsky
Amanda Cole
Amanda Curylo
Amanda D. Jock
Amanda Davidson
Amanda Dawn Bretzinger
Amanda Dittert
Amanda E. Venneman
Amanda Edwards
Amanda F. Wooten
Amanda Forman
Amanda Gabel
Amanda Godlove
Amanda Gottscho
Amanda Gross
Amanda Guinane
Amanda Hancock
Amanda Hartsell
Amanda Hebert
Amanda J.
Amanda Jo Montoya
Amanda Josephine Lombardo
Amanda Joy Ritter
Amanda K. Guzman
Amanda Kimbriel
Amanda Lake
Amanda Lamb

Amanda Lee
Amanda Leigh Patrick
Amanda M. McNally
Amanda M. Phlegar
Amanda Maceina
Amanda Marie Evans
Amanda Michelle Reed
Amanda Michelle Watkins
Amanda Montiel
Amanda Navas
Amanda R. Cammuso
Amanda R. Gribbins
Amanda Recker
Amanda Remo
Amanda Revier
Amanda Riccio
Amanda Riggs
Amanda Rubin
Amanda S. Johnson
Amanda Sassin
Amanda Sayer
Amanda Schade
Amanda Seamans
Amanda Shoemaker
Amanda Stubblefield
Amanda Torongeau Wilson
Amanda Vader
Amanda Vega
Amanda Virag
Amanda W. Elliott
Amanda Wilson-Salina
Amanda Wiskow
Amber "ACON" Murphy
Amber Andrist
Amber Barham Barrett
Amber Buchanan
Amber Clouse
Amber D. Derk
Amber Dawn Mathews
Amber Fathera
Amber Freeman
Amber Graning
Amber Helms
Amber Jaremko
Amber Jones Chamoun
Amber June Sypien
Amber Kay Stingel
Amber Krisell
Amber Lambrecht
Amber Lee

Amber Lynn Kuntz
Amber M. Davis
Amber Major
Amber N. Johnson
Amber P. Nielsen
Amber Perez
Amber Pritchett
Amber Pro
Amber Shaw
Amber Sunder
Amber the Hammer
Amber Tilley
Amber Vaughn
Amber Vu
Amber Webb
Amber Williams
Amelia Martinez
Amelia Vernon & Bubba
   Spears
America Behrens
America Epperson
Ami Blake
Amie Carey
Amie Dunn
Amy & Clinton Johnson
Amy A. Walters
Amy Ann Williams
Amy Baccus
Amy Bowyer
Amy Buchholz
Amy C. Capel
Amy C. Keough
Amy Carroll
Amy Catherine Varner
Amy Coleman
Amy Collins
Amy Dewar
Amy E. Goff
Amy Edwards
Amy Firestone
Amy G. Brown
Amy Graham
Amy Harbin
Amy Hardin
Amy Harkey
Amy Harmon
Amy Hartin
Amy Heathman
Amy Holtzinger
Amy Honer

Amy Is Awesome Freeny
Amy Jacobsen
Amy Jacobsen Leach
Amy Kass
Amy Kay Harrod
Amy L. Harrell
Amy L. Coon
Amy L. Roberts
Amy Lawson
Amy Lea Whitley
Amy Lee Gresham
Amy Leigh Connell
Amy Lynn Sheehan
Amy Lynne VanZandt
Amy M. Adams
Amy Marie Gross
Amy Marie Miller
Amy McGinnis
Amy Michele Mercer
Amy Morrow
Amy Nicely
Amy Noelle Culbreath
Amy Pearce
Amy Putney
Amy Rachelle Watson
Amy Rich
Amy Sowin
Amy Storms
Amy Swehla
Amy T. Soza
Amy Turner
Amy V. Lee
Amy V.P.
Amy Voss
Amy Williams
Amy Zimmerman
Ana Higgins
Ana M. Smith
Anahi Caldera
Analisa McKelvey
Analydia Pacheco
Anastasia E. Skiles
Anastasia Key
Andi Campise
Andi Horvath
Andie Wald
Andra Beyer
Andrá Rivolo
Andrea & Rosa Mendoza
Andrea & Tim Chiapa

Andrea Adams
Andrea Byrd
Andrea Caouette
Andrea Cartwright
Andrea Casey
Andrea Cordero
Andrea Driscoll
Andrea Dunger
Andrea Eisenhower
Andrea Glore Binsbacher
Andrea Kaljumaa
Andrea Kemp
Andrea L. Young
Andrea Lambert
Andrea Mendoza
Andrea Mosley
Andrea Perlwitz
Andrea Raffles
Andrea Valenzuela Schermer
Andrea Wentworth
Andrea Wilkes
Andrea Wilkinson
Andrea Wingett
Andrea Young
Andres Brigante
Andrew & Lindsay Huang
Andrew & Taylor Marshall
Andrew "Anders" Dorris
Andrew Bobal
Andrew Crain
Andrew Devlin
Andrew Folsom
Andrew Isenbart
Andrew J. Lea
Andrew Leonard
Andrew Mamone
Andrew Messina
Andrew Polchinski
Andrew R. Crawford
Andrew Veiga
Andrew W. Tisdale
Andrianna Cole
Andy Benfield
Andy Cross
Andy Halterman
Andy Pande
Angel Rose Conlon
Angel Van Horn & Joey Geib
Angela Baker
Angela Belding

Angela Brooks
Angela Dinkins
Angela Francoeur
Angela L. Gamlin
Angela McCaskill
Angela M.L. Johnson
Angela Mozingo
Angela Odom
Angela Oram
Angela Osika
Angela R. Noel
Angela Sinfellow
Angelena James
Angelica M. Robinson
Angelica N. Jusino
Angelica Salas
Angelina Fernandez-Romero
Angelina Floyd
Angelina Zeiher
Angelita Lopez
Angelyn Guzman
Angie Andragna
Angie Baker
Angie Dawson
Angie Fancher
Angie Jagers
Angie Keilhauer
Angie Stepp
Angie Tully
Angie Wiegmann
Anita R. Gingras
Ann C. Kielbasa
Ann Cook
Ann Sylvester
Anna & Evan Harasta
Anna B. Rubio
Anna Boyd
Anna Edwards Baxley
Anna Johnson
Anna Kirby
Anna Larriu
Anna M. Musial
Anna Markovich-Overdorff
Anna Mayberry
Anna McCorkle
Anna Robinson Harris
Annabel Raymundo
AnnaMarie Pellechia
Anne Bigler
Anne C. Stack

Anne N. Brunner
Annemarie Madaras
Annette & Gary B
Annette A. Romero
Annette D'Aurora
Annette M. Carrasquillo
Annette Miller
Annette Shepherd
Annette V. Saldivar
Anngela Gibson
Annie Adkins
Annie Beliveau
Annie Dougan
Annie Fuller
Annie Haider
Annie O'Reilly
Annika & Victor Romo
Annika & Wyatt Jensen
Ansley & Blake Maffei
Ansley Cotton
Ansley Louise Phillips
Anthony Caine Cardenas
Anthony Hernandez
Anthony J. Lenz
Antionette Joe
April Arviso
April Badger
April Campolito
April Douglas
April Duke
April Fivel
April Henley
April Holmberg
April McLemore
April N. Hampton
April Phillips
April Scott-Magante
April Sherrard
April Sperry
April Stevens
April Taylor
April Teichman
April Tomberlain
April Warner
Araceli Gaona
Aracely "Sally" Rios
Archey Family
Arely Alejandro
Ariana Sanchez
Arianna Chandler

Arica D. Caldwell
Ariel T.
Ariel Weishaar
Arika Scherzinger
Armando Lopez
Armstrong Clan 94
Ashlee Asselin
Ashlee Baucom
Ashlee Cordelo
Ashlee Earley
Ashlee Haley Johnson
Ashlei Bussell
Ashleigh Bloom
Ashleigh Buchanan
Ashleigh Gregory
Ashleigh M. Christopher
Ashleigh Rodriguez
Ashleigh S. McDonald
Ashley & Frank Rocchino
Ashley A. Rodriguez (ARod)
Ashley Ackelson
Ashley Ann Mooney
Ashley Ann Smith
Ashley Anne
Ashley Aschliman
Ashley B. Eisenhauer
Ashley B. Bess
Ashley Bender
Ashley Bess
Ashley Brewer
Ashley Brooke Thompson
Ashley C. Jordan
Ashley Carrillo
Ashley Christy
Ashley Cole
Ashley Cousins
Ashley D. Smith
Ashley Dean
Ashley Dempsey
Ashley Dunaway
Ashley Edwards
Ashley Elizabeth Whitt
Ashley Esch
Ashley Ferrante
Ashley Fields Shepkowski
Ashley Fregoso
Ashley Gattis, APRN
Ashley Gayton
Ashley Gerhardt Stuckey
Ashley Griffin

Ashley Hammer
Ashley Hartnett
Ashley Hasby
Ashley Ignacio
Ashley J. Burch
Ashley Jaclene Smith
Ashley Jelovic
Ashley Jensen
Ashley Karth
Ashley Kozlenko
Ashley Kreamer Cadena
Ashley Lee
Ashley Lovetere
Ashley Lynn Royea
Ashley M. Swaw
Ashley M. Drew
Ashley Majewski
Ashley Mayes
Ashley McMahon
Ashley McMath
Ashley Milan
Ashley Morgan
Ashley N. Craft
Ashley N. Henry
Ashley Nichole Hull
Ashley Nicole Atwood
Ashley Nicole Hendricks &
    Mr. Skybaby
Ashley Nicole Walker
Ashley Norwood
Ashley Olson
Ashley Ortiz
Ashley O'Steen
Ashley Paige Fusco
Ashley Palmerin-Garcia
Ashley Porter
Ashley Proctor
Ashley Renae Brawley
Ashley Rodriguez
Ashley Romero
Ashley Ruiz
Ashley S. Dodd
Ashley Schubert
Ashley Scott
Ashley Scott Joyner
Ashley Sengsouvanh
Ashley Sharpe
Ashley Snipes
Ashley Snyder
Ashley Stroke

Ashley Suarez
Ashley W. Michie
Ashley Wasson & Molly
  McElgunn
Ashley Whitmire
Ashley Zannini
Ashley, Kyler & Kaylee Morris
Ashli Evans
Ashlie & Matt McKenzie
Ashlie Schroeder
Ashlie Swainston
Ashlin Conley
Ashlyn Pugh
Ashlyn Reese
Ashton Hope Brown
Ashton Linnell
Ashton Strickland
Ashton Witt
Asia Means
Astrid Lesslie Martinez
Aubree Barnum
Aubrey D. Jackson
Aubrey Elizabeth Sanders
Aubrey Gould
Aubrey Griffin
Aubrey Jo Flores
Audra Burris
Audrey & Grayson Patrick
  Williams
Audrey Hessell
Audrey L. Schmidt
Audrey Pendley
Augie Graf
Aujiné Burt
Austin & Tia Showalter
Austin Blair
Austin Chandler Troy
Austin Harris
Austin Lee James
Austin Mayo
Austin Parker
Austin Rion
Austin Swartz
Austin Weaver
Autumn Cazeñas
Autumn Ringelstein
Autumn Wallace
Awna Irish
Azannette C. Padilla
Azsure Alderson

B IS FOR BRAVERY
B.J. Moore
Baby Whitling
Bailee Reiter
Bailey & Travis Sorsby
Bailey Balcer
Bailey Connor
Bailey Frazier
Bailey Lawrence
Bailey Schalk
Bailey Sergent
Bailey Trobaugh
Bailie Somnentag
Bandie Mundwiler
Barb & Brian W
Barb Applegate
Barb Betts
Barb Moye
Barbara Blankenship
Barbara Gera da Silva
Barbie McEachern
Barton & Crystal
BCB
Bea Lindsay
Becca Birge
Becca Cresap
Becca Dill
Becca Lamb
Becca Quisenberry
Becca R. Morgan
Becci Nace
Beckey Pearson & Kyle
  Hartmann
Becky & Jeff Bier
Becky Brents
Becky Chaklader
Becky Downer
Becky Eschner
Becky Evans
Becky Hinchley
Becky Horning
Becky LaBella
Becky Lynn
Becky Oleson
Becky Spanbauer
Becky Stokes
Becky Vanderhoff
Becky Wortman
Bekah Laine
Belinda Lopez

Bella Dudding
Ben & Jessi & Scarlett Reel
Ben Hein
Ben Melton
Ben Petri
Ben Winter
Benjamin Drewry
Benjamin J. Wadsworth
Benton Beasley
Bernadette (Bernie) DeBrango
Bernadette D. LeDoux
Bernie Hernandez IV
Berta Wesselman
Best Mom Ever Cindy Stolz
Beth Babcock
Beth Blodnick Herron
Beth Clark
Beth Davis
Beth Hall
Beth Kimper Coronado
Beth Leavitt
Beth Plumley
Beth Rehbehn
Beth Schneider
Bethann Monegro
Bethany & Michael Berardelli
Bethany Denlinger
Bethany Dillon
Bethany Eisenhart
Bethany Freeman
Bethany Grace Feltner
Bethany J. Castillo
Bethany Lane Scaggs
Bethany Laws
Bethany Sumpter
Bethany Teahan
Bethany Wolfe
Betsy C. Gentry
Betsy C. Keller
Betty Harper
Betty Piña
Beverly Giddens
Bex Crouse
Bianca & Carlos Silva & Chris
  Zarate
Bianca Agnello
Bianca Angoori
Billee Lynn Willson
Billie-Ann Bruce
Billy Lees

Bitantevera
BJ Southers
Blaine Bensken
Blaine Hamilton
Blaire Chatterton
Blake & Elisabeth Chapman
Blake Bettis
Blake Guenther
Blake Warren
Bobbi Brown
Bobbi Jo Marceno
Bobbie Haddad
Bobbie Moseley
Bobbie Pearson
Bobbie Purkey
Bobby Irwin
Bobby Kerns
Bobby Llanas
Bobi DeLancey
Bobi Sessions
Bonnie Sandra Price Meale
BoomBoom & the 6'ers
Boston Beckwith
Brad & Karen Scarberry
Brad & Keri Johnson
Brad Felkner
Brad Fuhrmann
Brad Kavan
Brad Lowery
Brad Massey
Brad Robertson
Braden D. Salazar
Braden Kober
Bradley Jacob Fehner
Bradley S. Parks
Brady Van Auken
Brand Morris Bailey
Brandi Davis
Brandi Diedrich-Roling
Brandi Dilday
Brandi Evans
Brandi Garrett
Brandi Leigh Calococci
Brandi N. Davidson
Brandi Paige Shifflett
Brandi Reiland
Brandi S. Coffman
Brandi Squires
Brandi Twaddle
Brandi Valentin

Brandi Veith Staloch
Brandi Webster
Brandi Whited
Brandon & Jamie Davis
Brandon Broadwater
Brandon Clay
Brandon Cummins
Brandon G. Dickinson
Brandon Greve
Brandon Griffey
Brandon Horvath
Brandon Leo Kemp
Brandon McCollum
Brandon Passon
Brandon Schluterman
Brandon Truong
Brandon Wilkins
Brandon, Holly, & Emerson
  DeWitt
Brandy Andrew
Brandy Beck
Brandy Bennett
Brandy Czech
Brandy Jo Martinez
Brandy Libby
Brandy M. Davis
Brandy S. Bonner
Breana Arvin
Breana Trottier
Breanna Brintnell
Breanna Emenhiser
Breanna Gambrell
Breanna Hinton Branch
Breanna Schaaf
Breanne Meggers
Bree Smith
Breelyn Hand
Brenda A. Zarate
Brenda Dehn
Brenda Howard
Brenda Jo Milligan
Brenda Luebrecht
Brenda Medina Sawyer
Brenda Montanez
Brenda Puapuaga
Brenda Scafidi
Brenda Zarate
Brenden Huddleston
Brennan Phillips
Brent Bargen

Brent Meister
Brent Michaels
Brentnee Tefteller
Brett Little
Bri Skye
Brian & Angie Reed
Brian & Lori Myrback
Brian Baty
Brian Bowman
Brian Dabbs
Brian De Jesús
Brian F. Martinez
Brian Forrest Brock
Brian L. Schultz
Briana Ashley Holland
Briana Burk
Briana Scott
Brianna Bonnet & Nikki
  Bergen
Brianna Cardoza
Brianna Dorsey
Brianna Hannigan
Brianna L. Moreault
Brianna Maglio
Brianna Palacioz
Brianna Sampson
Brianna Taylor
Brianne Guers
Bridget Pierson
Bridget Rose
Brielle England
Brienn Klahn
Brigette Burr
Brigid & Maura Maltagliati
Brigitte Achorn
Brinn Marie Torans
Bristol Gawronski
Britnee Manger
Britt R. Smith
Britta Oakley
Brittaney Torres
Brittani Burkhartsmeier
Brittani Labrecque
Brittani Thibodeaux
Brittany A. Ward
Brittany Aerni
Brittany Anderson
Brittany Ann Edwards
Brittany B. Schoengarth
Brittany Bailey

Brittany Bast
Brittany Bay
Brittany Bryant
Brittany Chaisson
Brittany Chrisco
Brittany Clark
Brittany Coone
Brittany Dixon
Brittany Donofrio
Brittany Faith Brown
Brittany Foley
Brittany Friedhofer
Brittany Hegwood
Brittany Hopkins
Brittany Kadra
Brittany Keelan Doyle
Brittany Killion
Brittany L. Weld
Brittany Land
Brittany McClung
Brittany Muzzey
Brittany Nguyen
Brittany Parcell
Brittany Renée Coleman
Brittany Rudy
Brittany Shickell
Brittany Stein
Brittany Stinson
Brittany Stluka Lassiter
Brittany Stovall
Brittany Welch
Brittany Womble
Brittney A. Quam
Brittney Ann Trower
Brittney Logan
Brittni Bordic
Brittnye Jarrell
Britton J. Barnum
Brooke Bowenschulte
Brooke Davis
Brooke Eaton
Brooke Helsel
Brooke Henning
Brooke Johnson
Brooke M. Conn
Brooke Matarese
Brooke Moreland
Brooke Olson
Brooke Pierce
Brooke Renae Alexander

Brooke Roane
Brooke Smith
Brooke Sudderth
Brooke Welton
Brooke, Zae & Evy
Brooks Gilpin
Brown Cordero
Bruce Rader
Bryan D. Paugh
Bryan Wellman
Bryanna Grimes
Bryce & Lori "Lowee" Galston
Brynn Fowler
Bryson & Shelby Stringer
Bryson, Will, & Ali
Brytanie McKay
BSLC Compton
Bucky McCoy
Butch Hendricks

C IS FOR CONVICTION
C&K Hagerty
C. Claire Starcke
C. Epperson
Cade Morris
Caden Jace Salazar
Caden Mason Casto
Cady Jones Waite
Caitie Price
Caitlin Baker
Caitlin Bond
Caitlin Burns
Caitlin Callahan
Caitlin Garza
Caitlin Holland
Caitlin JuAire
Caitlin Kelch
Caitlin O'Laughlin
Caitlin Reynolds
Caitlin Smith
Caitlin Thomas
Caitlyn Bailey & Chelsea
  Bradley
Caitlyn Isabel
Caitlyn Luecke
Caitlyn P. Blair
Caitlyn Ripp
Caitlyn Zuschlag
Caity Frisbie
Caleb & Logan Bailon

Caleb, Deirdre, & Bao Goare
Cali Knepp
Callaway McMichael
Callie Janosky
Callie Littleton
Callie Poland
Callum & Landon Steinke
Cally Mackrell
Calyn Posey
Camat Ohana
Cameron & Daniel Medlin
Cameron Argoe
Camilla R. Jesko
Camille Johnson
Camille Sellers
Camille Vetzel
Campbell Pierce
Candace Kuxhouse
Candace R. Hagan
Canden Byrd
Candice Crain-Radojits
Candice Ford
Candice Miller
Candie Lynn Cowden
Candy June Thompson
Candy Lucas
Candyce Floyd
Cara Bonomo
Cara Cusson
Cara Holt
Cara Rhoades
Cara Rodriguez
Cara Street
Carey Odden
Carl Weatherbee
Carla Goss
Carla Johnson Pierce
Carla Miller
Carla Roberts
Carla Summers
Carla Unberhagen
Carla Wersonick
Carla Workman
Carla Y. Rivera
Carleen Spicer
Carlos Mejia, R.
Carlos Tapia
Carly Colwell
Carly Earp
Carly Garrett

Carly Goldsborough
Carly Hatfield
Carly Kinton
Carly M. Caracciolo
Carly Sunshine
Carly Tinkler
Carly Tucker
Carly Young
Carlyn Machado
Carlyta Saldaña
Carmen Cragin
Carmen Hendricks
Carol Ann Frederick
Carol Hagensick
Carol Lambert
Carol Sacco
Carole McAuliffe
Carolina Estrada P.
Caroline Bloom
Caroline Brinson
Caroline Carter Davis
Caroline McAbee
Caroline Ondrey
Caroline Pacl
Caroline Phillips
Caroline Simpkins
Caroline Wilson
Carolyn Argue
Carolyn Ciotti
Carolyn Harris
Carra Carrillo
Carri McQuerrey-Funk
Carrie Bauer
Carrie Belknap
Carrie Cyr
Carrie Eisengrein Blair
Carrie Feyerabend
Carrie Flaugh
Carrie I. Gamble
Carrie Jo
Carrie Key
Carrie Sammons
Carrol Smith
Carson & Kinsley Wyrick
Carson Ragsdale
Carsyn Chase
Cary Ann Chandler
Caryn Carreiro
Casalyn Prieto
Casandra & Paul Casares

Casey Abshure
Casey Crozier
Casey Dew
Casey Ellison
Casey Frith
Casey Greene
Casey Jensen
Casey Kinton
Casey L. MacRae
Casey Mcbryde
Casey Minor
Casey Newman
Casey Price
Casey R. Rowan
Casey Sconyers
Casey Vettleson
Casey Zarr
Casie Conlon
Casie Winchell
Cassandra Beth
Cassandra Bone
Cassandra Kiger
Cassandra Kornacki
Cassandra Mae Mixon
Cassandra Sullivan
Cassedy Lopez
Cassidy & Eliza
Cassidy Beisser
Cassidy Orton
Cassidy S. Cooley
Cassie Hampton
Cassie Loewenberg
Cassie McCoy
Cassie Medina
Cassie Smith
Cassie Willett
Catalina Sanchez Escobedo
Catherine & Gregory Leach
Catherine A. Shield
Catherine E. Galway
Catherine Gobble
Catherine Kingston
Catherine Marie Hurst
Catherine Mustoe
Catherine Zink
Cathy Coussons
Cathy Ginette Reynolds
Cathy Herber
Cathy Hudson
Cathy Hunter

Cathy Kruger
Cathy L. Block
Cathy Rayhill
Cathy Rhodes
Cathy Thaxter
Cathy Wachter
Cathy Walsh
Cathy Westberg
Cati Funderburk
Catie & Andrew Orr
Cayci Peel
Cayden & Hannah
Cayla Bercaw
Cayla Marie Hurst
Cecilia Rico
Cecily Garcia
Celina Vigil Mandonado
César González
Chad & Kaley Johnston
Chad Curry
Chad Daniels & Family
Chad Harris
Chad Hastings
Chad Hunter Wells
Chad King
Chad Merryman
Chadsey Family
Chanda Lovelace Courtney
Chanda, Dylan, & Colton
   Fikes
Chandalyn Chrzanowski
Chandler Rose Secory
Chandler Wildeman
Chandlyr McClure
Channelle Steffen
Channing Wedel
Charis Koehl
Charlee Mozelle Howard
Charlene Draper
Charlene Williams
Charles Jerome Concepcion
Charlotte Chaffin
Charlotte H. Whatley
Charlotte J. White
Chase Bowen
Chelbelle
Chelcee Pollock Findley
Chelcye Matticks
Chelse Chavez
Chelsea Alicata

Chelsea Alspaugh Watlington
Chelsea Connel
Chelsea Edwards
Chelsea Etelka Nagy
Chelsea Gerberding
Chelsea Jacobs Edwards
Chelsea Matlock
Chelsea McGillen
Chelsea O'Neill
Chelsea Richenberg
Chelsea Robinson
Chelsea Slocum
Chelsea Spoonamore
Chelsea Teubert
Chelsea Walker
Chelsea Wallace
Chelsee Crockett
Chelsei Cogdill
Chelsey Ayers
Chelsey Cox
Chelsey Hernandez
Chelsey Lee Cox
Chelsey Vettleson
Chelsey Waswick
Chelsi Hill
Chelsie Grogg
Chelsie Lawrence
Chelsie Norris
Chelsie Rosen
Cher W.
Chérie Parker
Cherise Fegan
Cherri McClure
Cheryl A. Balsamo
Cheryl A. Savard
Cheryl Bertrand
Cheryl C. Martin
Cheryl Cain
Cheryl Ford
Cheryl Horton
Cheryl Hurson
Cheryl Kim
Cheryl McLane Black
Cheryl Otwell
Cheryl Quintana
Cheryl Riedlinger
Cheryl Vandergrift
Cheyenne Denice Howard
Chief Peter
Chloe Hamlin

Chloe L.
Chow Saelee
Chris & April Daley
Chris & Christy Breyman
Chris & Janel Welch
Chris & Jen S.
Chris & Lora Lee Clinton
Chris & Mollie Heinz
Chris Abrego
Chris Cannon
Chris Geldof
Chris Hunt
Chris Proschko
Chris Rogge
Chris Stasaitis
Chris Thomas
Chris Torres & Family
Chris Witte
Chrissy Bohanan
Chrissy Cooper
Chrissy Fawcett Sanders
Chrissy Ford
Chrissy Thomas
Christ Freier
Christi & Joe Velasquez
Christi Abney
Christi Henthorn
Christi McCorkle
Christi Ponton
Christi Robertson
Christian T. Birch
Christian Zoe Moore
Christiane Patry
Christianne Newby
Christin Adney
Christin Bell
Christina Brookshire
Christina D. Combs
Christina Deb
Christina Hansen
Christina Hewitt
Christina Howe
Christina Iñiguez
Christina Jarvis
Christina Lafreniere
Christina M. Rodriguez
Christina Naomi Perez-Gaspar
Christina Ovalle Nogay
Christina Pirson
Christina Pringle

Christina Rowland
Christina V. Shores
Christine "The Machine"
    Magsino
Christine Armentrout
Christine Bouck
Christine C. Perez
Christine Clingan
Christine E. Keating
Christine Gray
Christine Green
Christine Hearn
Christine Hicks
Christine John
Christine Kane-Duncan
Christine Martinez
Christine Masters
Christine Ponton
Christine Shook
Christine Tidmore
Christine Youngberg
Christopher Clark
Christopher Hancock
Christopher J. Ortega
Christopher Marvin Martin
Christopher P. Renaud
Christopher Vaughan
Christy Ann Clark
Christy C. Weihe
Christy Cooper
Christy Ellis
Christy Floyd
Christy Grummons
Christy Howar
Christy Hutchins
Christy Johnston
Christy Lawler
Christy Lynn Sanderson
Christy M. Lumpkin
Christy Maynard
Christy Meredith
Christy Oliver
Chrystal Cover
Chrystal Hobbs
Chrystal Watts
Chuck Clarke
Chuck Hester
Chuck Wincek
Chyristal Inman
Cicely Brooke Hislop

Cienna Toso
Cindi Offerman
Cindy A. Robinson
Cindy Coates
Cindy Colby
Cindy Conger
Cindy Davis
Cindy Duncan
Cindy Evert
Cindy Hickman
Cindy Hyatt
Cindy Lee Sibert
Cindy MacRae
Cindy Meier
Cindy Posey
Cindy Pratt
Cindy Rae Gonzales
Cindy Slaughter Leimkuehler
Cindy Solano
Cindy Stites
Cindy Strickland Melzer
Cindy West
Cindy Zdunkewicz
CJ Barone
CJ Cavazos
CJ Wallingsford
Claire Doyle
Claire Tritschler
Clara Zamora Gonzales
Clare V. Grover
Clarissa Marie Magliochetti
Claudia Arguelles
Claudia Davis
Claudia M. Miller
Claudia Torres
Clay Peevyhouse
Clay Shook
Clayton & Brenda Lynch
Clayton Lynch
Clinton Carraway
Cloey Allison
Codi Forney
Cody Clark
Cody Elizabeth Ryan
Cody Fuller
Cody Gregory
Cody Jeanette Dixon
Cody Miller
Cody Siebold & Nicole Dinkel
Cody Wilkins

Colbi Martin
Colby B. Simpson
Coleen F. Perry
Colette Razey
Colleen Bartsch
Colleen D. Plante
Colleen Echterhoff
Colleen Jazdzyk
Colleen Kennedy
Colleen Kurilla
Colleen M. Butler
Colleen Pulsford
Colleen S. Good
Colleen Smith
Collette Dice
Collin Bigart
Colton Owczykowski
Connie Berry
Connie Brown
Connie Bythrow
Connie Campbell
Connie M. Dosch
Connie McDowell
Connie Partin
Connie Smallwood
Connie Swofford
Connie Wegenka
Connor & Olivia Copley
Conolley A.
Constance Schmitt
Consuelo Martinez
Cora Pearl Swallows
Coral E. Pennington
Corey S. Pacheco
Corey Thomas Egger
Cori-Bell
Corrin Brockschmidt
Corrina Guitron
Cortney Carlson
Cory & Juanita Aleman
Cory & Miranda Parks
Cory Dennis
Cory Scott Peterson
Cory Svejkovsky
Coryl Martinez
Coryl Rose Martinez
Coty Moyers
Courtlyn Morse
Courtney Ann
Courtney Chroeung

Courtney Dale Clamp
Courtney Davis
Courtney Goober
Courtney Green
Courtney Johnson
Courtney K. McCann
Courtney Kaufman
Courtney Knowles
Courtney L. Dixon
Courtney Leigh Whitby
Courtney Longino
Courtney Lorenzo
Courtney M. Chambers
Courtney M. Berry
Courtney M. Robey
Courtney Michele Brown
Courtney Nash
Courtney Neff
Courtney Patterson
Courtney Piggott
Courtney Pratt
Courtney Priess & Alexis
    Werner
Courtney Runyan
Courtney Smith
Courtney Staves Adams
Courtney Thomas
Courtney Worrall
Courtnie Marie Evans
Courtnie Miller
Craig M. Bailey
Craig Stutzman
Craig Wiggington Jr.
CrayCray Cook
Crellin Judie
Cresta Duin
Cris Waters
Crissi Stamper
Cristen Hughes
Cristi Lloyd
Cristina Lopez
Cristina Sifuentes
Cristine Waters
Crystal A. Griego
Crystal A. Ruiz
Crystal Amber Curas
Crystal Blankenship
Crystal Blaylock
Crystal Bonds
Crystal Brahm

Crystal Doreen Nall
Crystal G. Tedrow
Crystal K. Earp
Crystal Kaczynski
Crystal Magni Palomino
Crystal Matile
Crystal Midwood
Crystal Mlynsky
Crystal Rose Allmon
Crystal Rothman
Crystal Scott
Crystal Zitnay
Crystalrose Gonzalez
Crystalyn R. Jensen
Crystie Bonner
Crysty Terminella
Currier O'Neal
Curtisfam5
Cyd Shepard
Cyndi Brannan
Cyndi Wagner
Cynthia Cort
Cynthia Frescas
Cynthia L. Brown
Cynthia Larsen
Cynthia Machado Martinez
Cynthia Nguyen
Cynthia Sifuentes

D IS FOR DEDICATION
D. Metcalf
D.J. Chrisman
Dag Duenas
Daina Goman
Daisy Kay
Dakota Allen Leo Schell
Dakota Dallas
Dakota Enriquez
Dakota Michael Delver
Dakota Reed
Dale Allen Beck
Dalene Threeton
Dalton Dice
Dalton J. Magilke
Dan Clark
Dan Lowther
Dan Rufenacht
Dana & Austin Meyer
Dana Chamblee
Dana Hood Villanueva

Dana Kirkhart
Dana M. Howarth
Dana Marie Woods
Dana Marshall
Dana Messer
Dana O
Dana Skidmore
Dana Suftko
Dana Tamayo
Dana Vande Hey
Dana Waldron
Danaka Crosley
Danalle Rabecki
Danasha LaTanya Hill
Dani Stempinski
Daniel Anderson
Daniel Buerges
Daniel Cardozo
Daniel E. Torres
Daniel Jacob Walker
Daniel Michalik
Daniel Thomas Marion
Daniel Watson
Daniela Horvath
Daniela Mondragon
Daniela Rodriguez
Daniela S. Torres
Danielle & Eddie Kelly
Danielle Aguilar
Danielle Bada McMath
Danielle Bouchard
Danielle Butler
Danielle Case
Danielle D. Phillips
Danielle Day 33
Danielle Doherty
Danielle Doyle
Danielle E. Guerrero
Danielle Ely
Danielle Foster
Danielle Frueh
Danielle Irene Smith
Danielle L. Jones
Danielle Lasiter
Danielle Linehan
Danielle Margolin
Danielle Miranda
Danielle N. Guidry
Danielle O'Brien
Danielle Orr

Danielle Penix
Danielle Rogge
Danielle Sanok
Danielle Stacy
Danielle Sweazea
Danielle T. Brown
Danielle Tedrowe
Danielle Tufano
Danielle Uribe
Danley Hyer
Danyall L. Miller
Dara Horn
Darci Lowe
Darci Stando
Darcy Abell
Daria Collins
Dario Aluisi
Darla Knutson
Darlene Michelle Stone
Darrell Ida
Darren Langley
Darrien Menezes
Daryl & Kandy Hirt
Dave and Laurie Loeffler
Dave Boyd
Dave Hunter
David & Ashley Lane
David & Megan Aldridge
David & Sarah Muir
David & Sonia Ortiz
David A. Carter
David A. Dawson
David A. Sanchez
David Albers
David Green
David Hassay
David Lenzmeier
David Linney
David McPeters
David Rodriguez
David S. Allen
David Wittlich
Dawn Calderon
Dawn Day
Dawn Fairfield
Dawn Gallup Graf
Dawn Hoffmann
Dawn Holland-Williams
Dawn M. Despaw
Dawn M. Simonsen

Dawn M. Farrell
Dawn M. Palacios
Dawn Marie Bucher
Dawn Michelle Robinson
Dawn Muchmore Henning
Dawn Philomena Nowlin
Dawn Remsburg
Dayna Downs
Dayna Patzner
De'Sha Hudkins
Dean Hancock
Deana Neis
DeAngelo & Cheryl Aguirre
DeAnna Cassat
Deanna Lauren Deeter
Deanna Leslie
DeAnna Parker
Deanne Schleiden
Deb & Sherry Roysdon
Deb Bohlken
Deb Coleman
Deb Jones
Debbe Cardoza
Debbe Wilson
Debbie Bates
Debbie Clements
Debbie Freer
Debbie Garcia
Debbie Giesel
Debbie Leitschuh
Debbie Meyer
Debbie Olson
Debbie Oudemans
Debbie Poetsch
Debbie Sandridge
Debbie Schenk
Debbie Stiles
Debbie Washburn
DebFred
Debi Jean Caldwell
Deborah Bennett
Deborah R. Robbins
Debra A. Edwards
Debra Brindley Hallett
Debra Cole
Debra Flores
Dee Hill
Dee Lanza
Dee Moss
DeeAnn Bredgaard

DeeJae Brewster
DeeJay Henderson
Deena Carroll
Deena Lewis
Deidra Lynn
Deidre Burke
Deirdre Cordova
Delma Lindsey
Deltah Mayfield
Denée Tacherra
Deneen Fayette
Denise Ann Kom
Denise C. Finn
Denise Johnson
Denise Lambert
Denise M. Massie
Denise Reyes
Denise Walker
Denise Watson-Quinalty
Denise Weber
Denise Wiggins
Denise Williford
Dennette & Gafoa Soliai
Derrick Hackett
Desiree Brooks
Desiree Dartez
Desiree Lynne
Destiny Foster
Destiny Low
Destiny Marcus
Destiny Terry
Devin Bradley
Devin Lewallen
Devin Michelle Dick
Devon Marie Wilson
Devonna Peterman
Dexter McDaniel
Deyanira Garcia
Deziree Dusso
Diana & Victor Arredondo
Diana Beirne Smart
Diana Chroeung
Diana De Leon
Diana Gilmore
Diana Goman
Diana Heise
Diana Henderson
Diana J. Hauser
Diana L. Vara
Diana LaVertue-Boston

Diana Ledoux
Diana Lesh
Diana M. Klesel
Diana Martin
Diana Sofia Guerrero
Diane Beyman
Diane Biederman
Diane Dixon
Diane Fritts
Diane Phillips
Diane Taylor-Glotfelty
Diane Verchio
Dianna Barnes
Dianne Laheta
Diego Hernandez
Dina Mooneyhan
Dina Trantham
Dixie Lee Ford
Dixie Lobmeyer
Dixie R. Linkel
DJ Duke
DJ Palombo
Dodo Estrada
Dominica Massey
Donielle Aluisi
Donna & Chris "We appreciate
    you!!!" Seaman
Donna aka CDNCountryGal
Donna Baird
Donna Barkley
Donna Block
Donna Clouser
Donna Gammon
Donna J. King
Donna Jean McKinney
Donna LaMarre
Donna Magan
Donna Sandoval
Donna Singletary
Donna Tsoukalas
Donna Tsoukalas
Donnalee Lucy Ferron Mille
Doreen Muck
Dorey Jimmo
Dorijean Kurtz
Dorothy L. Munos
Dorothy Morris
Dorothy Thompson
Doug Driver
Doug Hoogeveen

Douglas Speer Jr.
Dr. Chantal J. Rozmus
Dr. Dana E. Klush
Dr. Fran P. Riddick
Dr. Kelsa Reynolds
Dr. Rachel L. Spreng
Dr. Tracy A. Parks
Drew & Kimberly Hix
Drew & Sarah Hulsey
Drew Milot
Drew Thomas Dingler
Drew Zanella
Duanita Helm
Dustin "Big-D" Johnson
Dustin Crane
Dustyn Carroll
Dwight Forbush
Dylan "HodgePodge" Hodge
Dylan A. McCreary
Dylan Benson
Dylan Chadwick
Dylan Dykes
Dylan Hines
Dylan J. McDonough
Dylan Payne & James Burke
Dylan Shaddox

E IS FOR ENERGY

E. Lauren Hunt
Eagan
Earl D. (Butch) Roe, Jr.
Early Iannello
Eddie Kellam
Eddie Sorrell
Edgardo (Eddie) Rodriguez
Eileen Isenhoff
Elaine M. Oliver
Elaine McMillan
Elena Kaplan
Eli Hardegree
Elias Angel Tovar
Elida Contreras Urrutia
Elisa Green
Elisa Labra
Elisa Ramos
Elise de la Pena
Elise Taylor
Elise Vuillemont
Eliya Shabanov
Elizabeth Anne Peterson

Elizabeth Annette Aguirre
  Ward
Elizabeth Batten
Elizabeth Borling
Elizabeth Chrisco
Elizabeth Courtney Recchio
Elizabeth Drown
Elizabeth F. Cogbill
Elizabeth Fako
Elizabeth Flint
Elizabeth Grimaldi
Elizabeth L. Bruce
Elizabeth Lahman Serdynski
Elizabeth Mae Edwards
Elizabeth Meares
Elizabeth Parham
Elizabeth Payne Burns
Elizabeth Sipe
Elizabeth Sohns
Elizabeth Stone
Elizabeth Velasquez
Elizabeth Weinerth
Elizabeth-Anne Lutrell
Ellen E. Schneider
Ellen O'Malley
Ellen Schneider
Ellie Breidenbach
Ellie Holmes
Ellie Parsons
Elliott James Brandt
Ellyson Manuel
Elmer Cortes
Elvis Hasanović
Eme Lundy
Emi Spicher
Emilee Mitchell
Emilia & Allison Berrena
Emily & Aiden DeCap
Emily B. Ratcliff
Emily Bogner
Emily Bouldin Smith
Emily Corbin Fuller
Emily Dalton
Emily Decorah
Emily Devlin
Emily Eubanks
Emily Gadra
Emily Golden
Emily Goldsmith
Emily Hewitt

Emily Iacovelli
Emily Inhofe Diebold
Emily Izzy-Ava Smith
Emily J. Radford
Emily Kate Duvall
Emily Kochan
Emily Kraft
Emily LaCroix
Emily Mahoney
Emily Martin
Emily Maultsby Barnes
Emily McKibben
Emily Meadowcroft
Emily Merriman
Emily Mongiello
Emily Morrison
Emily Osborn
Emily Partridge
Emily Putney
Emily R. Clark
Emily Sane
Emily Schubert
Emily Shumaker
Emily Solo
Emily Swartz
Emily Tatro
Emily Velez Garrett
Emily Zimmerman
Emma & Charles Hanus
Emma Brown
Emma Catherine O'Brien
Emma Helmick
Emma Mitchell
Emma N. Wingfield
Emma Nicholson
Emma Renee Kinder
Emma Sainer
Emma Schmidt
Emmalee West
Emmie Chandler
Eric Aaron Pulido
Eric E. Scheumann
Eric Lewis, CPA
Eric Wazelle
Erica Barragan
Erica Bennin
Erica C. Khilling
Erica Davis
Erica Easton
Erica Greene

Erica Hoffmann
Erica Long
Erica M. Aguilar
Erica Mallard
EricHeatherBrandonEllie
Ericka Barsenas
Ericka Helfer
Ericka J. Blodgett
Erik & Eileen Montelongo
Erika Carlson
Erika D. Ferrales
Erika Day
Erika Dunn
Erika Honeyman
Erika Jenkins
Erika Keller
Erika Slagle
Erika Thurman & Michelle
  Krause
Erika Zulema Gutierrez
Erin Ashleigh Swain
Erin Authier
Erin Beat
Erin Bertocchi
Erin Burdick
Erin Compton
Erin Crane
Erin E. Paul
Erin Faulkner
Erin Greenwood
Erin H. E. Gorski
Erin Haugh
Erin Havard
Erin Homann
Erin K. Ebert
Erin Kahley
Erin Kammers
Erin Laney
Erin Lee Smith
Erin Lintzenich
Erin M. Arnold
Erin M. Sanders
Erin Marie Loveless
Erin McCurry
Erin Molloy
Erin Murray
Erin Nickel
Erin O'Leary
Erin P. Arnold
Erin Paige Neville

Erin Peters
Erin Ress
Erin Rigney
Erin Sexton
Erin Swain
Erin Wetzel
Eryn Harris
Esmeralda Casanova
Esmeralda Gutierrez
Espi Partida Fletes
Esther Gaines 3G
Ethan & Jakob Emerson
Ethan Kaiser
Eugene Medlin
Eunice Landrum Mullins
Eva Joyce
Evan & Monica St. Romain
Evan Joseph Penberthy
Evan Silbert
Evin Ege
Evonne Villarreal
Ezra Loza

F IS FOR FIGHT
Fancy Nancy Gibbons
Feather Sneed
Felicia Christy Tarin
Felicia M. Zapata
Felipe Valdivias
Felisha A. Sargent
Felisha Marie Lees
Fiona J. Keegan
Fiona O'Shea
Fletcher Family
Fletcher Mangum
Florence Cherry
Forrest Spieler
Frances Hedrick
Frances Villarreal
Franchesca Carrasco
Frank A. Conway
Franki Vallejo Jr.
Franklin Cammack
Franklin5
Future Mr. & Mrs. Hiebel

G IS FOR GRIND
Gabby Velez
Gabi Abbott
Gabriela Coreas Carranza

Gabriella Foristal
Gabriella Silveira
Gabrielle Maloney
Gabrielle Walther
Gaby Gutierrez
Gage & Cole Whited
Gail L. Harris
Galina Minayev
Galyean Ann
Garbutt Family
Garrett R. Bell
Garrett Rippy
Gary & Carey Norton
Gasper Olvera
Gavin Gorrell
Gavin Hauspurg
Gayle Higgs
Gaylon Ryan
Gene Halbrooks
Genesis Ashlock
Genevieve K.M. Warner
George L. Hartzell Jr.
George Lanterman
George W. Spady IV
Germain & Noelani Puente
Gianna Gabriela DeLeon
GiGi
Gila Craig
Gilbert & Thatiane Gonzalez
Gillian Paige Kemp
Gina Boilini
Gina Brooks
Gina Dertinger
Gina Gruver
Gina Marie Eliser
Gina Paulina Merritt
Gina Pecoraro
Gina Pilnacek
Gina Powell
Gina Rosemary Murphy
Gina Spangler
Gina Suhadolnik
Ginny Dorsch Nipper
Ginny Oswald
Giny Draper
Gisselle Diaz
Glenda Gandy
Glenda Hoffman
Gloria "Ed" Marano
Gloria Davila

Goose Galatolo
Gordon Desteli
Grace Chambers Coppedge
Grace Huston
Grace Manly
Grace Mayberry
Gracie Loren Guy
Granger Stefanko
Grant St. Cin
Grant Weathers
Greg & Jennifer Rush
Greg "TJ" Fleming
Greg Dunn
Greg Millard
Gretchen Jolie Peavy
Gretchen Simon
Greyson Barrett Hill
Greyson Varley
Griffin Hamby
Guadalupe Lawrence
Gumblegirl
Gwen Ertmann

H IS FOR HEART
Haeley Keitel
Hailey Armour
Hailey Hagerty
Hal Atzingen
Haley Almonrode
Haley Austin
Haley Bourne
Haley Burns
Haley Hungate
Haley Louwien
Haley McDaniel-Brill
Haley Rebekah Williamson
Haley Sims
Halley A. Black
Hallie & Jimmy McElvery
Hanna L. Brown
Hanna Stevenson
Hannah & Mattielyn Long
Hannah Alise Myers
Hannah Alto
Hannah Bohde
Hannah Burkhart
Hannah Dunn
Hannah E. Walker, Esq.
Hannah Elise Hogan
Hannah Elizabeth Ford

Hannah Elizabeth Lim
Hannah Garner
Hannah Gawrys
Hannah Hoffman
Hannah K. Bruce
Hannah Platko
Hannah Renee Andrews
Hannah Sue Hopkins
Hannah Swartwood
Harlene Wilson
Harley Hoffman
Harli Fountain
Harold Eddy
Harold King
Harrison Frizzell
Harrison T. Hughes
Hattie Nicole
Hayden & Hailey Zehring
Hayes Rufenacht
Hayley Barnett
Hayley Koenig
Hayley Wetzel
Haylle Hurley
Hazel Grace Ross
Hazel_TheFrenchy
Hazne
Heather & John Smith
Heather & Kayleigh Leavell
Heather A. Long
Heather Andrews
Heather Ann Nizzio
Heather Anne Hall
Heather Ashley
Heather Brady
Heather Bugg
Heather Cadwell
Heather Dauphin
Heather Day
Heather Engle
Heather Evans
Heather Gjertson
Heather H. Murphey
Heather Hardy
Heather Hendrickson
Heather Jean Abdo
Heather Joann Hoyt
Heather Justen
Heather Kelley
Heather L. Michaels
Heather M. Kelly

Heather M. Knotek
Heather M. Moretti
Heather Marie (Hays) Brown
Heather Marie Parker
Heather Marks Loving
Heather McKean
Heather Meleski
Heather Miller
Heather Nicole Smith
Heather Odem
Heather Poling
Heather Richardson
Heather Rodgers
Heather Ruggles
Heather Snakenberg
Heather Swinney
Heather Vaughn
Heather Walker
Heather Walls
Heather Wells
Heather West
Heather White
Heather, Robbie & Blake Satter
Hector Escalera
Heena Jivan
Heidi Cadiere Hill
Heidi Casas
Heidi Castro
Heidi Hill
Heidi Holloway
Heidi J. White
Heidi Leach
Heidi San Filippo McBurney
Heidi Sands
Heidi Whitney
Heileigh Miller
Helen Baker
Helen Parks
Helena R. Bodine
Henry Ros
Hilary Nekvinda
Hilda Hughes
Hillari Peugh
Hillary Garcia
Hillary Gutierrez
Hillary Ionson
Hillary Jo Heaton
Hillary O'Brian
Hillary Usher
Hobie Harris

Hogan & Pippa Hennings
Holden Hartley
Hollie Rich
Hollis Pyper Voyzey
Holly B. Dickman
Holly Bate
Holly Brown
Holly Davies
Holly Davis
Holly E. McGee
Holly F. Caldwell
Holly Hollingshead
Holly Hood
Holly K. Guidry
Holly Lee Mann
Holly Schmidt
Holly Shaffer
Holly Thompson
Holly Walker
Hope Caton
Hope Hutchison
Hope Johns
Hope Runde
Hope Smith
Hughes Family
Huie Library Henderson St.
    Univ.
Hung Le
Hunter Shelby
Hurt Family Carpool

I IS FOR INTUITION
Ian SpottedBear
Idella Mansfield
Imelda & Ezekiel Ruiz
In Memory of Claude Kindle
    (KEPK)
Indy Urzua
Intern Brendan
!rene Castillo
Iris Nayeli Urbano
Isabel Gaucin
Isabel Hamm
Isaiah Benavidez
Isela Casas
Isela Yvette Cardenas
Israel Segura
Iveta Wegricht
Ivette C. Rufino-Lopez
Ivonne Barancik

J IS FOR JOY
J&B Wright WPS
J&D Sollid
J.D. McNeill
J.L. Valentine
J.R. Sartain
J'aime Allbee
Jack Harrison Luke
Jack Southall
Jacki Waugh
Jackie Campbell
Jackie Chrisp
Jackie Crowley Mannato
Jackie Cruse
Jackie Duran
Jackie Gualtieri
Jackie Hayes
Jackie Hitt
Jackie Jacques
Jackie Macias
Jackie Price
Jackie Seeman
Jackie Sherrell
Jackie Sigvertsen
Jacklyn Rudd Islas
Jackson & Taylor Kenney
Jaclyn Eckert
Jaclyn O'Neil
Jaclynn Fuller
Jacob Coronado
Jacob Grandmaison
Jacob Hafner
Jacob Mauldin
Jacob Reed
Jacob Rehm
Jacqueline (Jack) Sweeney
Jacqueline Benfield
Jacqueline Emiko
Jacqueline Fernandez
Jacqueline Leigh Serany
Jacqueline Maldonado Snell
Jacqueline R. Warner
Jacqueline Siems
Jacquelyn Wilson
Jade Johnson
Jade Marie Wooten
Jade Treviño
Jade Weber
Jaime Foret
Jaime Hayes

Jaime L. Salemi
Jaime Pohlman
Jaime Valim
Jaimee Roy
Jaimie Kaye Brackett
Jaimie Saucedo
Jake & Megan White
Jake Russ
Jake Stinson
Jalen & Madilyn Fenty
James & Brittany Sikes
James A. Meyers
James Buckmeier
James Gerds
James Ronald Allen Jr.
James Sigmon
James Taff
Jami Ashley
Jami L. Drees
Jami Martin-Westbrook
Jamie & Matthew Gaddis
Jamie Baker
Jamie Boiles
Jamie Buehrle
Jamie Collins
Jamie Fassler
Jamie L. Bennett
Jamie Lenae Reed
Jamie Lentz Hedges
Jamie Leslie
Jamie Lynch
Jamie Lynn Navarro
Jamie M. Hurtgam
Jamie M. Boiles
Jamie Martino
Jamie McCarrick
Jamie Morin
Jamie N. Baker
Jamie Olson Donovan
Jamie Pryor
Jamie R. Neally
Jamie Rucker Skaggs
Jamie Ryerson
Jamie Stoops
Jamie Urner
Jamie Woz
Jamie, Ali, & Evan DeRubeis
Jan Kessler
Jan Kraeske
Jan Ruggiera

Jana Beebe
Jana Grohman
Jana Hubbard
Jana McClure
Jana Rose & Chris Jamail
Jana Shackelford
Jana Ulaga
Janae Azevedo
Janae Hendrix
Jane Elizabeth Turney
Jane Grollmus
Janeé Carden
Janelle Goodwin
Janelle Schweitzer
Janet & Aaron Sitler
Janet Couoh
Janet Ellis
Janet Goodwin
Janet L. Stewart
Janet Olander
Janet Pesl
Janet Williams
Janice Hataway
Janice Misla Haupt
Janie Wadsworth
Janine Noetzel
Janine Palmer
Janis Lampa
Janna Carroll
Janna Stock
Jaqueline Lopez Agundez
Jared & Breanna Gaschow
Jared Nakatewa
Jared Upshaw
Jaren Rodriguez
Jasmine Leonard
Jason & Elizabeth Martz
Jason & Jessica Scott
Jason & Kasey Benson
Jason & Oletta Ulibarri
Jason "Cavi" Cavanaugh
Jason A. Padua (JPad)
Jason Beegle
Jason Laplant
Jason Obara
Jason Plum
Jason Sullivan
Jason Underwood
Jason Withers
Jasper-Lynn Broadhurst

Javier Ramirez
Jax Williams
Jaxson & Raylend Steele
Jay Imming
Jayce Voeck
Jayci Begley
Jayden Ethan Madison
 Woodall
Jaymie Netterfield
Jayne Kathryn Denson
Jayson Brinkley
JD Hurst
Jean Bailey Robor
Jean Bird
Jean Jones
Jean Knowles
Jean Morgano
Jean Romano
Jeanette Granger
Jeanette L. Harwell
Jeanette Villa
Jeanna Louise Morris
Jeanna Martin
Jeanne Graham
Jeanne Guillen
Jeannie Green Brakefield
Jeffrey Barnard
Jeffrey J. Dicksey
Jeffrey Phillips
Jen & Cody Darling
Jen Conover
Jen Douglas
Jen Eldred
Jen Etcher
Jen Heinrichs
Jen Jones COS
Jen Kaiser
Jen Koehler
Jen LeFebvre
Jen Parrish
Jen Russo
Jen Ryder
Jen Taylor
Jena Shepard
Jena Willingham
Jenesa Stonko
Jeni Rooney
Jenn Bauguss
Jenn Bridwell
Jenn Romey

Jenn Samet
Jenn Schnee
Jenn Stanwick
Jenna & Chris Monaldi
Jenna & Dickson Howell
Jenna DeLeon
Jenna Dunne
Jenna G. Morgan
Jenna Hazelbaker
Jenna Leigh Davis
Jenna Leigh Rice
Jenna Looney
Jenna Miller
Jenna Morgan
Jenna Phelps
Jenna R. Turner
Jenna Schaff
Jennah Bailey
Jennah Hershey
Jenni Cook
Jenni Marie McGuire
Jenni Waidman
Jennie Forrest
Jennifer & Alex Rockwell
Jennifer & Hannah
 Barczykowski
Jennifer & Xander Vangelist
Jennifer A. Barbee
Jennifer A. Hudon
Jennifer A. Kittel
Jennifer Acevedo
Jennifer Anne Craig
Jennifer B. Goddard
Jennifer Ballance
Jennifer Bertucci
Jennifer Brackman
Jennifer Bruce
Jennifer Buentello
Jennifer Bushlack
Jennifer C. Wilson
Jennifer Case
Jennifer Cook
Jennifer Cornett
Jennifer Cox
Jennifer Crawford
Jennifer Crum
Jennifer Davis
Jennifer Delman
Jennifer Denise Brooks
Jennifer Dickens

Jennifer Drozdowski
Jennifer Eagleson
Jennifer Elaine Wolken
Jennifer Ellington
Jennifer Fagan
Jennifer Ferrand
Jennifer Flury
Jennifer French Rodgers
Jennifer Furrow
Jennifer Garcia
Jennifer Geordge
Jennifer Georgy
Jennifer Giacomino
Jennifer Goheen
Jennifer Goldberg
Jennifer Gomez
Jennifer Green Martin
Jennifer Hebding
Jennifer Holliday
Jennifer J. Tafoya
Jennifer Jackson
Jennifer Kathleen Ruiz
Jennifer Kay Leach
Jennifer Keegan
Jennifer Kevin Pham
Jennifer Kleinheksel
Jennifer L. Whiteley
Jennifer L. Messerschmidt,
     CPA
Jennifer LeAnn McQueen
Jennifer Lee Cooley
Jennifer Lewis
Jennifer Lucy Garcia
Jennifer Lynn
Jennifer M. Peña
Jennifer McClain
Jennifer McDonald
Jennifer Medford-Smith
Jennifer Molony
Jennifer Myers
Jennifer Neff
Jennifer Nessen
Jennifer Nicole Brown
Jennifer Petty
Jennifer Pfanenstiel-Cammarn
Jennifer R. Conway
Jennifer Rector
Jennifer Rinando
Jennifer Roth
Jennifer Sanchez

Jennifer Santoy
Jennifer Smith
Jennifer Stockwell Woelke
Jennifer Stout Cole
Jennifer Thornton
Jennifer Thorson
Jennifer Trail
Jennifer Urbaniak
Jennifer Vangelist
Jennifer Veronique Campa
Jennifer Warren-Jones
Jennifer Watson
Jennifer Whitehurst
Jennifer Zortman-Kershaw
Jenny Araujo
Jenny Bartlett
Jenny Benzine
Jenny Boisseau
Jenny Boykin
Jenny Cart
Jenny Clemens
Jenny D. Cook
Jenny Folsom
Jenny Garza
Jenny Holmgrain
Jenny L. Evans
Jenny M. Messinger
Jenny Patty
Jenny Queen
Jeremiah Bernal
Jeremy & Stephanie Wilson
Jeremy & Sylvia Reyes
     Hamilton
Jeremy Brislin
Jeremy Hinojosa
Jeremy Hogg
Jeremy Leon Chua
Jeremy Marlar
Jeremy Montoya
Jeremy Todd
Jerod Scott Moody
Jerred Harris
Jerrell & Erica Carr
Jerusha Wirth
Jes Sullivan
Jesica Childress
Jess C.
Jess Durand
Jess Parizek
Jess Rohling

Jess Warr
Jess Yost
Jesse & Sara Harlan
Jesse Lee Phelps
Jesse McGrady
Jesseca Aregger
Jessi Bieker
Jessi Garcia
Jessi McCorkel
Jessica & Noe Davila
Jessica (Franchis) Kessler
Jessica A. Parker
Jessica Alling
Jessica Annai Flores
Jessica AnnaLee McElroy
Jessica Barrero
Jessica Brodock
Jessica Brooke McCoy
Jessica Brooke Tirado
Jessica Budd
Jessica Burgess
Jessica Burtner
Jessica Church
Jessica Conway
Jessica Crosby
Jessica D. Alvarez
Jessica D. Castro
Jessica Dawn Plowman
Jessica Devine
Jessica DeWitt
Jessica Doswell Parr
Jessica Elizabeth Roberts
Jessica Engle
Jessica Festervand
Jessica Firsch-Wilson
Jessica Fones
Jessica Fox
Jessica Frigillana
Jessica Garton
Jessica Giovengo
Jessica Gusman
Jessica Heinrich
Jessica J. Cummins
Jessica J. McCool
Jessica Jacobs
Jessica Jordan
Jessica K. Smith
Jessica Keeley
Jessica Koster
Jessica Krabbe

Jessica L. Maslak
Jessica L. Cole
Jessica L. Diklich
Jessica L. Domingue
Jessica L. Hrubes
Jessica Lambert & Bradley & Layla Cannon
Jessica Lauren Hille
Jessica Ley, CCRP
Jessica Litvack
Jessica Lowry & Ray Bernstein
Jessica Luckett
Jessica M. Kyser
Jessica M. Lacey
Jessica M. McGowan
Jessica Marie Moses
Jessica Massengale
Jessica Mooberry
Jessica Moos
Jessica N. Porter
Jessica Navarro
Jessica Osborne
Jessica Parker
Jessica Pogue
Jessica Reed aka Future Mrs. Bones
Jessica Reynell
Jessica S. Allen
Jessica S. Leggett
Jessica Schladt
Jessica Schlager
Jessica Schmelzer
Jessica Snelgrow
Jessica Sparks
Jessica Stock
Jessica Terrell
Jessica Thompson
Jessica Tremblay
Jessica Upchurch
Jessica Weinberg
Jessica Willms
Jessica Winders
Jessica Yarber
Jessica Zoll
Jessie & Billy Gates
Jessie & Irma Ruiz
Jessie Benson Wagemann
Jessie Clark
Jessie Krabbeler
Jessie Lynch

Jessie Rae Vaughn
Jessie Wagemann
Jessye Hanson
Jestine Arnold
Jiji Nash
Jill & Emily Silva
Jill Anne Farrow
Jill Eno
Jill Euchner
Jill Fry
Jill Oldroyd
Jill Peterson
Jill Schwab Hays
Jill Thomas
Jill Weber & Barb Nannelli
Jillabella
Jillian Ackerman
Jillian Arensmeyer
Jillian Christine Jackson
Jillian Delosreyes
Jillian Gustin
Jillian Hall
Jillian Holmberg
Jillian K. Williams
Jillian McCarthy
Jillian Skokowski-Foster
Jim Richard
Jimmy B. Duke Junior
Jimmy L. Bank
Jimmy Matthews
Jingle Jangle
Jnet Jones
Joahna Sizemore
Joan Petty
Joanie Hearn
JoAnn Sifuentez & Mona Gutierrez
Joanna Barnes
Joanna Cotton
Joanna Winters
Joanne Werstlein
Joannie Shrum Borden
Jocelyn Vasquez
Jodi Anderson
Jodi Schweitzer
Jody A. Klemens
Jody Hawkins
Jody Lynne Marquardt
Jody Pecena
Jody Richards

Joe & Nicole Redd
Joe & Nicolle Cobuccio
Joe & Tricia & Joey Arnold
Joe Evans
Joel & Ann Marie Box
Joel Bradtmueller
Joel Cooper Henderson
Joel Dominguez
Joel, Laura, & Ryan
Joey & Pamela Dollar
Joey Curtis
Joey Owens
John & Jaclyn Deslate
John & Kendell Iko
John & Tracey Casciano
John Bruce
John Farrell
John Fry
John Gabriel
John Gray
John Iannaccone
John L. Carlson Jr.
John M. Rodriguez
John McGill
John Paul Bigouette
John Reddy
John W. Mahaney
Johni Flores
Johnny Clark
Johnny Farias
Johnson Twins
Joleen Fregia
Jolena Peachee
Jolene Chowdhury
Jolene Rae Maressa
Jon & Jacob Farley
Jon Wittoesch
Jonalyn Whetzel
Jonathan Blackburn
Jonathan D. Burgett & Family
Jonathan Evans
Jonathan Reiss
Jonathan Snaith
Jonathan Soto Osorio
Jonathan Thomasson
Jonathan True
Jonathan Wolff
Jonathon D. Briegel
Joni Altman
Joni Cheeves

Joni Marie Liverman
Joni Prince
Jordan & Rosa Deere
Jordan Allen
Jordan Ballou
Jordan Beal
Jordan Biester
Jordan Carter
Jordan Doss
Jordan Glosser
Jordan Hagarty
Jordan Halvorsen
Jordan Haney
Jordan Jackson
Jordan Paxton
Jordan Russ
Jordan Skelton
Jordan Tranbarger
Jordan Vaughn
Jordan, Meaghan & Magnolia
  Perceful
Jordanne Barr-Adamczyk
Jordon B. Pierce
Jordon McKay
Jordyn Ledyard
Jordyn Wells
Jorge Rojas
Jose L. Rodriguez
Jose Villanueva
Josef & Petra
Joseph Colurciello
Joseph Herbert
Joseph Nelson
Josh Morris
Joshua Acevedo
Joshua Anthony Good
Joshua D. Eatmon
Joshua Donald Johnson
Joshua Freed
Joshua J. Brockman
Joshua Jacobs
Joshua Radford
Joshua Ray Bryan
Joshua Rizer
Joshua Schulz
Joshua Warner
Joshua Wills
Josie Gentry
Josie McGuire
Journey Faye Windscheffel

Jovie Elleck Brown
Joy Guy
Joy Haisch
Joy Mehojevich
Joy Taylor
Joyce Dugre
Joyce Gillcash
JP Turner
JR Cornejo
JT Booth
Juan Hernandez
Juan Pablo Risso
Juanell Renee Ramirez
Juanita Hoff-Benson
Juanita Vásquez
Jude Diaz
Judi Harvey
Judy L. Robertson
Judy McClure
Judy Moulder
Judy Nauta
Judyth Montevilla
Jule Becker
Julee (Donaldson) Winings
Jules Russel
Juli
Julia C. Walker
Julia Diaz
Julia Himmelman
Julia McDonald
Julia Morgan
Julia Watt
Julia Wright
Juliana Cabrera
Juliana Sandoval
Julianna Daugherty
Julie & Izzy Maxwell
Julie A. Elbl
Julie A. Fischer
Julie A. Larkin
Julie Ann Howard
Julie Ann Martin
Julie Butler Martin
Julie Colvin
Julie Crytzer
Julie Denney
Julie Felton
Julie Gray
Julie Hanson
Julie Hayes

Julie James
Julie Keener
Julie McCoy
Julie Messick Clinkingbeard
Julie Nichole Burgart
Julie Nicole Jones
Julie Pepin
Julie Pham
Julie S. Martinez
Julie T. Cao
Julie Wheeler
Juliette Jones
Julio Lopez
June Bell
Justin & Amber Davis
Justin & Andrea Dew Family
Justin & Christy Rozinek
Justin & Jill Cornette
Justin & Melissa Thomas
Justin & Rachel Smith
Justin & Sarah Long
Justin & Taylor Adams
Justin Bales
Justin Boatman
Justin Case Larson
Justin Ealy
Justin Hein
Justin Kirk
Justin Riley
Justin Shimminger
Justine J. Haas

K IS FOR KNOWLEDGE
K. Kelley Floridino
K. O'Connor
K.R. Greenie
Kabriell Gideon
Kaci Kozik
Kacie Minchew
Kacy "The Sanch" Stanfill
Kacy Darnell
Kady Louise Ross
Kaela Phillips
Kaelie Jager
Kaenan Nix
Kaileigh Boitnott
Kailey Mae Kucavich
Kaili Prevatt
Kaitlin Collins
Kaitlin Greenberg

Kaitlin Leanne Smith
Kaitlin Reid
Kaitlin Wolfford
Kaitlin Yoder
Kaitlyn & Jordan Weber
Kaitlyn & Shawn
Kaitlyn Biggs
Kaitlyn Bleier
Kaitlyn Crawford
Kaitlyn Deal
Kaitlyn Isabella Moody
Kaitlyn Ricci
Kaitlyn Rose Walker
Kaitlyn Serene de Graauw
Kaitlyn Thompson
Kaitlyn Varnado
Kaity Kurilla
Kala Nevil
Kala Wright
Kaleb Lynn Jerry
Kaleb Smith
Kaleigh George
Kaley Short
Kali Welchons
Kalie Walker
Kalli Lochner
Kallie Nauholz
Kalyn Elpers
Kamden Kelley
Kamdyn Marku
Kami J. Trammell
Kami Ripley
Kami Rose Weidenbacher
Kami Steichen
Kamie Crim
Kammi Pearson
Kandace Parson
Kandice Gamotan
Kandice Sage
Kandy F. Lundy
Kansas Messina Girls
Kara Adrian
Kara Cervantes
Kara D. Davis
Kara E. Trujillo
Kara Leighan Landry
Kara McAtee
Kara Miller
Kara Steil
Kara Tumbleston

Kara V. Fox
Kara Wasielewski
Karah Frank
Karalee Griffith
Kara-Leigh Parritt
Karen A. Strauss
Karen A.L. Morin
Karen Ann Foley
Karen Burch
Karen Burrell
Karen Clemente
Karen Duffy
Karen E. Edwards
Karen E. Kibler
Karen Heimiller
Karen Holmes
Karen Horner
Karen James
Karen Kattengell-Noonan
Karen Kline
Karen L. Hill
Karen L. Pasquarette
Karen Loiacano
Karen Mawyer
Karen Mofield
Karen Muster
Karen Ryan
Karen S. Tisdale
Karen Sanchez
Karen Suckling
Karena Kaye Scholten
Kari Dawn Murray
Kari Zucca
KariLyn Gebhard
Karin A. Banks
Karina Gonzalez
Karina Orellana
Karina Villarreal
Karisma Silacci
Karl Carlson
Karla A. Martin
Karla C.
Karla Delgado
Karla Green-McCorkle
Karla Valenzuela Grajeda
Karla Whitcomb
Karleigh Rose Gutierrez
Karli Binkowski
Karli M. Bridges
Karlie K. Beach

Karly Rose
Karolanne Trogdon Martin
Karri Parker
Karrie Bruman
Kasey Bennett
Kasey Cummins
Kasey Curmode
Kasey Ellen Blore
Kasey Lee Smart
Kasi M. Ducote
Kassandra J. Bosley
Kassidy Carpenter
Kassie & Daniel Lowe
Kassie Heise
Kassie Wobbe
Kat Hoffman
Kate Adamson
Kate Black
Kate Campbell
Kate Elliott
Kate Evans
Kate Geiszler
Kate King
Kate Murray
Kate Raney
Kate Rutledge
Katelin Womack
Katelyn Charlie Richardson
Katelyn N. Faherty
Katelyn Walsh
KateLynn Albers
Katelynn Mansukhani
Katharine Fish
Katharine Smorodin
Kathee Wilkey
Katherine (Kate) DeMean
Katherine Bostick
Katherine Bozanich
Katherine Jordan
Katherine O'Maley
Katherine Rauscher
Katherine Walker
Kathleen Benesh
Kathleen E. Young
Kathleen Noble
Kathleen O'Connor
Kathleen Van Poucke
Kathrin Brown
Kathrine Harvey
Kathryn Drake

Kathryn Schulte
Kathryn Smith
Kathryn Sumner
Kathy Andrews
Kathy Benesh
Kathy Hedgepeth
Kathy Hurst
Kathy Jackson
Kathy Jernigan
Kathy Labus
Kathy Metzger
Kathy Northup
Kathy Oliver
Kathy Renee Salazar
Kathy Selley
Kathy Sternke
Kathy Strickland
Kathy Todd
KathyJen Moss
Kati Cox
Kati Hunter
Kati Michelle Prinz
Katie Argotsinger
Katie Arp
Katie Barbieri
Katie Barnes
Katie Bedward
Katie Berlon
Katie Billstrom & Lisa Malone
Katie Bowman
Katie Burrell
Katie Copley
Katie Edwards
Katie Hackett
Katie Hufford
Katie Jaimes
Katie Jones
Katie Kessler
Katie Landi Jordan
Katie Leining
Katie Lowe
Katie Lyn Richard
Katie Lynn Mangum
Katie Neff
Katie O'Neil-Dreher
Katie Petersen
Katie Roberts
Katie Rose Davidson
Katie Sanders
Katie Schings

Katie Schuett
Katie Shanklin
Katie Traas
Katie Wang
Katrina E. Burr
Katrina Hicks
Katrina Lighthart
Katrina Loader
Katryna Goodreau
Katy Theos
Kay Bowman
Kayce Rittman
Kaycie Clark
Kaydence Lee England
Kayla Benally
Kayla Bodine
Kayla Boyd
Kayla Brewer
Kayla Casper
Kayla Childers
Kayla Clem
Kayla Conger
Kayla Crawford
Kayla DeCriscio
Kayla Hatfield
Kayla Hauer
Kayla J. Haydock
Kayla Jackson
Kayla Jo Nichols
Kayla Kemp
Kayla Lane Williams
Kayla Latta
Kayla Lenhardt-Price
Kayla M. Winkle
Kayla M. Gatz
Kayla Manders
Kayla McCollum
Kayla Moran
Kayla Morel
Kayla Nicole Roberts
Kayla Null
Kayla Palczewski
Kayla Potts
Kayla Rafkin
Kayla Singer
Kayla T.
Kayla Timmerman
Kayla Yarbro
Kayla-Ann Pickering
Kaylan Moffett

Kaylan Sukhendra
Kaylee & Ryan
Kaylee Brook Thibodeaux
Kaylee Johnson
Kayley Borkowski
Kaylie Janssens
Kaylie Sellier
Kaylie Starch
Kaylin Earley
Kaylor Nelson
Kaytlin Nierman
KB
Kealy Jean Gray
Keeley Ward
Keely J. Jones
Keikilani Enosaran
Keith & Jennifer Moody
Keith (Brelaman) Breland
Keith Michael Kallina
Kelby Elam
Kelcy Barber
Kellan & Asher Kacere
Kellen Casey
Kelley Allen
Kelley Ann Gennity
Kelley Dixon Schwersinske
Kelley Hibbs
Kelley Votaw
Kelli Anderson
Kelli Barnat
Kelli Braquet
Kelli Clark Brown
Kelli Crouse
Kelli Farkas
Kelli Gravois
Kelli Hudson
Kelli J.
Kelli R. Raines
Kelli Tolocka
Kelli Western
Kelli Wilson
Kelli, Klara, & Finton Lane
Kelli-Beth Kellogg
Kellie Ann Barrett
Kellie Barnett
Kellie Miller & Patty Miguel
Kellie Thornton
Kelly & Connor Shank
Kelly A. Caesar
Kelly Baumgardner

Kelly Bitsilly
Kelly Bonatsakis
Kelly Brunson
Kelly Clow
Kelly Cothron
Kelly Covey
Kelly Dean Birge
Kelly E. Price
Kelly Hall & Wendy Brown
Kelly Hutto
Kelly Jo Hegg
Kelly Kestner
Kelly Kettner
Kelly Kinnear
Kelly Kuoppala
Kelly L. Reedy
Kelly Lynne Kolyer
Kelly McKee Austin
Kelly Molinaro
Kelly Moyers
Kelly N. Persky
Kelly Pate
Kelly Peak
Kelly Rosales
Kelly S.
Kelly Skibby
Kelly Wilson
Kelsey & Austin Kern
Kelsey & Gavin Norris
Kelsey A Baxter
Kelsey Adam
Kelsey Ambrose
Kelsey Ann Reed
Kelsey Bobbitt
Kelsey Carter
Kelsey Collins
Kelsey DeGhelder
Kelsey Erwin
Kelsey Helyer
Kelsey Jacobsen
Kelsey Jo Gerhold
Kelsey Jones
Kelsey L. Easley
Kelsey Lamke
Kelsey Lancon
Kelsey Luna
Kelsey McCartney
Kelsey McGuire
Kelsey N. Neill
Kelsey Naguszewski

Kelsey Pajonk
Kelsey Ridpath
Kelsey Rolando
Kelsey Rutledge
Kelsey Simons Sexton
Kelsie Adams
Kelsie Brien
Kelsie Klaus Harkins
Ken Tibbils
Kendra A. Coulson
Kendra Brown
Kendra Byers
Kendra Collier
Kendra Hutson
Kendra Jo Beattie
Kendra Redmer
Kendyl Tinsley
Kennedy Conn
Kenny Moore
Kenny Y.
Kenslei Krippner
Kera Mondez
Keri Bowman
Keri Koncak
Kerilynn Jagger
Kerri Jones
Kerri Overbeck
KerriAnne Corbett Cooper
Kerry Kaufman
Kerry Langford
Kesa Larson
KETC
Kevin Browning
Kevin Cauldwell
Kevin K. Ho
Kevin Lamm
Kevin Pham
Khai Eshenko
Kiesha Baker
Kiley Commerford
Kilie Payne
Kim & Tim Wilkerson
Kim Babcock
Kim Ball
Kim Bolden
Kim Brooks Smith
Kim C.
Kim Cospelich
Kim Crossfield
Kim Davis

Kim Dodd
Kim Gunnoe
Kim Hamilton
Kim Haynes
Kim Hegwer
Kim Heitert
Kim Hulseberg
Kim Leslie
Kim Meier
Kim Ming
Kim Montez
Kim Montoya
Kim Scollo
Kim Tolander
Kimberlee Reed
Kimberley Bingle
Kimberley K. Hoffstatter
Kimberley Leehan
Kimberley Wooden
Kimberly & John & Caya
   Allen
Kimberly & Makenzie
   Franklin
Kimberly A. Manuel-Espinosa
Kimberly Bellamy
Kimberly Betts
Kimberly Bradsher
Kimberly Dull
Kimberly Faye Rogers
Kimberly Frelo
Kimberly Fritz
Kimberly H. Valentine
Kimberly Hughes
Kimberly Lamb
Kimberly MacNeill
Kimberly Miller
Kimberly Ming
Kimberly Ray
Kimberly Stanley
Kimberly T. Oliver
Kimberly VanHorn
Kimberly Walton
Kimberly Westmoreland
Kimberlyn Fitts
KimBradyShandleyMary
Kimi Reinert
Kindal Carney
Kindra Reese
Kindra Sublett
Kinzie Hill

Kira Mohler
Kira René Crafton
Kiri Gomez
Kirsten Cabral
Kirsten L. Graham
Kirsten Neff
Kirstie Harris
Kirstin Kurilla
Kirti P. Loper
Kit Doughtie
Knoxley G. Fleming
Kobster
Kodi Elizabeth Davis
Kody Bostian
Kone, Aimee, & Peyton
  Boriboun
Konnor Carter
Kori Barber
Kori Lynn
Kourtnie Craig
Kris Wachala
Krista Gruhn
Krista Jones
Krista Reed
Krista Tippett
Kristal Roe
Kristeen Thurman
Kristen Beasley
Kristen Boykin
Kristen Bradley
Kristen Cabral
Kristen Chaz Nichols
Kristen Davis
Kristen Deslauriers
Kristen Gallimore
Kristen Goudreau
Kristen Hayden
Kristen Joy Duke
Kristen Kulbick
Kristen L. Williams
Kristen Leigh
Kristen M. Wofford
Kristen M. Golding
Kristen Marcel
Kristen Moore
Kristen Mullins
Kristen N. Grant
Kristen Palumberi
Kristen Schaff
Kristen Woods

Kristi Benrud
Kristi Bisbee
Kristi Byrd
Kristi Fogelquist Gadwah
Kristi Howe
Kristi Hromek
Kristi Johnston
Kristi Kertz
Kristi L. Epps
Kristi McNeely
Kristi Moore
Kristi Muir
Kristie Crawford Allen
Kristie Rossi
Kristin Carter
Kristin Craddock
Kristin Gallant
Kristin Garrett
Kristin Holman
Kristin Krawczyk
Kristin Lynch
Kristin Menefee
Kristin Milheiser
Kristin Murdoch Larson
Kristin Murrow
Kristin N. Clark
Kristin Podojil
Kristin Primm
Kristin Rind
Kristin Rogers
Kristin Strand
Kristin Sullivan
Kristina (Tina) Hamm
Kristina A. Whitmore
Kristina Allen
Kristina Berry
Kristina Bradbury
Kristina Chappelle
Kristina Groves
Kristina J. Groves
Kristina LeMire
Kristina Misiaszek
Kristina Westphal
Kristine Kessler (Future Mrs.
  Miranda)
Kristine Newton
Kristy Anderson
Kristy Anne-Garbacz
  Concepcion
Kristy Inacio

Kristy Mascho
Kristy Mazotti
Kristy Palady
Kristy W.
Krystal "KayBee" Burgess
Krystal Kollaja
Krystal Ludeman
Krystal M. Garcia
Krystal San Miguel
Krystal Voeck & Jayce Voeck
Krystin Goode
Krystle Braumann
Krystle Dawn Herzog
Krystle McDade
Krystle Smith
Krystyl Rufenacht
Kyah K. Gorin
Kyla Holland
Kyle Basham
Kyle Dettra
Kyle Dodd
Kyle Goodwin
Kyle Jackson
Kylee Looney
Kyleigh R. Saunders
Kyler Smith
Kylie Dennison
Kylie Moseley
Kylie N. Cheney
Kylie Nolting
Kylie Rice
Kylie Stouder
Kymberly Becenti
Kymberly Zuba
Kymberlyn Warner
Kyndel L.
Kyra Jane Boalch
Kyra L. Johnson

L IS FOR LEARNING
L80Gen
Lacee Amos
Lacey Denton
Lacey Jane McKnight
Lacey Johnson
Lacey Rowe
Laci Kent
Lacy Mulcahy
LaDonna Newton
LaDonna Thurston

LaDoris Garley
Laina Howell
Lakyn Pfliiger
Lana Parr
Lana Rainey
Landen & Payton
Landon & Addyson Sellier
Landon & Preston Hardister
Landon Blackburn
Landon Wilkey
Lane Truman
Lanette
Laney Lewellyn
Lani Bower
Lani LeStourgeon
Lara Coleman
Lara Griffin
Lara Manire
Larissa Jo Flores
Larry Rankin
Larson Foster
Laura Andrews
Laura Ann Gryder
Laura Ann Salinas
Laura B. Vancura
Laura Beard-Jones
Laura Beaton
Laura Begeske
Laura Brooks
Laura C. Bryan
Laura Casas
Laura Daum Benson
Laura E. Lewis
Laura Haushalter
Laura Hegeman
Laura Hess
Laura Hubbard
Laura Karnes
Laura Kinney
Laura Kinsey
Laura L. Ward
Laura Leighton
Laura Metzler
Laura Miller
Laura Murray
Laura Neigh
Laura Pearce
Laura Polis
Laura R. Williams
Laura Tonche

Laura Vellutini Rider
Laura Wylie
Lauran Mabry
Laurel Anderson
Lauren Adams
Lauren Anderson
Lauren Argenbright
Lauren Bach Moss
Lauren Bates
Lauren Behn
Lauren Blaquiere
Lauren Bouthillier
Lauren Bradley
Lauren Brizendine
Lauren Chumbler
Lauren Colson
Lauren Coward
Lauren Cunningham
Lauren Davis Buck
Lauren Denise Scott
Lauren DeVries
Lauren E. Ross
Lauren Fisher
Lauren Fountain
Lauren Frances Klimczyk
Lauren Garcia
Lauren Garner
Lauren Gurley
Lauren H.
Lauren Haller
Lauren Hilton
Lauren Jackson
Lauren Joseph
Lauren K. Redus
Lauren Klimczyk
Lauren Knight
Lauren Knox
Lauren Koble
Lauren Lange
Lauren Levey
Lauren Loper
Lauren M. Mitza
Lauren M. Garcia
Lauren M. Smith
Lauren Millner
Lauren Moritz
Lauren Morris Earley
Lauren Morrison
Lauren Nelson
Lauren Nichols

Lauren Pimentel
Lauren Preston
Lauren Randolph
Lauren Renae Joseph
Lauren Rook
Lauren Salvaggio Bennett
Lauren Schultz
Lauren Settle
Lauren Shannon
Lauren Shingleton
Lauren Spinella
Lauren Strange
Lauren Sudberry
Lauren Tommy Adams
Lauren VanWinkle
Lauren Wall
Lauri Rowland-Hill
Lauri Vaughn
Laurie Couey
Laurie Esther Sandoval
Laurie Hampton Woods
Laurie L. Coghe
Laurie Luedtke
Laurie Stotts Eller
Laurie Wade-Woodson
Laurie Webber
Lawrence Standingwater
Laydie Craver
Layla Jade Ross
LB Solomon
Lea Ann Eickelschulte
Leah A. Harris
Leah Rock Murphy
Leah Victoria Chandonnet
LeAn J. Bortvit
Leandra Doornbos
Leandro Molina
LeAnn Coker
Leann Davis
LeAnn McDaniel
LeAnne Robinson
Leanne Smith
Lee & Molly Bibb
Lee Ann Lewis
Lee Hill
Leeann Yogerst
LeeAnna Jimenez
Leena DeLand
Leena Love
Leigh Ann Patterson

Leigh Anne Biggs
Leilani Cardinoza
Leisha Liann
Lenna Morgan
Lesa Helton & Melody Wilson
Leslee Horning
Leslee Horning & Neal
  Quigley
Leslee Malone
Lesley January
Leslie A. Vladu
Leslie Ann Waldrop
Leslie Anne Liotta Rogers
Leslie Bass
Leslie Dawn Sanders
Leslie Hess
Leslie Hindman
Leslie King
Leslie Michelle Montemayor
Leslie Rhoades
Leslie Stanfield Bingham
Leslie Stokes
Leslie Stout
Lesly Avaritt
Leta D. Walton
Lexi Barber
Lexi Curl
Lexi Hill
Lexi Jadoff
Lexie Kuhfeldt
Libby Dietrich
Ligeia Pennington
Liina Alas
Lilly Carroll
Lilly Diorio
Lilly Ivens
Lily April
Lily Longacre
Linda Dayana Morales
Linda Diane Domebo
Linda Hogan
Linda Vias
Linda X. Ju
Lindsay A. Gin
Lindsay Bass
Lindsay Blair Fisher
Lindsay Burnett
Lindsay Fletcher
Lindsay Head
Lindsay Jackson

Lindsay Kopp
Lindsay McCammon
Lindsay Meyer
Lindsay Pavlovich
Lindsey "The Pimpin Joy
  School Counselor" Smith
Lindsey A. Grubb
Lindsey Basile
Lindsey Beasley
Lindsey Clark
Lindsey Clausen
Lindsey Douan
Lindsey E. Murphy
Lindsey Fruge
Lindsey Graf
Lindsey Johnson & Josh
  Buckner
Lindsey Lloyd
Lindsey Mechalik
Lindsey Ortmann
Lindsey Rebello
Lindsey Ryan
Lindsey Skowlund
Lindsey Stroud
Linh T. Nguyen
Linsey Denning
Linz Pafford
Lisa A. Ellis
Lisa Acker
Lisa Aitchison
Lisa Anne Nobles
Lisa Anne Peacock
Lisa Baker-Runk
Lisa Biles
Lisa Burton Wilson
Lisa Cameron
Lisa Caravello
Lisa DeGregorio-Zautner
Lisa Foote
Lisa Frisk
Lisa from the 'Stadt
Lisa G. Pepe
Lisa Gott
Lisa Hewlett Harris
Lisa J. Garcia
Lisa K. Cummings
Lisa Kirk
Lisa M. Boland
Lisa M. Collins
Lisa M. Albert

Lisa M. Long
Lisa M. Starn
Lisa Marks
Lisa Martine & Nina Martinez
  Castillo
Lisa McDaniel
Lisa Melchiorre
Lisa Peluso Couto
Lisa Renae Blackman
Lisa Rico
Lisa Sealey
Lisa Shaw
Lisa Sutliff
Lisa Tripodi
Lisa Weatherholt Engelskind
Lisa Weiland
Lisa-Marie Fitch
Lissette Grubb-Reyes
Liv Jennings
Live Love Nashville
Liz Arp
Liz Barnett
Liz Bell
Liz Hensel
Liz Hyke
Liz Lerma
Liz Moore
Liz Paris
Liz Rappa
Liz Sesock
Liz Zore
Lizette CP
Lizz Jonse
Lizzie Truman
Lizzy Cruz
Lochlan E.M. Smith
Logan Argabright
Logan Enright
Logan Gorrell
Logan Metesh
Logan Shea Atwell
Loni Tullos
Lora & Ellienora Sisk
Lora Yates
Loren Martinez
Lorenda Littlefield-Bolinger
Lorey Bowles
Lori A. Klock
Lori Ann Spadafora
Lori Anne Brown

Lori Berdos
Lori Davis
Lori Foster
Lori Gonneville
Lori Joy Mosier
Lori Kahley
Lori Leake
Lori Lynn Arthurs-Miller
Lori Majerus
Lori Queen
Lori Salyer
Lori Saucier
Lori Sciabbarrasi
Lori Speer
Lori Tissue Batko
Lori V. McLamb
Lorissa S. Duval
Lorrain FS Meek
Lorri L. Meriam
Lorrie Fleming
Louis J. Kulick
Louisa Maddox
Lucas Loughmiller
Lucas Orosco
Lucia Sapiens
Lucinda Simpson
Lucy Ann Eggleston
Lucy D. Carter
Luis Anthony Robles
Luke Mojica
Luna Aguayo
Lydia C. Jennings
Lydia Sophia Camargo
Lydia Williams
Lyla Dean
Lynda & Eric Phillips
Lyndsey Eisenhardt
Lyndsey Evans
Lyndsey Hill
Lyndsey Lindemann
Lyndsey McQuillen
Lyndsey Perkins
Lyndsy McIntyre
Lynette M. Bailey
Lynette Torrey
Lynn McGregor
Lynsey Cannon
Lynzi Brown
Lysette Lopez

M IS FOR MOMENTUM
M&M Richardson
Mabry Family
Macee Garcia
Maci Malone
Mackenzie Milliman
Mackenzie Secrest
Mackenzie Winterowd
MADDEN ROSS
Maddie Fink
Maddie Nash
Madelyn Halstead
Madelyn Marie Smith
Madelynn Legaspi
Madison Allen
Madison Economos
Madison Gravitt & Micale
  Costa
Madison Grover
Madison Hanson
Madison Keisker
Madison Nalewanski & Jessica
  Harmon
Madison Nicole Dugger
Madison Osborn
Madison Palmer
Madison Tullis
Mads Rutherford
Maegan Flynn
Maeghan Korte
Magan Cook
Maggi Kettler
Maggie Beardsley
Maggie Bryant
Maggie Combs
Maggie Edenfield
Maggie Hill
Maggie Lauren Lewis
Maggie M. Mueller
Maggie MacDonald
Maggie Robbins
Maggie Scheele
Maggie Sladick
Maggie Volz
Maghan B. Horne
Maghan Horne
Maiden Gomez
Makala Diercks
Makynna Meegan

Maleah Fick
Malinda Cline
Malisa Reel
Mallory Homb
Mallory Knape
Mallory Slade Brame
Mallory Tine
Mallory Z. Douraghi
Manda Fowler
Mandi Courson
Mandi Mosser
Mandi Mueller
Mandy & Kyler Willson
Mandy Backlund
Mandy Isbister
Mandy Quam
Mandy Salazar
Mandy Shelton
Mandy Skelton
Mandy Tichawa
Manny Rivera
Manuel Lechuga
Mara Demel
Marah K.
Marc Simmons
Marc Waltz
Marci Donoho
Marci Garcia
Marci Hargroder Saboe
Marci Hood-Anderson
Marco A. Zamarrón
Marcus Mirus
Marcus Yepez
Margaret A. Suddarth
Margaret Francois
Margaret Galewski
Margaret Shride
Mari Johnson
Maria Kelly
Maria Robledo
Maria Sarcinelli
Maria Wagemester
Mariah Baltierra
Mariah Lynn Hill
Mariah Sexton
Mariah Shealy
Marian Mally
Marianela Olivas-Sandoval
Maribel G. Jaimes

Maribeth & Travis Sullivan
Marie A. Miller
Marie Ann Baker
Marie Gardiner
Marie Johnson
Marie Mayer
Mariel "Mayo" Beesting
Mariel & Leanne Potter
Marievic Villanueva
Marijo Kandel
Marina Alvarado
Marion Doughty
Marisa Lawson
Marisa McLeod
Marisa Mineo
Marisa Samuelsen
Marisa Vera
Marisol Garcia
Marisol Kengin
Marisol Maldonado
Marisol Tijerina
Marissa Chavana
Marissa Conley-Poush
Marissa Fox
Marissa Hintz
Marissa Lutrus
Marissa Marie Rovensky
Marissa Martinez
Marissa Mucho
Marissa Niven
Marissa Psaila
Marissa Rios
Marissa Torsiello
Maritza Gamboa
Maritza Huerta
Marixssa Martinez
Marjorie Queen
Mark & Lacey Jaye Hayes
Mark Argo
Mark Cadence Dupes
Mark Zellner
Marlen A. Moreno
Marlen Moreno
Marlena & Brittany Aviles
Marlena Anderson
Marlo Pound
Marsha (Aiken Motorcycle)
Marsha Finlason
Marta Frank

Martee J. Harris
Martha Barela
Martha C. Glasgow
Martha Holmes Miller
Martin Garcia
Martricia Teller
Marty Kurtz
Marvin Leon Shilling
Mary & Greg Cols
Mary Alex Crawford
Mary Ann Kimbrell
Mary Belcher
Mary Berthiaume
Mary Beth Prince
Mary Briguglio
Mary Catherine Miller
Mary Cay Gross
Mary Cupp Hall
Mary Elizabeth Hill
Mary Elizabeth Thrower
Mary Garant
Mary Hane
Mary Jacobs
Mary K. Lucero
Mary Kathryn Reed
Mary Lynn & George Waite
Mary McCool Adkins
Mary Nunes
Mary Rebecca Miller
Mary Stufano
Mary T.
Maryann Elizabeth Harmon
MaryBeth Tyndall
Maryclare Garant
Masen Harvey
Mason Hegeman
Mason Phung
Matt & Erin Colburn
Matt & Olivia Oppelt
Matt Campbell Kinsley
    Campbell
Matt Dye
Matt Ely
Matt Farbo
Matt Garten (aka
    musicnutmatt)
Matt Smith
Matt Tighe
Matthew & Janie Bergin

Matthew "Big" Adamson
Matthew A. Jafari
Matthew Beauregard
Matthew D. Easley
Matthew E. Anderson
Matthew R. Barrett
Matthew S. Morgan
Matthew Stalnaker
Matthew Suls
Matthew Thomas
Matthew Warren
Maureen & Elizabeth Long
Maureen Johnston
Maureen Karavolis
Maureen Kitson
Mayderet Portesgil
Mayra Nevarez
McCahen Schweitzer
McKendry Fiorentino
McKenzie Benefield
McKenzie Jo Couey
McKenzie Scott
McKenzie Solomon
Meagan Edwards
Meagan Moore
Meaghan A. Copeland
Meaghan Messmer
Meaghen Weaver
Megan & Michael Welch
Megan & Steven Dessler
Megan Airgood
Megan Amrein
Megan Baccamazzi
Megan Breaux Ochoa
Megan Buettner
Megan Cipollone
Megan Claiborne
Megan Craig
Megan Cresci
Megan Delaney
Megan Dollarhide
Megan Duke
Megan E. Sowada
Megan E. Wesselman
Megan Elizabeth Aubrey
Megan Elizabeth Davis
Megan Foreman
Megan G. Morgan
Megan Gage

Megan Gipple
Megan Heinen
Megan J. Genz
Megan Jane Allred
Megan Junod
Megan LeFaiver
Megan Loeffler
Megan Marx
Megan McGivern
Megan Mertz
Megan Nelson
Megan Nicole Missick
Megan Pavia
Megan Pehl
Megan Preston
Megan R. Hanson
Megan Raible
Megan Ramsey
Megan Richardson
Megan Richtsmeier
Megan Roediger
Megan Seebeck
Megan Smith
Megan Somerville
Megan Sutliff
Megan Thrower
Megan Vliet
Megan Warren
Megan Wild Bowlsbey
meganhurst225 &
  tannerscogin226
Meghan "Merg" Miller
Meghan D. Perez
Meghan E. Lemmings
Meghan Leigh Lyons
Meghan McNeelege
Meghan Tahmaseb Peeler
Meghan VanderHamm
Meghan Widner
Meghann E. Junge
Meghann Searcy
Meghanne Kerr
Mel Baldwin
Melanie & Ryan North
Melanie Hoerchler
Melanie Lewis
Melanie Nicole Zamora
Melanie Peak
Melanie Reichert
Melanie Salazar

Melanie Wright
Melena, Leila & Sir Demestihas
Melinda "Muh" Lindsey
Melinda Banteah
Melinda D'Ambra
Melinda King
Melinda Smith
Melissa (Rogers) Todesco
Melissa Ahonen
Melissa Anderson
Melissa Ann Hernandez
Melissa Armenta
Melissa Banuelos
Melissa Barricella
Melissa Benitez
Melissa Bethea
Melissa Bierman
Melissa Billings
Melissa Brattlof
Melissa Cahoon
Melissa Carey
Melissa D. Forrest
Melissa Diane Fenner
Melissa Fanning
Melissa Feltner
Melissa Funk
Melissa Garrett
Melissa Garza-Perry
Melissa Hatcher
Melissa Hug
Melissa Jarrett
Melissa Johnson
Melissa Keener Hudson
Melissa Kelly
Melissa Klein
Melissa L. Rahfeldt
Melissa M. Carrillo
Melissa Maya
Melissa Owens
Melissa Pocius
Melissa Rogers Todesco
Melissa S. Lundy
Melissa Schmoll
Melissa Siegel
Melissa Stevens
Melissa Stoltenberg
Melissa Thompson
Melissa Vasquez
Melissa Westcott
Melissa White

Mellissa Cominsky
Mellissa Webster
Melody L. Salter
Melody Smith
Melony Sleeper
Memo Macias
Mercedes Galvan
Mercedes Garcia
Mercedes R. Rodriguez
Meredith Albers
Meredith Austin
Meredith Barnes
Meredith Bosso
Meredith Henderson
Meredith M. Ralls, Esq.
Meredith Schneider
Merissa Munson
Mia G. Hollingshad
Micaela Wright & Jace Hansen
Micah Fry
Micah Goodman
Micahel Cornejo
Michael & Selina Páramo
Michael Dana
Michael Flaherty & Julie
  Putnam
Michael G. Perkins
Michael Gay
Michael Grove
Michael Hines
Michael Justice Phillip Betts
Michael Peplow
Michael Privette
Michael R. Musto
Michael Redmond
Michael Scott
Michael V. & Nayeli A. Garcia
Michael Womack
Michael, Lori & Hope Alfano
Michaela M. Soto
Michaela Wahl
Michala Miihlbach
Micheal Myers
Michele Como
Michele Dedmon
Michele Detmer Flohre
Michele Eisenberg-Bezotte
Michele Ennis
Michele Hackel
Michele Livingood

Michele Rice & Autumn
   Oestringer
Michelle "Mixitup-Mich"
   Lubbert
Michelle A. Gavin
Michelle B. Smith
Michelle Bennett
Michelle Bousquet Banks
Michelle Braughton
Michelle Bryant
Michelle C. Lanterman
Michelle Carman
Michelle Carmona
Michelle Carpenter
Michelle Castaneda
Michelle Cole
Michelle Copley Webb
Michelle Crawford
Michelle Davis
Michelle Donato
Michelle Findley
Michelle Graham
Michelle Hollingsworth
Michelle Jarrell Ranes
Michelle Jay Jones
Michelle Jones
Michelle Joy Begay
Michelle Joyce
Michelle K. Marshall
Michelle Kam
Michelle Kinney
Michelle Krause
Michelle L. Eisenhauer
Michelle L. Goodwin
Michelle Lee Conner
Michelle Medrano Shillinglaw
Michelle Merrill
Michelle Morrow
Michelle Nofziger
Michelle North
Michelle Nuss
Michelle Pieprzica
Michelle R. Hinojos
Michelle Rath
Michelle Rosana Gonzalez
Michelle Roy
Michelle Starr Munday
Michelle Stine
Mick Bodenheimer
Mickelle Cota

Micki Gutierrez
Mickie Smith
Miguel Romero Jr.
Miguelito Walrath
Mikaela & Emelie Cissell
Mikayla Baker
Mikayla Cook
Mikayla Metrick
Mike & Alicia Raskett
Mike & Cindy Hoehner
Mike & Jennifer McKay
Mike & Megan Showalter
Mike Benz
Mike Gorsuch
Mike Kapetanovic
Mike Molloy
Mike Privette
Mike Quick
Mike Silverman
Mikhaila Rene Berry
Miki Prieto
Miles Cooper
Miles Hogge
Millet Sibal
Mindi Laine Brown
Mindy Feltmeyer
Mindy Garrison
Mindy Garza
Mindy Schumacher Grabau
Mindy Wilson
Mirabella Grace Carrara
Miranda Bailey
Miranda Bradford
Miranda Cooper
Miranda Garcia
Miranda Goforth
Miranda King
Miranda Monger
Miranda Trobiani
Mireya Haneke
Miriam Castro-Gutierrez
Miriam Cooper
Miriam Lamagna
Missy Blackburn
Missy Goldstein
Missy Hurst
Missy Melin
Missy Wetherington
Mister Edrobo
Misti Cisco

Misti Jade Hair
Mistie Hobbs
Misty Adams
Misty Dashiell
Misty Dierschke
Misty Duncan
Misty Mercer
Misty Moore
Misty Riley Brinson
Misty Snyder
Mitchell Smielowitz
Mitzi Mills
Mitzie Beaver
Mitzie Danielle Beaver
Mollie Rae Garrett
Mollie Reigle
Molly & Alivia Tutt
Molly C. Hall
Molly Ervin Person
Molly Estes
Molly Irwin
Molly Islam
Molly Jordan
Molly K. Pollard
Molly Luke
Molly May
Molly Mead
Molly Metras
Molly O'Gara
Molly Pawelski
Momma Record
Mona A. Jones
Mona Gutierrez
Monica A. Corbett
Monica A. Arroyo
Monica Cunningham
Monica Handwerger
Monica Heneghan
Monica Johnson-Raney
Monica Lynn Gonzalez
Monica M. Hanson
Monica Nicole Brack
Monica Perez
Monica Rochelle Apodaca
Monica Tupa
Monica Wieand
Monica Yarborough
Monika Cearley
Monika Troike
Monique Eaton

Monique M. Parra
Montana & Montgomery
  Landphier
Moore Tsabari
Morgan A. McCallum
Morgan Arnce
Morgan Clark
Morgan Cowles
Morgan Estell
Morgan Fox
Morgan Johnson
Morgan Jones
Morgan K. Felder
Morgan K. Smith
Morgan Little
Morgan McGee
Morgan Mescan
Morgan Rose Malizia
Morgan Vines
Mr. & Mrs. Morrissey
Mr. & Mrs. Scalderon
Mr. & Mrs. Timothy Jean
  Belley
Mr. & Mrs. Tony Thomas
Mr. & Mrs. Trevor Bluth
Mr. & Mrs. Vasquez
Mr. Kris Rivera
My BFF Bet Montez

N IS FOR NEGOTIATION
Nachely Martinez
Nan Harrison
Nancy Anderson
Nancy Bones
Nancy Ciffolilli
Nancy Dimas
Nancy Lively
Nancy S. Sherrill
Naomi A. Martinez
Naomi Garzon
Natalie Almanza
Natalie Guthas & Casey
  Ackerman
Natalie Hobart
Natalie Kelley & Will Chesney
Natalie Newman
Natalie Sandhaus
Natasha A. Mulford
Natasha James
Natasha Merritt

Nate Kerstetter
Nathalia Brockman
Nathan C. Wallace
Nathanael William Minor
Naxiely G
Neena T. Cavazos
Nena West
Nery O. Gouldner
Nicholas J. Peterson
Nicholas Kyle
Nicholas Raymond
Nicholas Schaub
Nicholas Van Dorn
Nichole Breau
Nichole Fox
Nichole Goulet
Nichole Jackson
Nichole Nickerson
Nichole Paige Seibel
Nichole Patterson
Nicholle Buckley
Nick & David Woodcock
Nick & Melissa Velarde
Nick Curtis
Nick Esquibel
Nick Paul
Nick Wendrick
Nicki Chadwick
Nicki Clem
Nicki Plummer
Nicole & ETSU Girls
Nicole A Tapia
Nicole Bilbrough
Nicole Buster
Nicole Carden
Nicole Convis
Nicole F. Fontenot
Nicole Ferrell
Nicole Gabaldon
Nicole Girard Rollins
Nicole Gwinner
Nicole Hahn
Nicole Higginbotham
Nicole Hopwood
Nicole King
Nicole Kraft
Nicole L. Brandt
Nicole Lucas
Nicole Lyman
Nicole McCabe

Nicole McPeak
Nicole Mello
Nicole Negrete
Nicole Osorio
Nicole Parsons
Nicole Resch
Nicole Reynolds
Nicole Rodriguez
Nicole S. Crowell
Nicole Scelzi
Nicole Scott
Nicole Silberstein
Nicole Stokes
Nicole Swartzman
Nicole Zeiher
Nicolet LaVeau
Nika Rowan
Niki Elizabeth
Niki Lee
Niki Tipton
Nikki Addair
Nikki Braun
Nikki Butt
Nikki Dugas
Nikki Hall
Nikki Hugh
Nikki K. Sargent
Nikki Nichols
Nikki Sokulski
Nikki Taylor-McClinton
Nikola Visic
Nikolas Gabel
Nikole Wynn
Nina Muskalla
Nina Star Galvan
Noah Fodness
Noelle Wiehe & Heather
  Sinda
Norine Correa
Norma C. Federico
Norma L. Quintero

**O IS FOR
OPPORTUNITIES**
Odessa Thompson
Odie Matthews
Odis Jones
Okey Wilson
Olivia Bobbitt
Olivia Bowers

Olivia Grimaldo
Olivia Kane
Olivia Laurin
Olivia Lynn Gutierrez
Olivia M. Picard
Olivia Makenzie Poysti
Omar Castillo
Omar Escalera-Mendez
Omar Villanueva
Oscar Dylan Diaz
Oscar ReRucha

P IS FOR PRACTICE
Page Moore
Paige Bushey
Paige Drane
Paige Foley
Paige Lane
Pam Brown
Pam Marchant
Pam Mixon
Pam Morley
Pam Prestridge
Pam Remon
Pamela J. Williams
Pamela Lannoy
Pamela Lea Savini
Pamela Martin
Pamela Shepard
Party Of 5
Pascale Nelson
Patricia A. Clarkson
Patricia A. Pierce
Patricia Cromer
Patricia Elders
Patricia Jones
Patricia Tullos
Patricia Walker
Patrick & Heidi Gitschlag
Patrick & Kristal Leach
Patrick Benjamin Lee
Patrick Brooks
Patrick Dorman
Patrick Hernandez
Patti Brock
Patti Gettemeier Hellrung
Patti Hutzel
Patty Giovingo
Patty Lee
Patty Rizzo

Patty Salinas
Paul J. Zarella, Jr.
Paul W. Tull
Paula "BTEAM" Torrez
Paula B.
Paula Burgdorf
Paula Kim
Paula L. Jean
Paula Nowatzke
Paula Rek
Paula Snell
Paula Sparrow
Paula Turner
Pedro E. Garcia-Melendez
Peggy DuCote Spruill
Peggy James-Pearson
Penny DeHaven McCreery
Penny Lane
Penny Lister
Penny Sourivong
Pete Guertin
Peter Anthony Peter Polis
Peter Gilbertson
Peter McGowan
Peyton Elizabeth Gaston
Peyton Tedder
Phil Holland
Philip Wayne Walther
Phillip Greenberg
Phyllis Frisch
Phyllis Naegeli
Pierce Johnson
Pierre Goria
Piper Utt
Polina Skaggs
Presley Lowe
Priscila Sandoval
Priscilla Chila Gomez
Priscilla Salas
Pvt Sample

R IS FOR REPEAT
R&A Crouch
Rabae Lidgett
Rachael Childers
Rachael Raymond
Rachael Spears
Rachael Thomae Pompura
Rachael Vronch
Racheal Pickens

Racheal Singleton
Rachel Alvarado
Rachel Ann Davis
Rachel Bevell
Rachel Bower
Rachel Bryson
Rachel Dallas Rose
Rachel Doran
Rachel Erin
Rachel Farris
Rachel H. Schroeder
Rachel Hinson
Rachel Jacobs
Rachel Julia Carbajal
Rachel L. Otwell
Rachel LeBlanc
Rachel Maier
Rachel Marie Correll
Rachel Mason
Rachel Moore
Rachel Morgan Hall
Rachel Munn
Rachel Nichols
Rachel Nilsen
Rachel Parker Humphries
Rachel Reaves
Rachel Renee Waddell
Rachel Roark
Rachel Sayers
Rachel Siditsky
Rachel Sizemore
Rachel Sowder
Rachel Stockton
Rachel Thacker
Rachel Thrasher
Rachel Tidmore
Rachel Towns
Rachel Uhas
Rachel V. Bull
Rachel Weeks
Rachelle Howard
Rachelle Mathis
Rachelle Pelletier
Raelynn Barnhill
Rafael & Sarah Magana
Ragan Riddle
Rahul Chaturvedi
Raiden Weldy
Raider Keenan
Raimey Ann Escoto

Raina Sheferaw
Rainey Fisher
Rainy M. Lowery
Ralph Hart, Jr.
Ralph Quidone III
Ralph Rianda
Ramirez Family
Ramirez Family 13/143
Ran Rodriguez
Randi Burt
Randy & Krissie
Randy Hinojos
Raul Montes
Ravin McCabe
Ray & Amanda Nuckoles
Ray Delgado
Raya Dane
Raymond H. Martinez
Raymond J. Fabian
Raymond Smith
Rea Lynn
Reagan Clarkson
Reagan Gear
Reagan Stith
Reanna Ramey
Reba Stoddard
Rebecca Baehrend
Rebecca Baych
Rebecca Cooper
Rebecca Crook
Rebecca Dawn Wareham
Rebecca Garza
Rebecca Hastings
Rebecca Kuan Khadimally
Rebecca L. Beasley
Rebecca L. Thompson
Rebecca Marie Garcia
Rebecca Martinez
Rebecca McLean
Rebecca Molinar
Rebecca Ward
Rebecca Warwick
Rebecca Whiteside
Rebekah Marie Lee
Rebekah McGuire
Rebekah R. Murphy
Red Caufield
Reece Renteria
Reese & Riley Jackson
Regina Allen

Regina Boston
Regina Thiry
Rena Magnuson
Renae Willey
Rene Woolley
Renee Broughman
Renee Estell Wills
Renee Hurn
Renee Johnson
Renee McAlister
Renee Smith
Renee Taylor Jauregui
Renee Vogel
Renee Wolk
Renee Eads
Rhagen Panyik
Rheadon Remy & Amy Jean
    Burkitt
Rhett C. Henley
Rhi Covington
Rhianna Holley
Rhiannon Helderbrand
Rhonda Ambrose
Rhonda Coots
Rhonda D. Phillips
Rhonda Kavan
Rhonda Pace
Richanne Kegans
Richard Baker Arnold II
Richard C. Stratford
Richard D. Morrison
Richard R. Frye
Richelle Ashley Smith
Richelle Ayers
Richie Ramsey
Richmond B. Dewan
Rick Garcia
Rick LaFave
Ricky Carrazco
Rikki Metcalf
Riley Arthur
Riley Elizabeth Yates
Riley Wilson
Rita M. Bernaldo
River Mount
Rizor Michael Clark
Rob Mignogna
Robert & Diane Bishop
Robert & Katie Dye
Robert & Kayla Dorsey

Robert Cummings
Robert Gerke
Robert Herrick
Robert Lopez
Robert Skidmore
Roberta Crain
Robin "Shy" Bullard
Robin Bottem
Robin Dennis
Robin Fetter
Robin Forester
Robin Graffius
Robin Lynch
Robin Strickland Greene
Robyn
Robyn Jennings Drumright
Robyn Ledbetter
Robyn McNabb Erwin
Robyn Wagner
Rochelle Dobson
Roczyn Sauers
Roger & Angela Gorbet
Roger Hill
Roger McMurtry
Rommie Cruz
Ronda Mason
Ronda Phillips
Ronnie Sparks
Ronnie Van Winkle
Rony Abbott
Rooooxanne
Rosa Olivia Perez
Rosa Wheeler
Rosana Christine Macias
Rose Bruner, ATX
Rose Cavanaugh
Rose Heffron
Rose Jackson
Rose Jenkins
Roshna Patel
Rosie Jakobeit
Rosie Sharkey
Ross Taylor
Roxanna Ferguson
R'Quoia Schlieper
Ruben Rueda
Ruby Lopez & Pearl Martinez
Rudy Ventura
Russell Pelech
Ruth Alvarez

Ruth J. Alvarez
Ruth Soto
Ryan & Leia Latham
Ryan & Lisa Maas
Ryan Brinker
Ryan Calabrese
Ryan D. Hagebusch
Ryan Deslauriers
Ryan E. Ketelhut
Ryan Gosse
Ryan Nicole Hoover
Ryan Shields
Ryan Sokol
Ryan Tucker
Ryan Vaughan
Ryan, Cole & Taylor
  Armstrong
Ryann Nicole Sanders
Ryann Stockman
Rylan Munson

S IS FOR SKILLS
S. Kade Stringham
Sabrina Galvan
Sabrina Moody
Sadaf Zendehdel
Sadie DeGiorgis
Sadie Harsey
Sadie Lynn Hackman
Sadie Mae Rigdon
Saleena Elizabeth
Salena Dominguez
Salena S.
Sam Bogaczyk
Sam R. Smith
Sam Reasor
Sam Robinson
Samantha "Coach" Schiavi
Samantha Baker
Samantha Bulmer
Samantha Chin
Samantha Deems
Samantha DeForest
Samantha Drescher
Samantha Elizabeth
Samantha Evans
Samantha Fairchild
Samantha Farnel
Samantha Ficco
Samantha Finley

Samantha Gillis
Samantha Green
Samantha Hillegass
Samantha J. Boch
Samantha J. Clement
Samantha Land
Samantha M. Heery
Samantha Monday
Samantha Nicole Dempsey
Samantha Puetz
Samantha Sexton
Samantha Seymour-
  Smallwood
Samantha Shaw
Samantha Tatterson
Samantha Teti
Samantha Weber
Sami Torres
Samii Jo
Samuel J. Gaston
Sandra Burns
Sandra de Arrigunaga
Sandra Guel Orta
Sandra J. Kinney
Sandra Jostes-Guerrant
Sandra Lee Saenz
Sandra Mancini Howe
Sandy & Billy Allen
Sandy Bryant
Sandy Castillo
Sandy Green
Sandy Haley
Sandy Jacobian
Sandy Jimenez
Sandy L. Patterson
Sandy Peeler
Sara & Carson Cochran
Sara & Jeffery Sanders
Sara "Bean" Gonzalez
Sara Ammann
Sara Burrow
Sara Carstensen
Sara Cooper
Sara Cornwell
Sara Davis
Sara Ebell
Sara Frank
Sara Gibson
Sara Gold
Sara Harvey

Sara Hosteng
Sara J. Bailey
Sara King
Sara Koppel
Sara Marler
Sara Marshall & Emily
  Kochan
Sara McClanahan
Sara Meeks
Sara Melow
Sara N. Jones
Sara Pack
Sara Reid
Sara Shahan
Sara Shea-Austin
Sara Soehlke
Sara Stapleton
Sara Taylor
Sara Weiand
Sara, Johanna & Alexa
Sarah A. Grow
Sarah A. Jackson
Sarah A. Mullane-Jackson
Sarah Ainsworth Johnson
Sarah Ann Emerson
Sarah App
Sarah Beadle
Sarah Brueggeman
Sarah C. Johnson
Sarah Castro
Sarah Catherine Orr
Sarah Chapie
Sarah Chappell
Sarah Cheney
Sarah Curylo
Sarah Danyelle Jones
Sarah Darr
Sarah Dotzel
Sarah E. Locke
Sarah E. Roark
Sarah Eliza Neff
Sarah Elizabeth Curlee
Sarah Faith Lubera
Sarah Flowers
Sarah Frank
Sarah G. Miller
Sarah Gadient
Sarah Goresch-Tronsdal
Sarah Hogge
Sarah Hughes

Sarah J. Nickles
Sarah J. Yodichkas "Yoda"
Sarah Jane Burfield
Sarah Jane Williams
Sarah Jo Rogers
Sarah Kuehl Manke
Sarah Lamb
Sarah LeHardy
Sarah Lucero
Sarah Lukat
Sarah Marie Jennings
Sarah Massucci
Sarah McGibbon, Lance Davis
Sarah Mendonca
Sarah Michelle Pettit
Sarah N. Coker
Sarah Peterson
Sarah R. Martin
Sarah Reed
Sarah Reynolds
Sarah Richardson
Sarah Sherman-Clark
Sarah Skidmore
Sarah Sprung
Sarah Stapley
Sarah Steinke
Sarah Taylor
Sarah Traynor
Sarah Traywick
Sarah Tucker
Sarah Ungvarsky
Sarah Zander
SarahAnn Smith
SarahElizabeth K.
Sarrah M.F. Dierks
Sasha D. Beritiech
Savanah Philpot
Savannah & Ryan Schaefer
Savannah Baker
Savannah Gwinn
Savannah Hastings
Savannah Leigh Parker
Savannah N. Morris
Savannah Nicholson
Savannah Paasch
Savannah Prine
Savannah Ruiz
Saylor Aspen Burgoyne
Scarlet Stiteler
Scarlett Hathaway

Scott & Pamela Saunders
Scott McDonald
Scott Poling
Scott Tavlin
Sean & Hannah Lucas
Sean "SeanP" Pigott
Sean Croell
Sean Ducey
Sean Kuehn
Sean M. Spitler
Selena Lynn Dunn
Selina J. Iseli
Selma Cardenas
Serah Farnell
Serena Robinson
Serena-Rose McVickar
Seryna Dawn Jackson
Seth Dupré
Severiana Varela
Shalini Vattes
Shallyn Mende
Shanda Chesnut
Shandy DeShae Nix
Shane & Mia Sparks
Shane Meche
Shania Bruce
Shanisty L. Radogna
Shanna Harrison
Shanna Helvey
Shanna Morin
Shanna Quiring
Shanna Zimmerman
Shannan Scott
Shannon & Steven Patrick
Shannon A. Credeur
Shannon Anguiano
Shannon Barrett
Shannon Connelly
Shannon Darnold
Shannon E. Stewart
Shannon Fleet
Shannon Hinrichs
Shannon Kay Leon
Shannon Keys
Shannon Lee Richardson
Shannon Lee Webster
Shannon Lindsay
Shannon McGregor
Shannon Pickrell
Shannon Reed

Shannon Sedotal
Shannon Shotliff
Shannon Smith
Shannon Zweifel
ShaRay Lawand
Shari Mangold
Shari R. Vickery
Sharilee Shults
Sharinda Hutton
Shariwaki
Sharon "Bunny" Adams
Sharon Boczkiewicz
Sharon Forrester
Sharon Justice Bull
Sharon Kopp
Sharon M. Pool
Sharon Salazar
Sharon Zwick
Shaulynn Dickson
Shaunda Revere Naquin
Shawn Chance
Shawn Foster
Shawn Reed
Shawn Sears
Shawn Zito
Shawna Bartlett
Shawna Diane Mattson
Shawna Sousa
Shawna Weaver
Shawnna Davison
Shea & Jennifer Suess
Shea Rhames
Sheila Beeson
Sheila D. Kaufert
Sheila E. Henry
Sheila Michaels
Sheila Thomas
Shelbi Alferd
Shelbi Ghosoph
Shelbi Robicheaux
Shelbi Spry
Shelby Davidson
Shelby Harkness
Shelby Laine
Shelby Larkey
Shelby Lynn Moore
Shelby Milby
Shelby Politte
Shelby Rae Errebo
Shelby S. Schroeder

Shelby St. Amant
Shelby Worthington
Shelby, Raney & Daulton
   Hagan
Shell Soraruf
Shelley Banning
Shelley Clark
Shelley M. Marquez
Shelley McGinn
Shelley Sawalich
Shelli Blanchard
Shellie Nicholson
Shelly Benoit
Shelly Byrd
Shelly Glasgow
Shelly Howard
Shelly L. Shepard
Shelly Marek
Shelly Perkins
Shelly Schaefer
Shelly Stephenson
Shelly Turner
Sheree Bradley
Sheri Bonini-Garboden
Sheri Hendel
Sheri Russell
Sherri Cousins
Sherri Hilton
Sherri Laisure
Sherrie Stanyard
Sherry Foster
Sherry G. Campo
Sherry Park
Sheryl Heizer
Sheryl Jervis
Shilpa Kaul
Shirley A. Curtis
Shirley A. Dawson
Shoncia Ball
Shonda Troutman
Shonna Epperson
Shonts Family
Sidney Paulson
Sidni Southerland
Sierra Sanders
Sierra Stieber
Simone Sanguinette
Sist Glendaklb
Skye Lynn Johnson
Skyler Adams

Skyler Barnes
Sondra Mojica
Sonia Steven Jackson
Sonya Eckenroth
Sophia A. Fuller
Sophia Cook
Sophia Rae Willis
Spencer & Caitlin Houk
Stacey Brimer
Stacey C. Monaco
Stacey Cruz
Stacey Duke
Stacey Gray
Stacey Swab
Stacey Vandling
Staci Johnston
Staci Olson
Staci Stepp
Stacia K. Shoults
Stacie Beatty
Stacie J. Bennett
Stacie N. Clayborn
Stacie V. Garcia
Stacy & Patrick Kirwin
Stacy Carnes
Stacy Fiore
Stacy L. Dreher
Stacy Latimer & Grant
   Latimer
Stacy Leverone
Stacy Lynn Miller
Stacy Mantei
Stacy Moore
Stacy Narvaiz
Stacy Ritter
Stacy Strba
Stacy Youngren
Starlynn Denae Singleton
Starr Smith
Stef Denby
Stefani Cubillas
Stefanie Drowns
Stefanie Leanne Santerre
Stefanie Osfolk Brown
Steph McNary
Stephanie "Fefi" Busto
Stephanie A. Cox
Stephanie A. Silva
Stephanie Abdallah
Stephanie Ann Anthony

Stephanie Ann Odom
Stephanie Barriga
Stephanie Bise
Stephanie Black
Stephanie Buzikowski
Stephanie Clatanoff Owen
Stephanie Creech
Stephanie Davis
Stephanie Elder
Stephanie Feeback
Stephanie Geoghan
Stephanie George Callie &
   Olivia Martin
Stephanie Gil
Stephanie Grossi
Stephanie Guffey
Stephanie Hewitt
Stephanie Hickerson
Stephanie Highley
Stephanie Hinderliter
Stephanie Hines
Stephanie Holtzapfel
Stephanie Howell
Stephanie Johle
Stephanie Johnson-Waco
Stephanie K. Barry
Stephanie L. Jones
Stephanie Lea Miller
Stephanie Lewis
Stephanie Lista
Stephanie Lynn Gonzales
Stephanie M. Carrasco
Stephanie Mahaffey
Stephanie Marie Evans
Stephanie McManus
Stephanie Midkiff
Stephanie Nastovska
Stephanie Owczykowski
Stephanie Patterson
Stephanie Pence
Stephanie Piña
Stephanie Pretzer
Stephanie R. Downs
Stephanie Ramirez
Stephanie Rickert
Stephanie S. Peterman
Stephanie Schafer
Stephanie Smith
Stephanie Sullivan
Stephanie Swanson

Stephanie Trujillo ATX
Stephanie Veden
Stephanie Vogel
Stephanie Wagner
Stephanie Wehmeyer
Stephanie Williams
Stephen Boger
Stephen Friedman
Stephen Gilbert
Stephen Lowery
Sterling Jones
Steve Alexander
Steve Shattuck
Steve Slocum
Steve Smith
Steven Blassingame
Steven J. Durila
Steven Van Der Steen
Steve-O Kahler
Storm Tyde Yost
Stormy McBride
Suanne Mestas
Sue Ann Licht
Sue Kane
Sue Roberts
Suheily A. Ramirez
Summer Florence
Summer Hammonds
Summer Lee Brown
Summer Mashburn
Summer Muno
Summer Shipp
Sunny Hall
Susan Aguirre
Susan Clooney
Susan K. Crawford
Susan McMahan McKinzie
Susan R. Nelson
Susan Schultz
Susan Soileau
Susan Stephens
Susan T. Peña
Susan Vitt
Susan Warne
Susie Jones
Suzanne Brackins
Suzanne Eller
Suzanne Henderson
Suzanne McKee
Suzanne Ross

Suzanne Tropea
Suzanne Zink
Suzi Baker
Suzie Rodriguez
Sybil Eggleston
Sydnee Carroll
Sydney Carella
Sydney Eidson & Lauren
  Burns
Sydney Jean Valentino
Sydney Kirby-Rohnow
Sydney Moore
Sydney Samolewski
Sydney Wann
Sylvia Mitchell
Sylvia Reyes Hamilton

T IS FOR TRAINING
T. Neil Butler
Tabatha Jones
Tabitha & Tyler Buss
Tabitha Carter
Tabitha Farley
Tabitha Ridge
Taffy Luther Sexton
Tahara Anderson
Tahia Washington
Taloen Olenick
Tamara Kraft
Tamara Urso
Tamaria Raleigh
Tambra & Cav & Mic McGaw
Tamela Pipes
Tammy Adkins
Tammy Brewster
Tammy Brown
Tammy Creswell
Tammy D. Creswell
Tammy Falco
Tammy Gregory Dixon
Tammy Heying
Tammy Jenkins
Tammy K. Larimore
Tammy Layne
Tammy Lee LeBlanc
Tammy Luttrell
Tammy Roney
Tammy S. Roesner
Tammy Suiter
Tana Conway

Tanah Reaves
Tanisha Kieper
Tanner Tillack
Tanner Waggoner
Tanner Williamson
Tanya & Jakary Greer
Tanya Baker-Murrey
Tanya DeLaRosa
Tanya Orlando
Tanya Rogers
Tanya Sampson
Tanya Yumi Pawlak
Tara Angelina Desko
Tara Creighton
Tara Davis
Tara Eisele
Tara Lee Slone
Tara Lee Walker
Tara M. King
Tara M. Reedy
Tara Olivier
Tara Pottichen
Tara Powers
Tara Tipple
Tara Warren
Taralyn Stearnes
Taryn Gladstone
Taryn Henry
Tasha Alexander
Tasha Brink
Tasha C.
Tasha Nickler
Tasha R. DeLeo
Tatiana Martinez
Tatum Hannon
Tawnisha Scantlin
Tawnya Naslund
Tawnya Tolsch
Tay M.
Tayler M. Beuth
Tayler Marie Lopez
Tayler Ramsey
Tayler Reitz
Taylor Barborek
Taylor Catherine Casey
Taylor Cutbirth
Taylor Devlin
Taylor Dix
Taylor Dover
Taylor Eubanks

Taylor J. Paulhamus
Taylor Kaatz
Taylor Kerns
Taylor Lambrinos
Taylor Larson
Taylor Leet
Taylor M. Johnson
Taylor Malbon
Taylor Marie Snavley
Taylor May
Taylor N. Kelly
Taylor Nicole Newkirk
Taylor O'Dell
Taylor R. Puckett
Taylor Rhett Mabie
Taylor Ross
Taylor Rowe
Taylor Royce-Pavlot
Taylor Ruffing
Taylor Sadlowski
Taylor Vaughn
Taylor Webb
Taylor Williams-DellAntonio
Taylor Wilson
Teah Obeidalla
Team Helstrom
Team Nunez OG
Tera Smith
Teresa Askren
Teresa Cantwell
Teresa Hiller
Teresa Holub
Teresa Jackson
Teresa L. Amerson
Teresa Lynn Evans
Teresa Palmore
Teresa Traci Tisserat
Teresa Zuehlke
Terese Call
Teri Irwin
Teri Isabell
Terra Evans
Terra L. Baker
Terri & Max Geritz
Terri Keith Smith
Terri McNellis
Terri Schneider
Terry L. Khoury
Terry Michael Snyder
Teryl Booth

Teryn Emas
Tess L. Kersten
Tessa Harris
Teylor Kirkpatrick
The Brockmeyers
The Buchman Family
The Chamy
The Collins Crew
The Don A. Harris
The Frohlings
The Godbouts
The Haddock Family
The Jacquez Family
The Jagger Girls
The Luker Family
The Magid Family
The McQuillin Family
The Oxford Family
The Pelache Family
The Rebisz Family
The Resor Family
The Schwartz Family
The Teresinski Family
The Thorne Family
The Villasenor Family
The Votaw/Friedman Family
The Wann Family
The Winkelpleck Family
Thea Meyer
Thera "Like Theraflu" Border
Theresa Cardoza
Theresa Carle
Theresa Ferguson
Theresa Orendain
Theresa Stewart
Theresa Wilson
Therese M. Roberts
Thomas Gunn
Thomas Kiger
Thomas Mieldzioc
Thomas P. Gray
Thomas Youngman
Tia D. Scott
Tiffanie Ann
Tiffanie L. Stevens
Tiffany & Russell Williams
Tiffany Asher
Tiffany Butler
Tiffany C. Pate Franks
Tiffany Conquest

Tiffany D. Bryant
Tiffany Dailey
Tiffany Dawn Schuman
Tiffany Edwards
Tiffany Garmon
Tiffany Garner
Tiffany Hash
Tiffany Held
Tiffany J. Fisk
Tiffany Jane Cline
Tiffany Jones
Tiffany Koos
Tiffany M. Rosser
Tiffany McMillan Odom
Tiffany N. Hines
Tiffany Pool
Tiffany Rismiller
Tiffany Rollins
Tiffany Scoggins
Tiffany See
Tiffany Sharpensteen
Tiffany Simmons
Tiffany the Moth-a Effin Kobee
Tiffany Walden
Tiffeney Johnson
Tige Azevedo
Tim Blanchfield
Tim Fife & Marvin Chavez
Tim G. Wymer
Tim Rogers
Timmy Guyette
Timmy Manning
Timothy M. Carpenter
Timothy O'Reilly
Timothy T. Manning Jr.
Tina & Alex Smith
Tina Albright
Tina Hartnett
Tina Holloway2
Tina M. Rogers
Tina O. Lane
Tina Walker
Tina Zeider
Tisha English
Tisha Lawrence
Tissie McClure
Tito & Diane Aquino
TJ LeBaron
Toai & Jessica Huynh
Tobias Mroch

Tobin Potts
Todd Gilvin
Todd Mitchell
Todd N. Taylor
Tom Karambela
Tomi Hebert
Tommy Wasiuta
Toni L. Kimes
Toni Lamas
Toni Lynn Battaglia
Tonia Mauer
Tonia Molino
Tonia Y. Deyo
Tony & Lindsay Rude
Tony Bolanos
Tony Douglass
Tony Douglass & Amy
   Tuschen
Tony P.
Tony Rodriguez
Tonya Burton Loy
Tonya Dawn Williams
Tonya Higgins
Tonya House
Tonya Morrison
Tonya Walker Beckum
Torey M. Guajardo
Tori & Mark Kokosko
Tori Bradsher
Tori Mickelson
Tori Rosendal
Tracey Hedrick
Tracey M. Byer
Tracey Schaub
Tracey Smith
Tracey Young
Traci M. Scullawl
Traci McFerrin
Traci Metcalf
Tracie A. Alfaro
Tracie D. Feight
Tracy Baumgart
Tracy Champagne
Tracy Frost
Tracy Johnson Popple
Tracy L. Bailey
Tracy L. Clark
Tracy Minchich
Tracy Morales
Tracy Warren

Tracy Wood
Travers McEntyre
Travis Jarrett
Travis Koehn
Travis Lee Mason
Travis McIntyre
Travis Perez
Travis Rathbun
Travis Weaver
Treena Stuart
Trena J. Lackey
Trent Satterwhite
Trenton Isabel
Trenton Tucker
Treven Hunter
Trevor & Danyell Lang
Trevor & Lisa Ducote
Trey & Ginger Bird
Trey Mullins
Tricia A. Ackermann
Tricia Colvin
Tricia Dushek
Tricia Fry
Tricia Moore
Tricia Stickrod
Trina M. Caraway-Grimes
Trina M. Grimes
Trip Ros
Trish Huelga
Trish Jackson
Trish Rodgers
Trisha Chambers
Trisha L. Dickshinski
Trisha Thompson
Trisha Voelker
Tristan & Terran Germann
Tristin Ranger
Troy & Destiny Howard
T-Roy Howard
Tucker & Greyson Kent
Twyla Johnson
Ty S. Reed
Tyler A. Moreno
Tyler Bercher
Tyler Brooks
Tyler Castro
Tyler Freye
Tyler Gray
Tyler Ian Monroe
Tyler Jones

Tyler Mazdra
Tyler Miller
Tyler Powell
Tyler Rodrigue
Tyler S. Boucher
Tyler S. Monson
Tyler Yoakum

U IS FOR UNDERDOG
UTJEN

V IS FOR VALUES
V. Ashley Dixon
Val Farley
Val Kirby
Val McCausland
Valarie Evans
Valecia M. Parker
Valeria Deyanira McCoy
Valerie A. Ducey
Valerie Anne Whittaker
Valerie Baker-Wray
Valerie C. Salcido
Valerie Dixon
Valerie Gallegos
Valerie Rae Davis
Valerie Schulz
Van Winkle Family
Vance & Emily Flores
Vanessa April Gonzalez
Vanessa Bongiovanni
Vanessa Mantei
Vanessa Mata
Vanessa Ramos
Vanessa Silvas
Vanessa Turley
Vee Bowman
Verdawn Hunt
Veronica A. Klodt
Veronica D. Barria
Veronica Fisher
Veronica L. Gency
Veronica Marie Morales
Vicki B. Smith
Vicki J. Braquet
Vicki L. Taylor
Vicki Wilken
Vickie & Alani Gonzalez
Vickie Lynn Szarmach
Vickie Saucedo

Vickie Scales
Victor & JoElda Trevino
Victoria Brooks
Victoria Browne
Victoria Di Stefano
Victoria Kinmonth
Victoria Lahrman
Victoria Myers
Victoria Oviedo
Victoria R.
Victoria Roth
Vikram Parolkar
Virginia A. Trevino
Virginia Blair Watson
Vivian Martinez
Vivian Mendez
Vivian Tejeda & David Tejeda
Vivian Villaran
Viviana Wyatt
Vivien Garcia
Vladi Rabinovich

W IS FOR WILLPOWER
Wade Arrington
Wade Brooks
Wahl Family (BEEB)
Wanda Bodey
Wanda G. Braddy
Wanda Wanie
Wayne Wilkins
Welthy Cunningham
Wendi Davidson

Wendy Baron Seagraves
Wendy Coco
Wendy Dixon
Wendy Gossett
Wendy Griffith
Wendy Hendrickson
Wendy McWherter
Wendy Musitano
Wendy Ogden West
Wendy Pilgrim
Wendy Urban
Wes & Eron Farris
Wes Thornton
Wesley Wright
Whitney Biggs
Whitney Brown
Whitney Carr
Whitney Dose
Whitney Hall
Whitney Hoskin
Whitney Overturf
Whitney Pewitt
Whitney Renae Mason
Whitney Safranek
Whitney Ward & Devin Ward
Wilbert J. Rodriguez
Will & Jessie Taylor
Will "Daddy" Daniel
Will Bynum
Will C. Smith
Will Gallegos
Will Weber

Will Young
William Thomas Fortunato
Winnie Poole
Winter & Kyle Bosanko
Wyatt F. Dennis
Wynona Danes

Y IS FOR YES
Yesica Rodriguez
Yoda Nero
Yolanda Buenavista Perez
Yolanda Munoz
Yolanda Sánchez
Yvette Paniagua Enriquez
Yvonne LaFrance
Yvonne M. Ray

Z IS FOR ZEAL
Zac Hollingshad
Zac W.
Zach Penny
Zachary Abe
Zackary Sanders
Zaira D. Moran
Zanny Love
Zayra Trujillo
Zephaniah Duby
Zoey Schmidt & Aunna
  Woods
Zoraya (pronounced zor-eye-
  ugh)